The Influence Economy

The Influence Economy

Decoding Supplier-Induced Demand

MAXIM SYTCH

OXFORD
UNIVERSITY PRESS

OXFORD
UNIVERSITY PRESS

Oxford University Press is a department of the University of Oxford.
It furthers the University's objective of excellence in research, scholarship,
and education by publishing worldwide. Oxford is a registered trade mark of
Oxford University Press in the UK and in certain other countries.

Published in the United States of America by Oxford University Press
198 Madison Avenue, New York, NY 10016, United States of America.

Library of Congress Cataloging-in-Publication Data
Names: Sytch, Maxim, author.
Title: The influence economy : decoding supplier-induced demand / Maxim Sytch.
Description: New York, NY : Oxford University Press, [2025] | Includes
bibliographical references and index.
Identifiers: LCCN 2024037176 (print) | LCCN 2024037177 (ebook) |
ISBN 9780197665152 (hardback) | ISBN 9780197665176 (epub) |
ISBN 9780197665183
Subjects: LCSH: Professions—Marketing. | Consultants—Marketing. |
Industrial procurement. | Consumer behavior. | Supply and demand.
Classification: LCC HD8038.A1 S98 2025 (print) | LCC HD8038.A1 (ebook) |
DDC 658.8—dc23/eng/20241205
LC record available at https://lccn.loc.gov/2024037176
LC ebook record available at https://lccn.loc.gov/2024037177

DOI: 10.1093/9780197665183.001.0001

Printed by Integrated Books International, United States of America

CONTENTS

Thank you for picking up this book. It will take you on a journey through the shadowy corners of the marketplace, where professionals whom we entrust with the well-being of companies—consultants, lawyers, or bankers—can guide companies toward choices and services that are unnecessary or even harmful.

As we explore the curious world of supplier-induced demand, I am going to ask you to keep an open mind. It is a detective story in which the clues are buried within the mechanics of professional services, waiting for us to uncover why well-intentioned advice can sometimes be our downfall. As we weave through the evidence, you will learn how supplier-induced demand takes shape, spawned from a combination of market forces, changes in the fabric of professional identity, and the intricate dynamics of buyer–seller relationships. It is like a dance where both buyers and sellers often move in perfect sync, yet neither often hears the music playing.

The insights we will gain, while cradled within the context of professional services, are mere echoes of a larger story unfolding across the landscape of our economy. This is more than an academic discourse; it is the unveiling of an invisible shift toward a world where others' influence nudges us toward decisions and consumption, which we might later question. And, I hope, that in this revelation lies the power to understand and reclaim the autonomy of our choices.

Inspired by the most common query I encountered during discussions about this book—"What is it about?"—I encapsulate the answer in the book's opening pages. Since my answer to this question was invariably free from academic citations and data presentations, you won't find any in the book's opening chapter, either.

From this point forward, the choice is yours. You may opt to set the book aside after reading the first chapter, hopefully taking away a few morsels of information to ponder. Alternatively, you can continue on a journey, page by page, chapter by chapter, delving deeper into one of the most fascinating and consequential dynamics of the modern economy. I preview all sections of the book in the opening chapter, so if a particular section ignites your curiosity, yet another approach is to navigate directly to those pages.

I hold two aspirations for this book. First, I aim for it to act as a catalyst, sparking rigorous scholarly inquiry into the complexities of supplier-induced demand and its broader implications for the influence-based economy. Second, over the years, I have witnessed my students, bright and full of integrity, venture boldly into the world of professional services—some to offer their expertise, others to seek it. These individuals are the architects and patrons of our marketplace, bearing not only their own ambitions but also the destinies of the organizations they serve. My hope, as this book finds its way into their hands—and indeed into the hands of buyers and suppliers at large—is to illuminate the undercurrents of supplier-induced demand and ignite a constructive dialogue among them to address this phenomenon.

Now I shall leave you to it and refrain from falling victim to the irony of promoting a book on supplier-induced demand.

CHAPTER 1

What is this Book About?

From the depths of our ever-expanding service economy, an intriguing phenomenon beckons us. It is a transformation of profound proportions: the relinquishment of demand ownership by the buyers themselves. No longer are they the architects of their own needs and wants. Rather, it is the service providers who shape the demand to which they cater. And there is more to this narrative. Not only are these services thrust upon buyers, but many of them prove to be unhelpful or even detrimental. This is the essence of supplier-induced demand, the villain and focal point of this book.

Within these pages, I embark on a mission to construct a framework that illuminates the intricate nuances surrounding the emergence and impact of supplier-induced demand. My argument is that supplier-induced demand arises from a volatile fusion of three main forces. First, we have *enabling market conditions*, which establish a fertile landscape—an opportunity structure—for supplier-induced demand to emerge. Second, the *institutional logics of action* exert their influence, molding suppliers' perspective of their own actions and sculpting their very identity. And last, we encounter *breakdowns in learning cycles*, which impede buyers (and sellers) from discerning the existence of supplier-induced demand and gleaning valuable insights from it (see Figure 1.1 for details).

I explore the phenomenon of supplier-induced demand in the context of professional services, which range from consulting, legal advice, and banking, to lobbying and marketing. Within this context,

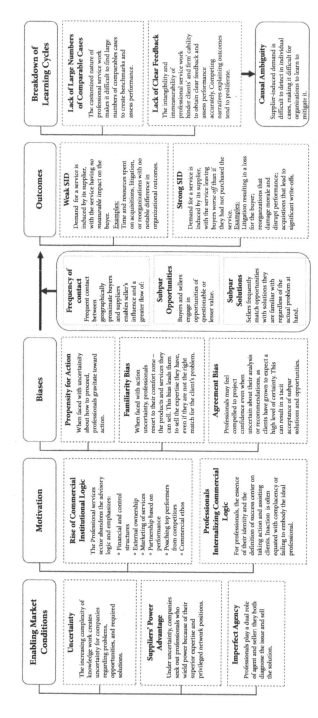

Figure 1.1 Theory of Supplier-Induced Demand

supplier-induced demand may assume multifarious guises, manifesting as superfluous reorganizations, frivolous lawsuits, and ill-conceived acquisitions. These seemingly innocuous actions may not only fail to yield positive outcomes but could potentially inflict detrimental consequences upon the buying organization. They could squander valuable resources, demotivate the workforce, disrupt business operations, and further engender a host of operational, legal, and financial setbacks.

Sellers of professional services, however, are not the malevolent force some may perceive them to be. Rather, the dynamics of supplier-induced demand in professional services exemplify a sweeping transformation in our economic landscape that is likely to affect many other economic sectors as well. In this introductory chapter, I synthesize the book's overall idea while pointing to specific segments further in the text for in-depth reading. It is in these detailed explorations that the argument truly unfolds. The crux of the book is that professional services, and our knowledge-based economy in general, bear witness to a significant degree of supplier-induced demand. It does not, however, manifest ubiquitously. Rather, supplier-induced demand emerges under specific conditions that buyers and sellers must learn to mutually recognize.

Understanding these conditions raises an air of alarm as our economy continues to evolve toward even more complex knowledge-based work. It is my hope that this book raises awareness and creates a call to action. What could ensue is a productive dialogue involving buyers and sellers of professional services about jointly mitigating the encroachment of supplier-induced demand.

THE OPPORTUNITY STRUCTURE: ENABLING MARKET CONDITIONS

Imagine yourself in the company rooms of the 1950s, where executives grappled with typewritten reports and contracts in a haze of cigarette smoke. In those bygone times, leaders dedicated their energy to highly tangible matters: how to drive down production costs or how to sell another batch of their product. Fast forward a mere few decades to see executives gathered to discuss the analysis of unprecedented amounts of data over videoconference. Their conversations now transcend yesterday's mundane concerns, delving into the realms of competitive strategies and intellectual property, contemplating the intricacies of acquisition synergies and the nuances of corporate diversification, and pondering corporate venture financing and the enigmatic art of commodity hedging. Behind these contrasting boardroom tableaus lies the deep transformation toward a knowledge-based economy.

Operating successfully in today's economy demands an unprecedented level of technical prowess. Finance executives must be fluent in sophisticated financial modeling and simulations, the ever-evolving regulatory landscape, and the expanding frontier of financial technologies, where blockchain and cryptocurrencies may hold court. Along with information technology professionals, these executives often help erect and navigate increasingly robust systems and controls, shielding against the perils of cybersecurity breaches and protecting data privacy. And they do all of this while navigating a complex web of environmental, social, and governance accountability and reporting.

Legal craft is similarly growing more sophisticated with each passing day, intertwined with the multifaceted tapestry of intellectual property, new forms of licensing agreements and contracts, and alternative avenues of dispute resolution. Today's legal personnel routinely traverse cross-border and multijurisdictional law, embracing the complexities of a global economy, often in the form of e-commerce and digital economic exchange. Operations, strategy, and human resource managers have and continue to face similar levels of complexity in their work.

Moreover, these specialized domains of organizational action necessarily converge, requiring even more sophisticated workers who can scaffold different areas of expertise. Indeed, nearly every pivotal corporate maneuver—whether it be a high-stakes litigation battle, a transformative acquisition, or a strategic reorganization—unfolds on the interstices of finance, law, strategy, human capital, information systems, and operations. In fact, these areas are often united by formidable enterprise resource management systems and sophisticated, cross-functional, matrixed governance structures. All these developments go hand-in-hand with advancements in data analysis and quantitative modeling, machine learning, predictive modeling, and the ever-evolving iterations of artificial intelligence.

The deepening and convergence of expert specialization in knowledge-based work, coupled with rapid technological advancement, lead to organizational activities of immense complexity. Chapter 3 reveals that this continually growing complexity of knowledge-based work weighs heavily on business leaders, leaving them grappling with a daunting sense of uncertainty. Indeed, it becomes challenging to discern the true nature of the problem or opportunity that lies before them and determine the most prudent course of action. Importantly, it becomes equally difficult to ascertain potential outcomes of undertaken interventions.

In that sense, the market for professional services defies the expectations of conventional competitive markets. Instead of buyers confidently seeking the best provider to meet specific needs, markets are shrouded in uncertainty. Buyers grapple with elusive questions: What do we truly need? How can we effectively address those needs? What outcomes might unfold from our choices? How do we even evaluate the outcomes? Organizational executives thus often find themselves wrestling with perplexing dilemmas. They ponder the need for yet another restructuring effort, question the merits of an additional debt offering, or contemplate whether a sale to a specific acquirer aligns with the best interests of their business. Or they may weigh their intellectual property strategy and the strength of their patents against potential infringers, assessing the viability of legal action.

You can probably relate to the difficulty of willingly embracing that uncertainty. It vexes us, disrupts our equilibrium, and brings discomfort, anxiety, and the sense that we've lost control. As you delve into the pages of this book, you will learn that uncertainty activates our amygdala, that ancient part of our brain primed for responding to threats and fear. It should come as no surprise, then, that humans are not content to flounder in uncertainty. Instead, we strive to mitigate its effects.

In such overwhelming circumstances, we instinctively seek solace in the counsel of experts. Working with experts evokes feelings of trust and compensates for the lack of information, both of which become power-ful remedies for reducing ambiguity in our decisions. Breakthroughs in neurological science have revealed that even our neurons and synapses function distinctively when we seek the guidance of knowledgeable individuals. In Chapter 4, you will learn that the meteoric rise of professional service firms stems largely from their unparalleled ability to assuage uncertainty in the eyes of their clientele.

Alongside the industry pillars of manufacturing, technology, and traditional services now stand towering giants, offering an entirely different breed of expertise: professional services. Familiar names, such as McKinsey and Accenture in consulting, Goldman Sachs and Morgan Stanley in investment banking, EY or PwC in the domain of accounting, and Kirkland & Ellis and DLA Piper in the legal sphere, have emerged as titans in today's economy. These and many other professional service firms have not only matched the scale and organizational complexity of corporations in more traditional sectors but, in many respects, have surpassed them. These pages begin to unravel the intricate dynamics of professional services, revealing a world in which three market conditions converge—uncertainty (Chapter 3), supplier power (Chapter 4), and imperfect agency (Chapter 5)—to create an environment ripe for supplier-induced demand.

Chapter 4 continues by exploring how every strand of the professional firms' DNA—be it the meticulous selection and development of personnel or the nuances of interactions with clients—has evolved to amass and radiate the advantage of expertise. Professionals are widely perceived as extremely capable experts. They are also deemed capable of cross-cutting relevant expertise domains to locate and synthesize germane, diverse insights to solve daunting organizational problems.

Beyond their advantage of expertise, professional service firms have acquired strategic positions within the intricate networks of information and economic exchange among companies. Chapter 4 also highlights that the partners of leading professional service firms command a surprising level of deference from even the most seasoned executives. These partners, by virtue of their connections spanning multiple sectors and industries, hold the power to shape the flow of business opportunities that course through their clients' companies. Remarkably, their wide networks of referrals can also exert influence even over the trajectory of corporate executives' careers.

The combination of expertise edge and unique network positions endows professional service firms with unprecedented power. It is the level of power that opens doors to an unparalleled ability to guide clients in understanding their business needs and the best ways to address them. Simultaneously, the same power compels clients to bow to the professionals' influence, deferring to their wisdom and counsel. Exercising this power is not as overt or forceful as one might imagine. Instead of envisioning a power struggle followed by submission, picture an almost imperceptible force that capitalizes on our ingrained tendencies to defer to those of high status and expertise.

In experimental studies, this influence is akin to the allure of a professionally dressed individual jaywalking confidently across a red light, effortlessly captivating our attention and prompting us to follow suit. Or consider research findings showing that we hesitate just a bit longer before honking at a luxury car stuck in front of us at a green light—the slight delay is born from our perception of its novelty and higher cost. These instances, seemingly unrelated to the world of professional services, provide a glimpse into the underlying dynamics at play. They reveal the sway that deference to status and authority holds over our actions, often operating below our conscious awareness.

Against this backdrop, professional service firms have assumed a remarkable dual role—a duality that takes center stage in Chapter 5. On the one hand, they act as advisors or agents. As trusted guides and repositories of knowledge, they assist their clients in navigating the multitude of opportunities and challenges their organizations face. Envision a sagacious consigliere who steers you through the treacherous waters of organizational management. On the other hand, these very firms find themselves in the role of sellers, promoting and vending their specific services.

Perfect agents, agency theory tells us, are a rare breed. Just think about the lengths we go to—in terms of contracts, board, or regulatory oversight—to ensure that senior executives dutifully represent shareholders' interests. What makes professional service providers particularly imperfect is precisely this odd fusion of agent and seller roles. Professional service firms absorb portions of their clients' decision-making authority, while simultaneously acting as purveyors of customized solutions to these very clients. Consultants, lawyers, and investment bankers are not mere conduits of opportunity assessment and strategic guidance. Conveniently, they also sell reorganization plans, litigation services, initial public offering facilitation, and merger and acquisition expertise.

THE MOTIVATION: THE RISE OF THE COMMERCIAL INSTITUTIONAL LOGIC

By now, some of you might be exclaiming, "I knew it! It all comes down to money!" And perhaps economists are shaking their heads, convinced that incentives have always held immense power in shaping behavior. Worse yet, some executives, when engaging in conversations about the book, were quick to mention some illustrative examples of brazen fraud in selling professional services.

But I caution against jumping to conclusions just yet. In this book's sixth chapter, I present a compelling counterpoint to the prevailing image of ambulance-chasing personal injury lawyers or conniving car mechanics "fixing" a perfectly functional vehicle. In the domain of professional services, long-lasting and deeply rooted relationships flourish between professional service firms and their clients. Partners accord priority to specific client accounts for years, creating a bond that extends far beyond fleeting transactions. While not uniform, these enduring relationships are remarkably prevalent in professional service work and continue to grow in their significance.

The dynamics in these embedded relationships differ significantly from dealing with a personal injury lawyer with whom you may never cross paths again. They are similarly a far cry from entrusting your car to a mechanic you visit once every few years. Research presented in this book indicates that these embedded relationships, which underpin transactions in professional services, provide a powerful deterrent to opportunism and unethical behavior. Instead, the involved parties are often motivated by a shared understanding and commitment to the relationship itself that transcends mere financial gain.

Therefore, it would be a grave mistake to attribute supplier-induced demand to professionals' intentional malice. In fact, you will discover that in professional services, the elusive nature of supplier-induced demand makes it difficult to detect; indeed, even suppliers themselves often remain blissfully unaware of its presence.

The narrative of supplier-induced demand presented in Chapters 6 and 7 thus veers away from conventional depictions of service professionals as driven solely by primal instincts, relentlessly pursuing self-interest, and venturing beyond legalities and ethics in their quest for personal enrichment. Instead, it offers a different perspective through which we can perceive these professionals—one that reveals their assimilation into a new institutional logic, a new paradigm of work. The esoteric term "institutional logic" helps us understand how undercurrents of workplace practices, norms, and cognitive perspectives intersect with our socialization at work. The change in institutional logic was so profound for professional services that it has reshaped the essence of what it means to be a professional. Within this new paradigm, the act of selling and catalyzing action is seen as a means to create value for their clients, their organizations, and ultimately themselves.

Chapter 6 serves as a time machine, transporting us back several decades to witness the remarkable metamorphosis of professional services. These once modest advisory groups, owned exclusively by contributing partners, stood as bastions of tradition. Seniority dictated promotions and tenure, with partnership bestowing a lifelong guarantee of employment. Poaching partners from other firms was considered taboo—an act that ran counter to prevailing professional norms. And the notion of advertising professional services seemed anathema, while discussions about growth, revenue, and profitability were alien to firms' hallways.

The winds of change have swept mercilessly through these hallways. Today's preeminent consulting, legal, and investment banking giants have grown into sprawling commercial entities, unrecognizable from their humble beginnings. They have flung open their doors to external ownership and, in some instances, have even become publicly traded enterprises. The path to partnership has changed dramatically, placing primary—if not exclusive—emphasis on an individual's ability to generate revenue and acquire clients. Today, underperforming partners face the looming threat of being replaced by revenue-generating stars poached from rival firms. Millions of dollars are poured into marketing initiatives, and professional firms' conference rooms hum with discussions of dollar figures and financial metrics. The phrase "eat what you kill" has firmly settled into the parlance of the profession, encapsulating the new ethos that has taken root.

As the commercial institutional logic gradually tightened its grip on professional services, it displaced firms' former emphasis on advising. The new commercial paradigm offered a different perspective on the profession, wherein professional success and value delivery became inseparable from actively serving clients. And, the more work undertaken for clients, the greater the perceived value delivered. With this logic, the sale of professional services became an occasion for celebration, elevating not only the expert professional service firms, but also their forward-thinking and innovative clients. Conversely, abstaining from engaging with professional service firms was often seen as a harbinger of complacency and a sign of falling behind the curve.

In Chapter 7, I contend that, more than any other group, professional service firms' employees find themselves uniquely susceptible to the transformative forces the commercial logic wields. Their identity is intricately intertwined with their work, with the two often becoming indistinguishable. Their waking hours, personal relationships, and sense of achievement revolve centrally around their professional accomplishments and career advancement. For professionals, their work is not just what they do, it is often who they are.

In the eighth chapter, I illuminate how, under enabling market conditions, the convergence of the commercial logic and identity transformation paves the way for supplier-induced demand to emerge. Biases play a significant role in this phenomenon. One such bias is the propensity for action. When faced with uncertainty about how to proceed, professional service firms tend to gravitate toward action. Action is perceived as the epitome of value delivery to clients. In contrast, inaction is seen as inertial and devoid of worth. It is crucial to note that this bias toward action diverges markedly from the traditional advisory logic, where refraining from action can be considered equally valuable. In this context, the decision not to reorganize, not to alter strategy, not to engage in litigation, or not to file for an initial public offering is often construed as creating value.

Imagine professional service firms as actors on a stage, driven by a deeply ingrained instinct to perform, to take action. This leads to a scenario in which a growing number of opportunities enter the consideration set of both the sellers and the buyers, leading to more opportunities being pursued. But here is the catch. As more opportunities come into play, it is inevitable that many of these opportunities are of questionable or lesser value. This problem becomes particularly salient when the fog of uncertainty rolls in, obscuring the problem, the desirable action, and the potential outcomes. And then comes the issue of compatibility. Often, opportunities are paired with solutions that are conveniently available in the professional service firms' sales repertoire, and thus are familiar to their employees. It's as if the answer was pre-decided, irrespective of the question. The end result? The quality of pursued opportunities and solutions diminishes.

The analysis of professional services through the lens of a changing institutional logic reveals that supplier-induced demand does not stem from service professionals engaging in cheating, unethical behavior, or deliberate deception of their clients. Rather, it arises from their pursuit of success and legitimacy as defined by the commercial institutional logic. It emerges as they actively embrace their professional identity and leverage their skills to promote their work, sincerely believing that doing so serves the best interests of their clients. Employees of professional service firms mostly adhere to the rules of the game. However, playing within the rules can, at times, yield disastrous consequences for their clients.

A discerning reader is sure to notice a recurring theme threading throughout this book. Supplier-induced demand does not rest solely on the shoulders of service providers; veritably, buyers also play a vital role in its emergence. A prevailing admission emerged through interviews with corporate executives: the problem also lies in their—the buyers'— incapacity to effectively engage with and manage professional service providers. In any transaction, a dyadic agreement exists for the exchange of goods and services. Therefore, understanding supplier-induced demand and its resolution must at least begin by acknowledging the roles both sellers and buyers play.

Take, for example, the expectations clients harbor regarding professionals' expertise, their presumed omniscience. Such expectations socialize and even pressure service professionals into levels of confidence in their recommendations that would otherwise be unmerited. Alternatively, clients may bring service professionals on-site merely to signal to investors that appropriate actions are being taken, to assuage the concerns of their board members, or to validate executives' decisions. Service professionals therefore find themselves at a client's office without a substantive purpose. In such situations, the convergence of enabling conditions and the ramifications of commercial logic make it especially likely that professional service firms and their clients would consider actions of low or dubious value. And when shrouded in uncertainty and clouted by professionals' power, decisions based on experts' particularistic narratives are more likely to resonate and be embraced readily by buyers, even to their detriment.

THE IMPLICATIONS OF SUPPLIER-INDUCED DEMAND

Supplier-induced demand manifests in a multitude of guises, varying in significance. On the more benign end of the spectrum, we encounter what I classify as the weak form of supplier-induced demand:

organizations allocating resources to extraneous accounting checks, legal discovery, consulting research, or banking due diligence. In essence, this takes the shape of misdirecting time and money toward tasks that offer little intrinsic value. However, at the other end of the spectrum, which is far more consequential, we encounter more potent manifestations of supplier-induced demand—the strong form. In these cases, companies embark on mergers and acquisitions, engage in lawsuits, or instigate reorganizations that disrupt the natural flow of work, corrode employees' morale, and outright erode value.

Let me paint you a picture from my own experience. I once worked with a behemoth of the corporate world—a Fortune 500 company—as it was sliced and diced by a renowned consulting firm in a major reorganization project. The exercise was like a surgeon's scalpel, cutting through the fibers of the company, leaving roles, workflows, and even people rearranged or removed entirely. The emotional toll was immense; it was as if the soul of the company was being stitched up on the operating table. In an anonymous survey I administered, a manager shared the heartbreak in a simple, devastating sentence: "*I cried twice today.*"

A year on, I circled back, hungry to know the fruits of such labor. "What came out of this grand reorganization?" I asked eagerly. The response astounded me. One of the company's senior leaders replied, "*We don't know.*" I blinked. How could this be, after all this cost and trauma to the organization? But the answer came that another reorganization was already underway, courtesy of the same consulting firm. The irony was not lost on me. It was as if the solution to the chaos was more chaos. This is the smoke and mirrors of supplier-induced demand. It is a story of a never-ending cycle in which the very people brought in to solve problems might just be the ones writing their next paycheck.

Now, bear with me. It is possible that both surgeries were necessary, and that the double dose of corporate medicine was the recipe for a healthier, more vigorous enterprise. Perhaps the company needed more time to realize the benefits of the reorganizations. Or maybe the company would have been even worse off without them. This is the puzzle of supplier-induced demand: it is really difficult to pinpoint in individual cases. Performance in the knowledge-based realm of professional services can be as challenging to measure as the richness of a painting. Many professional services projects are customized and adapted to each client's specific context, making comparisons among projects challenging.

And once the dust settles, everyone involved—the buyers and sellers alike—has their reputations hanging in the balance, fueling narratives that justify the expense and the effort poured into the project. So, we live in a world where the outcomes of professional service work are murky, and there is a cacophony of competing voices trying to make sense of what they have witnessed. To evidence supplier-induced demand and to understand when and how it emerges, one needs to step back and look at the patterns across multiple instances of professional service work, which is what this book aims to do.

The consequences of supplier-induced demand reverberate with significance. On the one hand, supplier-induced demand perpetuates the misallocation and squandering of buyers' resources, dealing a blow to their growth potential and competitive advantage. On the other hand, it redirects the attention and intellectual prowess of some of our economy's brightest talents—professionals within service firms—toward superfluous and potentially detrimental pursuits. The welfare implications of diminished economic growth loom large, particularly when we contemplate the risk of supplier-induced demand spreading to other sectors within our ever-expanding knowledge-based, service-driven economy.

This lens of the commercial institutional logic through which we view the motivation for supplier-induced demand presents complex implications for both society and the economy. It presents a mixed message that simultaneously restores faith in human nature, while rendering the mitigation of supplier-induced demand an arduous task. One begins to realize the futility of seeking perfect contractual safeguards and incentives for professional service work or crafting yet another set of ethics guidelines. Fervent enthusiasts advocating for the regulation of professional services on par with markets for cigarettes or sugary snacks will find themselves equally disillusioned. It becomes abundantly clear that professional services, in and of themselves, possess the capacity to deliver value to the clients who avail themselves of such services.

Professional services are not inherently malevolent products. The empirical evidence set forth in this book suggests that companies often reap tangible benefits from engaging with professional service providers. The true challenge lies in discerning the precise circumstances under which this value is least likely to materialize, owing to the pervasive presence of supplier-induced demand.

THE ARGUMENT BASE

At this point, I would like to step away from supplier-induced demand for a moment and discuss the evidentiary base that enables me to advance the claims in this book. The argument in this book essentially rests on three pillars, each reinforcing the argument in its own unique way. First, I embark on a thorough exploration and synthesis of a substantial body of pertinent empirical research spanning multiple disciplines. As you venture deeper into this journey, you will learn in Chapter 2 about the intellectual origins of supplier-induced demand in healthcare economics and the intriguing parallels it shares with the studies of credence goods. In subsequent chapters, I weave together insights from social psychology, sociology, and neuroscience—wisdom that unveils how expertise molds influence and power dynamics and how the tendrils of uncertainty shape human behavior. Much of this conversation is anchored in scholarly work that has meticulously examined the evolution of professional service firms over the past few decades, shedding light on their changing role within the contemporary economy. The academic terrain covered in this book is thus extensive. In fact, as I pen this section, I contemplate the arguments that would convince my editor that each of the hundreds of academic citations woven throughout this book is indeed essential.

Second, I infuse a significant element of fieldwork into these pages. My curiosity about the phenomenon and the sheer amount of time it took for this project to gestate led me to conduct more than 80 semi-structured interviews with both buyers and sellers of professional services. These interviews spanned the domains of consulting, legal, and investment banking services. In other words, I spent substantial time listening to partners in professional service firms, who sell their firms' services, as well as senior executives from a range of organizations who procure those services. The insights I gleaned from these conversations are complemented by countless hours spent observing events involving buyers and sellers of professional services, ranging from industry conferences to professional service firm alumni gatherings and development seminars. In studying legal services, I had the opportunity to observe intellectual property litigation firsthand, witnessing the dynamic back-and-forth in the courtroom. I have similarly witnessed multiple meetings in which consultants pitched work and delivered results to clients. I hope you find that the insights from the fieldwork add concreteness to what otherwise could seem like rather abstract dynamics of interpersonal and interorganizational interaction. This fieldwork is also my attempt to peek into the underlying behavioral dynamics that may be difficult to discern with quantitative analyses alone.

This brings me to the third and final edifice of the argument. This book features a detailed econometric analysis of the consumption of legal services in the form of intellectual property litigation (Chapter 9). Using data on hundreds of companies, thousands of intellectual property litigation services providers, and thousands of lawsuits, I establish the presence of supplier-induced demand empirically, quantify its magnitude, and understand its boundary conditions. As I detail in Chapter 9, several factors make this setting attractive for exploring supplier-induced demand empirically. Like many professional service sectors, it satisfies the enabling market conditions for supplier-induced demand and has been subjected to the relentless influence of the commercial institutional logic. A particular advantage of this setting, however, is that—by tracking litigation outcomes at scale—I can better pin down the organizational outcomes of consuming legal services, and hence assess the impact of induced demand on the buyers. This, as you will see, is not always easily accomplished in the explorations of supplier-induced demand.

WHAT DO WE LEARN?

The empirical results in Chapter 9 present evidence of a strong form of supplier-induced demand in legal services. Not only do companies procure more litigation services under the influence of external service providers, but they also engage in litigation that carries a lower probability of winning. And yet, supplier-induced demand is not uniform. It reveals itself selectively, only under a specific set of circumstances. Even within the field of intellectual property legal services, known for its profound uncertainty akin to other professional domains, the influence of suppliers manifests only in situations where uncertainty about the outcome of legal action reaches unusually high levels.

Moreover, supplier-induced demand appears to originate not merely from any service provider. Rather, it stems from those legal service providers that have regular contact with potential buyers. And, while capturing the exact instances of face-to-face contact empirically constitutes a tall order, I proxy it through the geographic proximity between the buyers and sellers. In other words, a distance that can be reasonably covered with a routine commute becomes our guide. It's the sweet spot that allows for frequent contact between buyer and seller, paving the way for the emergence of supplier-induced demand.

What emerges is a mesmerizing tango of possibilities. On the one hand, the buyers seeking guidance on potential opportunities or the best course of action find it easier to reach out to co-located providers. The proximate sellers, on the other hand, find it easier to take on an active role, reaching out and offering opportunities. It could be an investment banking firm extending a hand to a private company, enticingly whispering that they are ready for an initial public offering. Or a legal services firm taking the initiative, proactively suggesting that the time has come to enforce their client's intellectual property rights in a court of law. These conversations extend beyond the initial instance of purchase; they also influence how much of a given service should be consumed. For example, should a given lawsuit or reorganization continue? And for how long?

Proximity thus enables influence. When buyers and sellers of professional service firms are in close physical proximity, conversations are likely to be more frequent and face-to-face, even extending into social settings. These conversations have the potential to establish or strengthen long-lasting relationships between companies and their professional service providers. Within this nexus of frequency and intimacy, the pernicious effects of the commercial institutional logic and new professional identity come into play, leading to supplier-induced demand. The paradox lies in that the relational mechanisms, which are effective in preventing opportunistic pursuits and fraud, inadvertently create opportunities for supplier-induced demand by creating robust channels for influence.

If you are among the intrepid souls willing to venture deep into the data tables, you will discover some fascinating regularities. First, companies surrounded by external legal service providers in close physical space display a heightened propensity to initiate litigation. Relatedly, if a company chooses a proximate legal service provider as its counsel in litigation, the lawsuit that ensues tends to last longer and hence becomes more expensive for the company. Second, and consequentially, the increase in frequency and duration of litigation that accompanies working with proximate providers of legal services is not necessarily accompanied by legal success. On the contrary, companies embroiled in lawsuits under these circumstances are more likely to find themselves on the losing end. Taken together, these findings constitute evidence of the strong form of supplier-induced demand, in which excessive consumption of professional services can prove to be detrimental to the buyers. Importantly, these effects appear only in those situations when there is a particularly high level of uncertainty about the outcome of litigation.

WHY DON'T BUYERS (AND SUPPLIERS) LEARN?

At this juncture, readers may wonder why buyers fail to grasp the concept of supplier-induced demand and abstain from it. Considering the lack of benefits and the potential harm it poses, why does this phenomenon persist? After all, both individuals and organizations have the capacity to learn from past experiences and avoid repeating mistakes. One would naturally assume that armed with their ability to learn and adapt, organizations would effectively recognize and address the pitfalls associated with supplier-induced demand. However, as I elaborate in Chapter 10, the seemingly logical process of learning often stumbles when confronted with the practical realities of professional service work.

Within the realm of knowledge-based endeavors, evaluating outcomes and establishing a clear link between those outcomes and the work of professional service providers proved to be exceptionally challenging. In Chapter 10, I delineate the indispensable prerequisites that organizations must meet to learn effectively from experience. Among these prerequisites, two factors stand at the forefront: the presence of many comparable cases and clear performance feedback. However, the nature of professional service firms' work poses challenges to meeting these conditions.

Professional service projects are often sporadic or tailored to individual clients, thereby limiting the pool of comparable cases. Furthermore, each project is carried out within a distinct set of organizational and economic circumstances, which tend to evolve throughout the course of service delivery. The multitude of confounding variables is staggering, encompassing elements such as the fluctuating economic conditions and regulatory landscape, personnel turnover, the strategic actions of competitors, and the level of employee commitment to the work at hand. As demonstrated in the previous example involving a Fortune 500 company and as I will explain in more detail later in the book, it becomes exceptionally challenging to identify instances of supplier-induced demand due to these reasons. Consequently, causal ambiguity ensues, making it arduous to ascertain the precise forces that contributed to the observed outcomes.

In these situations, a multitude of explanations—competing narratives—vie for dominance. When a merger falls short of expectations, should we attribute it to a flawed acquisition decision or the acquirer's mismanagement of the integration process? If a lawsuit fails to achieve the desired outcome, should we question the decision to litigate or the choice of legal representation? Even the notions of what defines success and meeting expectations are subject to debate. It becomes incredibly challenging to envision the alternative scenarios that might have unfolded in the absence of a given acquisition or a lawsuit. For example, is it conceivable that a poorly executed acquisition still succeeded by depriving a primary competitor of the acquired company's vital resources? Or did a lost lawsuit serve as a deterrent, dissuading future wrongdoers from risking litigation and draining their time and finances on legal battles?

In Chapter 10, we will also delve into the challenges involved in measuring the outcomes of knowledge-based work provided by professional service firms. These firms often find themselves caught between a proverbial rock and a hard place. On the one hand, clients dismiss narrow measurements, arguing that success in a specific program may be detrimental to broader organizational performance. On the other hand, clients resist broader performance metrics, voicing concerns that such measures might inadvertently credit professional service providers for work they did not undertake.

In the aftermath of professional service work, an intriguing clash of narratives is fueled further by our deep-seated inclination to rationalize our actions and make sense of the observed outcomes. Service professionals and the buyers of their services may unconsciously resist acknowledging that a lengthy and labor-intensive endeavor has resulted in disappointment. Sunk costs, potential damage to one's reputation, and the fear of regret upon admitting failure stand in the way of producing clear performance feedback. In such circumstances, the natural inclination is to seek ways to reframe questionable outcomes in a positive light or shift blame away from one's own skills, efforts, or foresight.

The scarcity of comparable cases magnifies the lack of reliable and consistent feedback, erecting a substantial hurdle in identifying and tackling supplier-induced demand. It is also clear that these dynamics, which impede effective organizational learning, do not exempt the sellers of such services. In fact, the peculiar nature of supplier-induced demand, defying easy outcome measurement in individual instances, makes its detection and hence learning from it a challenge for both providers and suppliers alike.

CONCLUSION

The book's core aim is to expose the covert forces that have surreptitiously reshaped the buyer–seller relationship within professional services. Its message, which is alarming, resonates on two crucial and interconnected levels. First, supplier-induced demand emerges as a pernicious phenomenon, permeating the very essence of professional services. However, it is not a universally occurring phenomenon; rather, it manifests under specific conditions that this book illustrates. Second, understanding the conditions and motivations that foster such demand confronts us with a disconcerting truth: our knowledge-based and service-oriented economy drives buyers and sellers closer to, rather than away from, the clutches of supplier-induced demand. Moreover, the inner workings of supplier-induced demand suggest that it has the potential to smother other sectors of our economy under its weight.

Readers should refrain from hastily passing judgment on the realm of professional services, for this book is no sweeping indictment. I implore both sides of the debate to move beyond clichés that dismissively claim professionals create no value or that view this book as an outright assault on professional services. Neither of these stances holds true when we examine the evidence presented. The reality is far more nuanced and intricate. Professional services, in their entirety, offer indispensable benefits to organizations. However, the argument and evidence in this book shed light on the conditions under which the tendrils of supplier-induced demand unfurl, leaving clients and our entire economy worse off.

Chapter 11 shows that delving into the underpinnings of supplier-induced demand holds the potential to advance our understanding of theories pertaining to organizational boundaries, economic agglomeration, and the social embeddedness of economic actions. For years, scholars studying organizational boundaries have grappled with the elusive task of deciding which activities should be kept within the confines of an organization and which should be outsourced to external entities. Within these pages, a fresh perspective emerges, suggesting that the presence of conditions conducive to supplier-induced demand should be a crucial consideration when ascertaining the scope of organizational activities to be retained in-house.

Similarly, this book offers insights into a key constraint on the growth of economic clusters, such as the renowned Boston cluster or the innovation hub of Silicon Valley. The expansion of these vibrant centers of economic activity is intertwined with the increasing density of local professional service providers. Law firms, investment banks, and consulting firms and marketing agencies gravitate to these epicenters. This book draws a crucial connection between this density and the heightened risks associated with supplier-induced demand. By doing so, the book sheds light on a previously unexplored factor that impacts the growth and sustainability of economic clusters.

Unraveling the ascent of the commercial institutional logic within professional services transcends the stereotypical portrayal of ambulance-chasing lawyers and the surface-level narrative of mere incentive conflicts. The origins of supplier-induced demand run much deeper, as the commercial institutional logic permeates the essence of professionals' identity. Within this identity, stimulating demand becomes synonymous with delivering value and attaining success, often blinding both buyers and sellers to the presence of supplier-induced demand.

In the final chapter, I advance an argument that, instead of relentlessly pursuing foolproof fraud-detection methods or adopting a blanket skeptical stance toward professional services, there are other avenues worth exploring. This alternative approach focuses on understanding the precise preconditions and motivations that give rise to supplier-induced demand—the very essence of this book—and actively working toward transforming them.

I therefore suggest several strategies that buyers, sellers, and policymakers can consider to mitigate both the conditions that enable supplier-induced demand and the widespread impact of the commercial institutional logic. Consider, for instance, the power imbalance favoring professional service providers. I advise companies to evaluate the outsourcing of work to external professional service providers not solely based on managing immediate costs but also by understanding that transferring complex tasks outside the company's boundaries can gradually result in the erosion of critical in-house expertise. This, in turn, exacerbates knowledge and power disparities between clients and professional service providers, perpetuating the cycle of supplier-induced demand. The empirical evidence presented in this book leads me to advocate for the retention of certain tasks in-house, particularly those that are heavily veiled by uncertainties regarding the identification of problems, opportunities, and suitable solutions. Moreover, I identify the elements of organizational cultures that would be particularly desirable to cultivate in professional service firms so that they can buffer these firms from the pernicious influence of the commercial institutional logic.

All this said, let me be clear about one thing. If you hope that these and other related recommendations will surely eradicate supplier-induced demand in every transaction, you may find yourself disillusioned. Detecting supplier-induced demand is challenging—often, none of the parties involved are even aware it is occurring. Nonetheless, by modifying the context—the very stage upon which supplier-induced demand occurs—we can significantly reduce its instances.

CHAPTER 2

Meet Supplier-Induced Demand

At the turn of the 20th century, the British Empire fought the infamous Boer Wars for influence in South Africa. In a stunning blow to its self-esteem and indomitable global image, Britain suffered losses that were more than four times as high as those of the Boers. The aftermath of the costly conflict, in which newspaper reporters and pundits were on the prowl for a scapegoat, revealed an unexpected culprit for the unprecedented losses: public health (Dwyer-Hemmings, 2018). As it turned out, British army recruits were in exceptionally poor health. They suffered from malnutrition, respiratory impairment, defective hearing, and ringworm. Notably, this dismal state of health persisted as 40% of recruits nationally—and up to 90% in some towns—were rejected from military service for health reasons (Clare, 2016; Gilbert, 1965). The alarm was raised as the ambitions of a global empire clearly could not rest on such an unfit military. In the words of David Lloyd George, the presiding British Prime Minister, "You cannot conduct an A1 empire with a C3 population" (The Times, 1919). The British government sprang into action, starting several public health reforms. It mandated compulsory medical checks for schoolchildren, introduced a national insurance program, and supplied free school meals for those who could not afford them.

Among these initiatives was the government's endorsement of the "focus of infection" theory. Advocated by several elite, influential surgeons, this theory stated that tonsils—the small lymph nodes in the back of one's mouth—could be blamed for many infectious diseases, as well as other physical ailments and even mental underdevelopment. When presented by influential medical minds, such as George Ernest Waugh, a Cambridge-educated leading British surgeon, the theory seemed convincing. The thought was that infectious pathogens entered the body through the mouth, nose, and throat. Then, the pathogens accumulated in the tonsils, were swallowed, and subsequently propagated infections (Grob, 2007). Removing the tonsils seemed a necessary step to ending infections.

The tonsillectomy, a surgical procedure to remove the tonsils, thus gained prominence and popularity within the medical community. In the first half of the 20th century, it was performed on more than 80,000 British schoolchildren annually (Dwyer-Hemmings, 2018). It was perceived as a quick, safe, and easy procedure, capable of preventing anything from tuberculosis and cervical adenitis to respiratory infections and bad breath. Over time, the surgery became more technologically advanced and was performed by designated medical specialists known as otorhinolaryngologists. Notably, the entire surgical subspecialty of otorhinolaryngology—head and neck surgery—owes its birth precisely to the proliferation of tonsillectomies in early 20th-century Britain.

It was at this time that James Allison Glover, a World War I veteran and a newly appointed medical officer to the British Ministry of Health, began to study epidemics in public schools. He systematically collected data on treatments related to nasopharyngeal diseases, tonsillitis, and tuberculosis. Largely in response to the rapidly increasing popularity of tonsillectomies, Glover initially discussed the impacts of removing the tonsils and adenoids during early childhood and adolescence in 1932 at the centenary meeting of the British Medical Association in London. He followed this initial discussion with several research papers, all of which culminated in the notorious 1938 report titled, "The Incidence of Tonsillectomy among Children," published in the *Proceedings of the Royal Society of Medicine* (Storey, 2004).

To the surprise of the medical community, Glover's (1938) report documented a more than four-fold variation in tonsillectomy rates among British school districts. In an extreme comparison, a child from Soke of

Peterborough was 19 times more likely to receive a tonsillectomy compared to one living in Cambridgeshire. Glover's (1938) most disturbing finding, however, was that such significant variation in tonsillectomies from school district to school district did *not* matter. It did not matter for the incidence of runny ears, enlarged glands, or rheumatism. It did not matter for the relative incidence of otitis, deafness, or enlargement of cervical glands. It did not even matter for school attendance: children from school districts with a high incidence of tonsillectomies were just as likely to miss school as those who had a lower incidence of such procedures. Fundamentally, thousands and thousands of medical procedures were performed for no discernable benefit. Even worse, tonsillectomies were routinely accompanied by severe post-operative pain, which was known to be a "significant clinical problem" (Dhiwakar, Clement, Supriya, & McKerrow, 2008: 1). And, removing one's tonsils could result in major bleeding, which in certain rare cases was fatal (Carmody, Vamadevan, & Cooper, 1982; Krishna & Lee, 2001; Tate, 1963).

How could this happen? How could these unnecessary medical procedures that caused patients discomfort, or worse, be performed in such high numbers? Glover's (1938) analysis showed that the observed variation could *not* be explained by factors such as nutrition, unemployment, living conditions, or climate. Moreover, this variation did not correlate with the variability in medical or general dental services in the region. Indeed, some of the most extreme differences in the frequency of the procedure occurred in *neighboring* school districts. Unable to find any other explanation for the observed variation, Glover (1938: 108) concluded that, "variations of medical opinion on the indications for operation" caused the geographic variation in procedure rates.

Indeed, limited medical knowledge surrounding the procedure at the time left much room for doctors' discretion. To begin, the function of the tonsils in the early 20th century was largely unknown to the medical profession. Some, however, were raising doubts that the tonsils' function was just as likely to be important and protective against disease as causative of disease (Dwyer-Hemmings, 2018; McGavin, 1903). One surgeon likened this to military defense, suggesting that "tonsils were to health what Gibraltar was to British security in the Mediterranean" (Dwyer-Hemmings, 2018: 221). A Kentucky physician in the early 20th century similarly observed, "I think the very fact that we do not know the physiology of the tonsil ought to make us a little chary about doing needless operations" (Grob, 2007: 385).

In an 1888 evaluation of more than 2,000 children, W. Franklin Chappell (1889) identified 1,200 abnormalities, which included 279 enlarged tonsils. While he recommended that children receive medical examinations between the ages of 6 and 14, he did not include any recommendations regarding tonsillectomy. Moreover, there was little agreement within the medical field concerning the difference between "diseased," "enlarged," and "normal" tonsils (Editorial, 1928). Thus, throughout the early to mid-20th century, the determination of the need for tonsillectomy—and thus its realization—depended largely on the individual physician and the ideology common to their hospital or geographic area.[1]

Even more striking is later evidence from the 1950s and 1960s: merely ending up in a hospital for unrelated reasons could have been a reason for a tonsillectomy. One study from the 1950s indicated that children who had undergone appendectomy were twice as likely to undergo tonsillectomy (Binning, 1950). Another study on a large sample of children

---

1. The variability in physicians' views about tonsil evaluation lingered. One British study conducted in the 1970s showed nine color slides of child tonsils to a group of 41 ear, nose, and throat specialists, pediatricians, and general practitioners and—unbeknownst to the physicians—showed two slides twice. The study found that the average ability of the physicians to provide the same assessment for the twice-shown slide was only a little larger than chance (Wood, Wong, & Theodoridis, 1972). Another study carried out around the same time observed how specialists examined children for tonsillectomy indicators and how they made their decisions. In this work, medical sociologist Michael Bloor (1976) found that the specialists seemed to agree on the three crucial indicators for a tonsillectomy, namely enlarged cervical glands, pitted tonsils, and a flushed appearance to the anterior pillars that flank the tonsils in the pharynx. Physicians differed widely, however, in how they interpreted and applied these indicators in clinical practice. Specifically, some doctors looked for all three indicators to be present, whereas others viewed just one indicator as sufficient evidence of tonsillar infection and for tonsil removal. One doctor's sole criterion was observing "multiple enlarged cervical glands" or at least "two cervical glands so enlarged that they were clearly visible on the surface of the neck" (Collins and Pinch, 2005: 70).

in Newcastle found that boys under four years of age were seven times more likely to have undergone tonsillectomy if they had been circumcised (Miller, Court, Walton, & Knox, 1960). Glover (1938) also raised questions about the disconcerting finding that the surgery was more likely to be done on children whose families could afford it: tonsillectomy rates for children from wealthy families were more than three times as high as those for children from poor families.

Glover's (1938) seminal report is widely credited as the first scientific study of what has become known as *supplier-induced demand* (Evans, 1974; Fuchs, 1978; Grytten & Sørensen, 2001; Watts, Shiner, Klauss, & Weeks, 2011). Supplier-induced demand (SID) broadly refers to the increase[2] in the demand for a service or a good associated with the discretionary influence by its supplier. Three key elements of SID deserve a closer look.

First and foremost, such demand is driven by the supplier of a particular service. This means that the buyers' decision to obtain a given service or good, or more of it, is largely influenced by the supplier of that service. This was the case in Glover's (1938: 1232) report, in which the decision to perform or not to perform a tonsillectomy was linked to the "variations of medical opinion." Later research linked such variations to a physician's location or the practice inclinations of the physician's peers (Folland, Goodman, & Stano, 2016). In applying this to professional service firms, the focus of this book, one can begin to wonder about the role investment bankers, lawyers, and consultants play in inducing acquisitions and divestitures, litigation, or reorganizations for their clients.

Second, the increase in demand for a particular good or service is unrelated to the buyer's needs. In this respect, one can further differentiate

---

2. Some conceptualizations of SID posit a "change" in demand rather than an "increase" in demand following supplier inducement (Fuchs, 1978). The reference to change allows for the possibility that a supplier may choose to influence the buyer toward a *reduction* in demand for their service, such as when service providers look to avoid being overworked or prefer leisure to income. Because there is no systematic empirical evidence supporting the reduction-in-demand hypothesis, such discussions stay at the level of theoretical intuitions and fall beyond the scope of this book.

between strong and weak forms of SID. Strong SID refers to situations when the purchase of a service makes the buyer worse off than if they had not bought that service. Strong SID, for example, would describe the 3% to 9% of the patients who experienced bleeding because of the tonsillectomy. Financial write-offs following acquisitions, lost litigation, or reorganizations that disrupt ongoing business activities and suppress employee morale could also show strong SID. Weak SID, in turn, relates to procuring services that have no discernable positive or negative effect on the buyer. In these situations, buyers spend resources—time, money, or people—on needless things. The weak form of SID thus applies to patients who experienced no bleeding or pain and lived through their tonsillectomy, but remained no more protected from infections than people who did not undergo the procedure. In markets for professional services, weak SID could describe companies that complete acquisitions, litigation, or reorganizations with no detectable difference in organizational outcomes, such as revenues, market valuation, operational performance, or personnel retention.

Of course, distinguishing between strong and weak SID is a matter of degree, and I encourage research analysts to use their knowledge of the empirical context to draw such distinctions. The overarching aim should be to demarcate the degree to which the buyer's outcomes have improved, worsened, or remained unchanged as a result of obtaining the service or commodity. Importantly, as I argue later in this chapter and throughout the book, understanding whether *a given transaction* constitutes SID in markets for professional services—whether strong or weak—can be a tall order, and these determinations can be convincing mainly, if not exclusively, in large-sample studies.

Finally, SID is motive-agnostic. It may be tempting for some readers to leap to conclusions regarding why SID occurs and even dwell on its possible ethical underpinnings (Labelle, Stoddart, & Rice, 1994). I encourage you to refrain from doing so. As I explain in Chapters 3–8, the antecedents of SID can be surprisingly complex and include factors such as the market's enabling characteristics and the prevailing institutional logic in professional services.

INTELLECTUAL ROOTS OF SUPPLIER-INDUCED DEMAND

Following Glover's (1938) path-breaking study, the intellectual roots of SID can be traced to healthcare economics. Subsequent research demonstrated that the procedure rates of tonsillectomies, prostatectomies, and hysterectomies or the hospitalization rates for medical issues, such as back problems, gastroenteritis, and heart failure, generally exhibited a large degree of geographic variation in terms of treatment rate and are related more to the supply of the physicians than the need for the service (Watts et al., 2011). In a closely related argument, sometimes referred to as Roemer's law, Milton Roemer (1961) stated, "a hospital bed built is a filled bed," suggesting that the supply of medical personnel and hospital beds increases the use of medical services. Furthermore, research focused on the role economic incentives play revealed that obstetricians are over 50% more likely to perform a Cesarean delivery in geographical areas that incentivized them more heavily than natural births (Bogg, Diwan, Vora, & DeCosta, 2016). Even the duration of infants' stays in neonatal intensive care units, rather than regular hospital beds, was linked to varying hospital payment rates (Shigeoka & Fushimi, 2014). All this work raised concerns about patients' consumption of unneeded and even harmful medical services.

A germane stream of research in economics popularized the term "credence goods," which are defined as goods or services for which the seller knows more than the consumer about the quality the consumer needs (Darby & Karni, 1973; Dulleck & Kerschbamer, 2006). In essence, credence goods markets are characterized by information and knowledge asymmetries, in which expert vendors sell to uninformed consumers (Balafoutas & Kerschbamer, 2020). Using the example of repair services, Michael Darby and Edi Karni (1973: 69) explained credence goods as follows: "A consumer cannot fully evaluate the repair of a malfunctioning durable good or human being, since he is unfamiliar with the intricacies and peculiarities of the particular machine. Due to lack of knowledge of the inputs of repair services required to maintain given flows of ultimate services from a commodity, the consumer must purchase both information and repair services." Subsequent research ascertained similar dynamics in retail markets for computer and automotive repairs, financial advisory and insurance services, as well as political discourses about public infrastructure projects (Anagol, Cole, & Sarkar, 2017; Bucher-Koenen & Koenen, 2015; Kerschbamer, Neururer, & Sutter, 2019; Schneider, 2012).

An astute reader is sure to grasp an insight that is foundational to understanding the workings of SID markets, namely that the sellers do not just sell a given service. They also act as an agent, expertly advising buyers whether there is a problem to be solved or whether a given service is necessary in the first place. This dual role of an agent and a seller constitutes a significant deviation from the foundational view of competitive markets, in which buyers know what they need and subsequently choose from various available providers (Arrow, 1963). We will return to this and other characteristics of markets that enable SID in Chapters 3–5.

An eerie parallel appears concerning contemporary legal, consulting, financial, or marketing services, which have evolved to deviate significantly from the classic blueprints of competitive markets. In modern-day markets for professional services, companies' needs are often not clearly defined. It is not uncommon for executives to struggle with questions such as, "Is yet another restructuring really necessary?" "Do we really need another debt offering?" "Is a sale to this acquirer truly in the best interest of the business?" "Are our patents strong enough to merit suing the alleged infringer?" or "Would yet another marketing campaign make a difference?"

In such questioning moments, executives often turn to service providers for expert guidance and advice. Notably, though, it is also customary for service providers to approach clients proactively with their experience, knowledge, and potential offerings. Indeed, professional service firms—such as those offering financial, consulting, or legal services—play a key advisory function for organizational buyers and frequently position it as a source of competitive differentiation. Professional service firms are thus increasingly blurring the line between a seller, who is expected to make money selling a service, and an agent, who is expected to advise a client as to whether the service is necessary in the first place. In this book, you will discover that the proliferation of the commercial institutional logic that reinforced this dual role in markets for professional services has become one of the key precursors of SID in this sector.

To be fair, establishing SID empirically in medical services proved to be a thorny endeavor. A typical research design involved regressing the per capita frequency of a given medical procedure on the density of the medical specialists performing the procedure by geographical areas. This is often referred to as an "aggregated" research design. In such an analytical approach, which is often cross-sectional, establishing a positive effect of the density of medical professionals on the frequency of the medical procedure would be interpreted as proof of SID.

The conclusions of this work, however, were frequently contested due to the absence of patient outcome data. Without this information, even if the frequency of a focal medical procedure covaries with the density of medical specialists performing it, it is unclear what that means. Are the patients in the areas with low concentrations of physicians *under-served* relative to their medical needs? Or are the patients in areas with high concentrations of physicians *overserved*, thus being induced to consume a given medical procedure in excess relative to their medical needs (Carmignani & Giacomelli, 2010; Labelle, Stoddart, & Rice, 1994)?

Aggregate studies often fail to account for the fact that the per capita provision of medical services may be correlated with other factors, such as income, taste, education, or insurance coverage. The resultant omitted variable bias casts doubt on the validity of empirical inferences. Using geographic areas as units of analysis further invites measurement-error criticism because both patients and physicians can cross administrative borders in the consumption and delivery of medical services (Liu & Mills, 2007; Wilensky & Rossiter, 1983). In a comical variation of critiquing aggregated research designs, David Dranove and Paul Wehner (1994) found that variations in the regional supply of obstetricians induced the demand for childbirth, clearly an impossible outcome.

Moreover, research on SID has been criticized for the absence of clear theoretical assumptions and rigorous theorizing (Mohammadshahi, Yazdani, Olyaeemanesh, Akbari Sari, Yaseri, & Emamgholipour Sefiddashti, 2019). Some scholars have lamented the fact that many conceptualizations of SID have failed to systematically address the duality of sellers as agents and the corresponding knowledge and information asymmetries (Evans, 1974). Others have questioned the implicit assumptions about the target income suppliers are aiming to attain or maintain via SID (Folland, Goodman, & Stano, 2016). Some have puzzled over whether SID could translate into a change in the price of the offered services, rather than volume, and how consumers could perceive it in different contexts (Rizzo & Blumenthal, 1996). Yet others have been flummoxed by whether demand is knowingly induced, and what it could mean for the suppliers' morality (Labelle, Stoddart, & Rice, 1994).

Considering these critiques, this book aims to advance our understanding and rigor in studying SID. First and foremost, in the context of professional services, this book seeks to develop a robust theoretical conceptualization of SID. In doing so, it takes a deep dive into exploring the complex set of enabling conditions for SID. Second, this book applies a disaggregated company-level and relationship-level research design to studying SID in the context of firms' use of legal services. In this design, I track the propensity of a given company to consume intellectual property (IP) litigation services while controlling for an entire slate of the company's observable characteristics, such as size, profitability, and technological capabilities, all of which can affect the company's use of professional litigation services. I similarly account for a set of characteristics that describe the nature of the relationship between the company (the buyer of litigation services) and the intellectual property litigation external counsel (the provider of services). Finally, the data used in this book enable me to capture the duration and outcomes of the resultant litigation, thus getting substantially closer to understanding whether and under what circumstances the procured services are beneficial or detrimental to the buyers.

ARE SUPPLIER-INDUCED DEMAND AND GUMMY WORMS THE SAME?

Skeptics might wonder if the conversation about SID differs in any way from the discussion of marketing consumer products that are known to be detrimental to buyers. Think tobacco products, sugar-packed sodas, or neon-colored gummy worms. It is important to recognize that SID in the field of professional services constitutes a fundamentally different problem.

Most centrally, the services offered by professional service firms are *not* inherently detrimental to the buyers. The essence of these services—unlike that of tonsillectomies—is functional and value-adding. Mergers, acquisitions, and divestitures sold by investment banks serve an important function for reallocating capital investments and managerial control, which is essential for running more efficient and effective enterprises. External lawyers' litigation services perform a critical function of upholding property and other types of rights when the germane law is incomplete or when market mechanisms of dispute resolution are inadequate. And the rapid pace of changes in technology, consumer preferences, and competitive landscapes necessitates organizational change and operational improvements in which organizational consultants excel.

As a result, when buying professional services, companies hardly get the clarity of the detriment that comes with purchasing a pack of cigarettes. Quite the opposite: in most cases, there is an expectation of creating value. And professional firms' marketing efforts can be targeted at proactively uncovering and responding to clients' needs. By contrast, SID is unrelated to the buyers' needs and can be outright harmful. A major complication in this respect is that when buying a specific professional service or, in many cases, after the purchase is made, the buyer might have difficulty conclusively establishing the value it received from the supplier. Often, when viewed at the level of a discrete individual offering, rather than in large samples, it is plain impossible to establish SID. Indeed, few companies have the luxury of running controlled experiments, in which they could evaluate the outcomes of a service intervention to the counterfactual of what could have been, had the service not been procured, all of this while holding all other circumstances constant.

Consider in this respect that many services that professional service firms offer are customized to a particular enterprise, which axiomatically suppresses their comparability to offerings obtained by other companies. Even if such services are not customized, they are delivered in the unique context of a specific enterprise, with its peculiar history, culture, resources, and employee competencies. Under these circumstances, evaluating the outcomes of an offering relative to those of similar others becomes a Herculean task in the absence of large samples. It becomes equally challenging to assess whether the company gained or lost from the engagement: results that one could be tempted to attribute to a specific service intervention in many cases could be explained by a variety of confounding factors that occurred at the time. As experienced executives will tell you, ordinarily, there is no shortage of narratives explaining poor acquisition outcomes, which range from the validity of the decision itself, to its execution, to the changes in the market environment that coincided with the transaction.

Similarly, when asked how he evaluated whether an intellectual property litigation an external counsel steered was successful, a chief legal counsel commented that it is difficult to use any external benchmarks because "everything is so one-off." My fieldwork revealed that, in the absence of concrete measurement of outcomes, in-house counsel often rely on proxies in evaluating the quality of the work an external provider renders. Such proxies could include, in the opinion of one in-house legal counsel, whether the opinions are well-written so that "the opinion shows up clearly at the top of the document" or, in the words of another, whether "they [external counsel] make it easy for me to then go and implement that thing if it is actually necessary." Another in-house counsel commented on preferring documents that are not riddled with typos. These are all proxies of someone's expertise and competence, but they are hardly helpful in evaluating the quality of the legal advice received and of the ensuing legal outcomes.

One important element of SID, therefore, especially in professional service contexts, is that for a given transaction, the buyer often would not know if it has bought a "lemon." As I will explain in Chapters 7 and 8, the service providers may not always recognize a lemon sale, either. I am tempted to draw a parallel in this respect to the escalation of commitment. Escalation of commitment is a potent decision-making bias that causes leaders to continue to invest, often in incremental steps, in a failing course of action (Staw, 1997; Staw & Ross, 1989). This bias helps understand leaders' ongoing investment in failing research and development projects, underperforming personnel, and losing wars. Adding money to research and development (R&D) efforts, giving more time and different assignments to a struggling employee, or putting more military boots on the ground can be addictive.

And yet, while the escalation of commitment has been widely established in empirical and experimental research, it is often unknowable at the level of an individual project. Indeed, it is quite possible that yet another small R&D tranche will turn around a project and result in a breakthrough invention, that another three months of different assignments will prove the value of an underperforming employee, or that yet another infusion of troops will help a struggling nation at war attain its military objectives. The decision-makers just do not know for sure and do not recognize their actions as the escalation of commitment.[3] The same is often true for SID. So, unlike merely advising people to stay away from products that cause lung cancer or diabetes, the challenge requires understanding the conditions under

---

3. For a concrete example of the escalation of commitment, consider the dollar auction (Bazerman & Neale, 1992; Shubik, 1971). In this auction, participants bid for a $20 bill. The rules of the action are such that bidding starts at one dollar and continues in one-dollar increments; participants cannot jump-bid or top their own bid. The auction's winner gets the $20 bill, the runner-up pays his or her bid to the auctioneer. As the two highest-bidding participants get to the $19 and $20 bids, it becomes clear that the runner-up is incentivized to bid another dollar to try to regain $20, which creates an escalatory dynamic. Note the incremental nature of each investment decision, which makes escalation so enticing. By spending just one extra dollar, the bidder hopes to get $20 back. In my experience, participants easily get to a $50 price tag for a $20 bill, or even higher. When you see someone bidding $50 for a $20 bill, the escalation of commitment becomes obvious. It is not nearly as obvious in real-life situations.

which SID is most likely to occur and the motivations that drive it. It subsequently requires designing a set of organizational and market interventions that, on average, are likely to diminish the likelihood of SID and its negative effects, while not ruling out its occurrence in any given transaction.

SUPPLIER-INDUCED DEMAND AND ITS IMPLICATIONS FOR ORGANIZATIONS AND MARKETS

Understanding and learning to counteract SID carries profound implications for organizations and markets. Three implications are central. First, there are significant implications for the utilization of experts' capacity and social welfare. The paradigm of SID heightens concerns that a non-trivial share of professional services is wasteful or outright detrimental to buyers. In healthcare, for example, experts estimate that between 10% and 30% of all practices result in little to no benefit to the patient and can lead to poor patient outcomes due to adverse events resulting from treatments or unwarranted secondary tests, with potential for overtreatment of incidental findings (Grimshaw et al., 2020; Grol & Grimshaw, 2003).

Moreover, professional service markets, as I explain here, are moving *toward* rather than *away from* enlarging SID. Not only can SID undermine value for the buyer and limit its growth potential but also, when considered at scale, can result in inefficient use of economic resources and human capital, thus adversely affecting economic development and social welfare. Moreover, SID can coexist with unmet needs for professional services, as professional service firms' energy and resources are diverted from more pressing client needs. In extreme cases, suspicions of SID can contribute to widespread skepticism regarding professional services, prompting some buyers to either withdraw entirely from the market or significantly increase transaction costs in search of alternatives.

Second, the SID lens carries significant implications for theories of organizational boundaries. The choices of what organizational

activities should remain inside versus outside organizational boundaries constitute some of the most vexing questions in organization
theory and strategy. The lens of SID suggests there could be an entire category of costs and risks in organizational boundary choices
that are not accounted for by classic organizational perspectives on
transaction costs (Williamson, 1975, 1981, 1985), social embeddedness
(Gulati, 2007; Gulati & Nickerson, 2008; Uzzi, 1997), or organizational
resources (Barney, 1999; Lavie, 2006; Pfeffer & Salancik, 1978) and
that can have profound implications for organizational outcomes and
economies at large. One of the suggestions emerging from this lens is
that—in the presence of enabling conditions and motivations to induce
demand (detailed in Chapters 3–5)—buyers will be well-advised to consider absorbing the known transaction costs and move at least some of
the activities performed by professional service firms in-house. More
broadly, this perspective can spur organizational research and practice into considering the risks and consequences of SID when assessing
choices pertaining to vertical integration and the scope of organizational
activities conducted in-house.

Finally, one of the central arguments of this book, explored in detail in
Chapter 8, suggests that SID is particularly likely to occur with relationships where buyers and suppliers are closely located in physical space.
Propinquity helps explain the continuity of contact between buyers and
suppliers, in which it is easier for buyers to seek professional advice
and for suppliers to offer unsolicited services. In high-uncertainty situations, it is precisely such continuity of contact that results in SID.
This book therefore shows how companies can suffer from being in
close geographic proximity to the providers of specialized services. Because professional service firms tend to accompany agglomerations of
producers (Padgett & Powell, 2012; Saxenian, 1994; Suchman & Cahill,
1996), examining SID can therefore help uncover new constraints on the
viability and growth of economic clusters and industrial districts.

This book is situated in the context of professional service firms
interacting with organizational buyers. "Professions" are traditionally
defined as vocations based on applying a specific body of higher-
education knowledge, bound by professional norms or a shared code

of conduct (Abbott, 1988; Løwendahl, 2005).[4] Professional service firms, therefore, are described as knowledge-intensive organizations whose offerings include customized applications of highly specialized information and knowledge under the constraints of professional norms (Broschak, 2015; Greenwood, Li, Prakash, & Deephouse, 2005; Løwendahl, 2005). As such, professional service firms include purveyors of legal, accounting, management consulting, technology consulting, engineering consulting, insurance brokers, marketing and public relations, architectural, actuarial, computer design and software, information system and computer science consulting, as well as specialized design services (Løwendahl, 2005). Collectively, they comprise a massive share of the global economy and are expected to grow to seven-and-a-half trillion US dollars—roughly the combined size of present-day French, Indian, and United Kingdom economies—by 2026 (TBRC, 2022).

Moreover, the dynamics analyzed here are likely to extend far beyond professional services obtained by for-profit and nonprofit organizations. For example, the enabling forces of SID described in this book may well apply to the transactions requiring complex subassemblies and subcomponents or the provisions of specialized computer code. They may be equally applicable to individual consumers obtaining financial or medical advice, insurance, or education services. And they permeate the public sector, such as in governmental purchases of military services and equipment, infrastructure, public education, or healthcare services. Governments, after all, are collections of organizations in the form of various agencies, departments, and ministries (Haveman, 2022), which routinely transact with professional service firms and highly specialized suppliers.

One key argument made here, therefore, is that SID constitutes a significant force in the contemporary economy, and it is therefore imperative to understand the conditions under which it is most likely

---

4. The reference to "professions" in defining professional service firms is malleable: for example, some scholars question whether management consulting unequivocally qualifies as a profession, while not disputing the fact the management consulting firms sell professional services (Løwendahl, 2005).

to occur. The other, and perhaps a more concerning argument, is that the global economy has been evolving and continues to evolve toward, rather than away from, SID.

Three key dynamics account for this evolutionary trajectory. Organizational scholarship has aptly chronicled the first of these dynamics as the "shrinking core and expanding periphery" of organizations (Gulati & Kletter, 2005). This metaphor refers to organizations' moving many specialized services and complementary offerings outside organizational boundaries, focusing on the leaner core of organizational activities offered in-house. In addition to relying on legal, auditing, consulting, strategy, and financial advice from outside professional service providers, companies are shifting the locus of control over information technology, marketing, lobbying, commercial real estate, insurance, privacy, and cyber security services to reside in outside experts' hands. In parallel, many professional service firms have burgeoned into global powerhouses, surpassing the size and scale of major corporations. For example, taken together, PricewaterhouseCoopers and KPMG—leading tax and audit advisory firms—have grown to employ well over 500,000 individuals. Management consulting firms, such as Deloitte and Accenture, now boast of more than 400,000 and 700,000 employees, respectively. By comparison, an average Fortune 500 company employs just about 58,000 people (Fortune, 2022). The size and scale of operations of global law firms have similarly skyrocketed (Galanter & Palay, 1990).

In a parallel trend, companies' R&D, manufacturing, and marketing efforts are increasingly shared with scores of other companies, which led to the emergence of complex procurement and alliance networks supporting entire ecosystems of offerings (Gulati, 2007; Lavie, 2006; Sytch, Kim, & Page, 2022). The development of such ecosystems, in turn, created an endogenous push for developing even more complex offerings that rely on bringing together the dispersed expertise of the involved companies (Gulati & Kletter, 2005; Shipilov & Gawer, 2020). Professional service firms have prominently stepped in to steer the production and delivery of such offerings.

Second, specialized offerings are becoming increasingly complex, and their applications, inner workings, and outcomes are becoming harder and harder to assess for non-specialized buyers. The expertise gap between the sellers and the buyers will only continue to widen as sellers grow to incorporate highly specialized talent, volumes of data and sophisticated machine learning and statistical techniques, natural language processing and computational linguistics, and artificial intelligence and computer simulations. Consider an automobile driver's seat, which many of us may view as a rather simple commodity. It has evolved into an extremely complex product with haptics that can alert the driver with vibrations to lane departures or impending collisions, built-in massage, heating and cooling, or position memory read off the entering key fob. As such, a seat can have up to 450 different configurations, which requires deep engineering expertise and multiple computer chips. The seat has therefore evolved into a heavily distributed product with hundreds of subassemblies and specialized suppliers needed before it is finally shipped to the likes of General Motors or BMW.

Third, the rising complexity of the offerings, whose nature may be difficult for non-experts to understand, and the dynamism of the marketplace collectively contribute to the high and rising uncertainty about the relevance of some of these offerings. In our knowledge-based economy, it is becoming increasingly difficult to say with confidence what the problem is, how best to solve it, and how to evaluate the applied solution.

As I explain in detail in Chapters 3–5, these preconditions—coupled with the changes in the dominant institutional logic (Chapters 6 and 7) guiding professionals' work—work together to enable SID. This book, therefore, is as much an observation of SID as it is a call to action to avert the emergence of the influence-based economy, in which demand is driven by sellers' discretion rather than by buyer's needs. I therefore encourage future research and policy not only to follow suit in understanding and measuring SID, but also to drive organizational and policy change to mitigate it.

PROLOGUE: THE QUIETUS OF TONSILLECTOMIES

A 1952 editorial in the *Journal of the American Medical Association* marked the end of the focus-of-infection theory, which was responsible for the spread of tonsillectomies. It said that "many patients with diseases presumably caused by foci of infection have not been relieved of their symptoms by removal of the foci, many patients with these same systemic diseases have no evident focus of infection, and foci of infection are as common in apparently healthy persons as in those with disease." By the 1980s, both public and professional opinion vocally condemned the tonsillectomy procedure as a "dangerous fad" (Dwyer-Hemmings, 2018: 217). These days, medical professionals understand that tonsils form an important part of the human immune system, serving as early warning signs to fight infection. Located near the entrances to breathing passages, the tonsils detect the bacteria or viruses that may be absorbed into the bloodstream when humans breathe. When this occurs, the immune system is triggered to create antibodies to fight any potential infection (Collins & Pinch, 2005). This shift in medical understanding and public perception was catalyzed, in large part, by the work of James Alison Glover.

CHAPTER SUMMARY

Supplier-induced demand refers to the demand generated by the discretionary influence of the supplier, which is unrelated to the buyer's needs. In the weak form of supplier-induced demand, procuring an additional service may result in no change in the buyer's outcome relative to not doing so; in the strong form, the buyer may be left worse off. The intellectual origins of supplier-induced demand can be traced back to healthcare, where James Alison Glover, in the 1930s, uncovered evidence that the frequency of tonsillectomies—surgical procedures to remove tonsils from one's throat—varied greatly across different school districts and depended on the surgeons' discretion. Disturbingly, higher rates of tonsillectomy did not translate into improved health outcomes for schoolchildren. Studying supplier-induced demand in professional services has profound implications for organizations and markets. This is because the economy is moving toward, rather than away from, a higher level of supplier-induced demand, which can profoundly impact our understanding of managerial control, vertical integration, and the economics of agglomeration.

CHAPTER 3

Uncertainty

STRUCTURE AND AGENCY

Where does supplier-induced demand (SID) come from? Let me pause on the general for a moment, before dwelling on the specific. It will hardly surprise the reader that the comprehensive conceptions of social action involve the joint consideration of social actors—with their individual attributes, abilities, and motivations—and the surrounding social context. The surrounding social context can refer to the observable actions of others, social and physical structures interlinking people, or the institutions and norms guiding how people interact with one another. For example, something as fundamental as the decision to marry and the choice of a marital partner has been explained by people's economic needs (Bulcroft & Bulcroft, 1993) and specific partner preferences (Chiappori, Salanié, & Weiss, 2017). Notably, it has also been explained by the social networks in which people are embedded (Gopalkrishnan & Babacan, 2007), the prevailing social norms and legal regulations (Scott, 2000), or the mere geographic proximity to eligible marital partners (Bossard, 1932).

In sociological research and its intellectual descendants, the dualism of social actors and the surrounding context is often discussed under the rubric of agency and structure (Giddens, 1984; Sewell, 1992).[1]

1. The exact conceptions of structure and agency vary across theoretical perspectives. For Anthony Giddens (1984), structures broadly incorporate formal and informal societal rules that guide action and combine material and nonmaterial resources that affect social interactions and the distribution of power in social systems. And agency is viewed as action,

This research has gradually evolved from the conceptions of "oversocial-ized social action" (Granovetter, 1985: 483) and "rigid causal determin-ism" (Sewell, 1992: 2), in which structure is given nearly unconditional primacy over agency,[2] to a more deliberate consideration of the so-cial actors' abilities, resources, and motivations analyzed alongside the constraints and opportunities engendered by social structures (Gulati & Srivastava, 2014). Examples of attending to both agency and struc-ture can be found in network research that considers both structural constraints and actors' motivations in investigating network dynam-ics (Ahuja, 2000; Sytch, Tatarynowicz, & Gulati, 2012) or research that explicitly calls for attention to individual personality characteristics in examining the returns to social capital (Burt, 2022). Such dualism also appears in organizational theorists' unveiling of organizational and in-dividual actors' significant discretion when interfacing with legal and regulatory systems. Exemplifying such discretion, organizations strate-gically and purposefully shop for favorable legal jurisdictions, influence legal adjudicators and regulators to obtain advantageous decisions, and even shape the favorable regulations themselves (Edelman, Uggen, & Erlanger, 1999; Gao & McDonald, 2022; Rao, Yue, & Ingram, 2011; Sytch & Kim, 2021).

Psychological research has similarly upheld the importance of both the individual and the social context in explaining an array of ac-tions and outcomes. For example, the classic ability–motivation–opportunity framework used to understand action and its ensuing

---

independent of the motivations underlying it. In later network research, which drew inspi-ration in part from Gidden's (1984) reasoning, structures were conceptualized as concrete patterns of relationships interconnecting social actors, and agency was viewed as the en-actment and change of those structures by purposeful, intentional agents (Ahuja, Soda, & Zaheer, 2012; Nohria & Eccles, 1992: 13; Tatarynowicz, Sytch, & Gulati, 2016). In institu-tional research, structures are often viewed as entrenched cognitive and cultural schemas that could be enacted and contested by agentic social actors (Benford & Snow, 2000; Rao, 2008; Thornton, Ocasio, & Lounsbury, 2012).

2. Examples of this work could involve new institutional research (DiMaggio & Powell, 1983; Meyer & Rowan, 1977) or earlier conceptions of social and organizational action embedded in social structures (Burt, 1982, 1992; Lorrain & White, 1971). For example, Ronald S. Burt (1992: 4, 36), in his influential statement on how network structures shape individuals' pri-vate advantage, argued that an individual's "physical attributes are a correlate, not a cause of competitive success" and treated motivation and opportunity "as one and the same."

outcomes considers actors' abilities or capacity to perform an action, motivation to do so, and contextual factors that may enable or inhibit opportunities for such action (Blumberg & Pringle, 1982; Siemsen, Roth, & Balasubramanian, 2008; Sterling & Boxall, 2013). Such views evolved from the gradual coalescence of industrial and social psychology. While industrial psychology has understood individual outcomes as a function of selection and training that facilitates individuals' capacities to perform, social psychology research has highlighted the notion of motivation in performance and the role that social context plays (Siemsen, Roth, & Balasubramanian, 2008). The framework of ability, motivation, and opportunity has been broadly applied in understanding consumer choice (MacInnis, Moorman, & Jaworski, 1991), organizational decision-making (Wu, Balasubramanian, & Mahajan, 2004), harnessing and activating social and human capital (Adler & Seok-Woo, 2002), and knowledge management (Argote, McEvily, & Reagans, 2003). For example, consumer choice could be dissected through the consumer's ability to process the content of an advertisement, which could be aided by brand familiarity, and by their motivation to process the information. At the same time, consumers are constrained by the surrounding distractions that can shape the time and attention they can devote to a given ad (MacInnis, Moorman, & Jaworski, 1991).

While the diverse research streams just cited vary widely in their intellectual ancestry, levels of analyses, methodologies, assumptions, and terminology, the overarching focus is similar. Skilled, motivated actors navigate the world in which their actions can be enabled or constrained by the context in which they take place. Of course, the intellectual appeal of the agency–structure dichotomy could be deceptively simple. Anthony Giddens (1984), for example, brought to light the complex duality of structure and action, in which structures are produced and reproduced by reflexive individuals under the constraints of the structures themselves. This meant that neither structure nor agency could exist independently of the other (Gulati & Gargiulo, 1999; Gulati, Sytch, & Tatarynowicz, 2012; Sytch, Tatarynowicz, & Gulati, 2012). Empirically, this makes it a formidable challenge to isolate the impact of surrounding structures and institutions on action from potential forces. Similarly, it is often taxing in psychological research to tease apart ability, motivation, and opportunity. For example, how accurately one perceives the structure of social relationships could be explained by an individual's ability to observe relationships, one's motivation to do so, or by the quality of the information the individual receives from network connections (Casciaro, 1998; Casciaro, Carley, & Krackhardt, 1999; Yu & Kilduff, 2020).

At the risk of oversimplification, consider the saga of Elizabeth Holmes, the former CEO of the startup company Theranos. The startup engaged in inimitable deception and fraud: Theranos raised more than $400 million in investments and reached a $9 billion valuation, all on a non-functioning blood-testing product. Holmes, the face of the company and its key decision-maker, was sentenced to more than 11 years in prison for playing a central role in defrauding investors. This raises the question of what, exactly, precipitated her lies and deception? Is it her flawed morality coupled with the insatiable pursuit of wealth, status, and power? Is it the opportunity to make undetectable mistakes and exert influence, enabled by uninvolved and uninformed company board and investors?[3] Or is it the culture of Silicon Valley that normalizes entrepreneurial deception as exaggerated promises to customers and investors, pressuring entrepreneurs to "fake it 'til you make it"? Such a normative environment exceedingly rewards the "makers," letting the "fakers" painlessly move on to the next entrepreneurial opportunity (Carreyrou, 2018).

I do not claim to resolve the perennial person-versus-environment puzzle in this book with respect to understanding SID. Far from it. In fact, my data will not allow me to quantitatively pin down professionals' exact motivations underlying SID. Any empiricist will quickly recognize that as a Herculean undertaking. In setting up this part of the argument, however, I will instead rely on insights from my fieldwork,

---

3. In the words of Rupert Murdoch, who occupied a peculiar place in this scandal as both an investor in Theranos and an owner of the *Wall Street Journal* (the publication that was ultimately responsible for revealing Theranos's deception), "Of course it was fraud . . . But I only have myself to blame for not asking a lot more questions. One of a bunch of old men taken in by a seemingly great young woman! Total embarrassment" (Weaver, 2022).

which involved more than 80 semi-structured interviews with buyers and sellers of professional services, and extant research on professional services. This said, a disciplined understanding of how professionals and the buyers of their services interact within the mutually created work context is necessary. Developing such an understanding will not only help guide future research but also help develop effective countermeasures to SID.

Understanding both the person and their broader socio-professional milieu leads us to understand SID as a complex phenomenon that emerges from the combination of enabling market conditions and the motivations of the involved actors. This perspective helps us see when and under what circumstances SID is most likely to arise, pointing to the market conditions and institutional logics that can enable or inhibit it. Such an understanding curbs the unsubstantiated criticism that *all* professional services are worthless or value-destroying, just as it attenuates the unbridled enthusiasm about the role professional services play in the contemporary economy. This perspective similarly reveals the complexity of motivations behind SID, casting major doubt on whether professionals' blunt opportunistic pursuits are to be blamed. It also helps understand the role buyers play—yes, buyers—in driving and sustaining SID. Furthermore, it lays out a clearer foundation for organizational and policy remedies to counteract the influence-based economy. My hope, therefore, is that this multifaceted perspective can help guide future research on influence dynamics in various sectors of the economy and on its implications for organizations and social welfare.

I begin by analyzing the opportunity structure, or the attributes of the professional services market, which enables the possibility of inducing demand. There are three primary characteristics, or *enabling conditions*, for SID (see Figure 3.1). The first characteristic is the high and escalating levels of uncertainty that pervade much of professional service work. This significant uncertainty drives executives and corporate buyers to seek the guidance of experts. The second characteristic is the power and influence wielded by professional service firms over their clients, deriving from the professionals' superior expertise and network positions. Crucially, this edge in knowledge and expertise equips

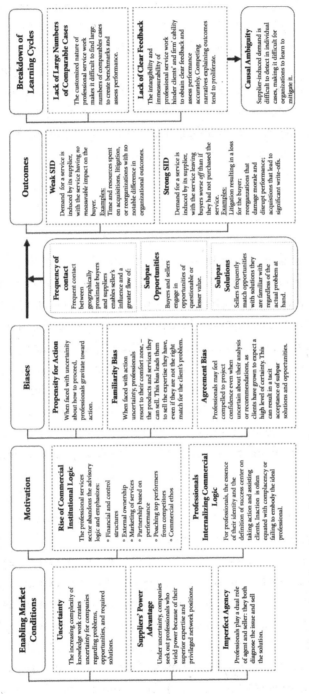

Figure 3.1 Theory of Supplier-Induced Demand

professional service firms to alleviate uncertainty for their clients. The third and final characteristic lies in the role of professionals as "imperfect agents" (Mooney & Ryan, 1993), who advise the buyer (the principal) on their needs as well as the optimal actions to fulfill those needs, while also selling the specific services to meet those needs. These conditions collectively represent a significant and expanding segment of professional services. Together, they foster an environment ripe for the seller's influence, which can give rise to SID. I delve into each of these conditions in detail, elaborating on their implications for SID.

RISE IN UNCERTAINTY

The role uncertainty plays in inducing demand can be linked to several interrelated dynamics. First, the degree of uncertainty in complex, knowledge-based work is often substantial and growing. Organizations are frequently uncertain about the challenges they face, the most appropriate solutions, and the methods to evaluate their efficacy. Second, it is precisely under conditions of uncertainty that people are more likely to seek out and rely upon experts' guidance. When needed knowledge and information are difficult to obtain and evaluate, people find solace in an expert's image and reputation. And third, within this context, professional service firms have emerged as key players in managing how organizations interface with uncertainty. They can both alleviate and induce uncertainty, thereby influencing the degree of control their clients experience. Collectively, these dynamics transform uncertainty into a sturdy foundation for experts' influence and the emergence of SID.

In principle, the views on what constitutes uncertainty vary across scientific fields. As Linda Argote (1982: 420) famously quipped, "there are almost as many definitions of uncertainty as there are treatments of the subject." Such diverse definitions typically relate to people's real or perceived inability to estimate the probabilities of future events, accurately predict potential outcomes of a decision, and assess cause-effect relationships (Milliken, 1987). Thus, most centrally, uncertainty pertains to the lack of pertinent information and knowledge and has therefore been described as a subset of unknowingness (Argote,

1982; Gaba & Terlaak, 2013; Packard & Clark, 2020; Townsend, Hunt, McMullen, & Sarasvathy, 2018).[4]

Uncertainty stems from many sources. It can emanate from the dynamism of the environment, which involves the rate of environmental changes or their unpredictability (Davis, Eisenhardt, & Bingham, 2009; Packard & Clark, 2020). For example, companies can experience uncertainty related to future changes in regulations, rates of taxation, macroeconomic policies, or political regimes (Henisz & Delios, 2001, 2004). The incompleteness of laws, rules, and regulations, and the variability in their enforcement, can also give rise to uncertainty (Edelman & Suchman, 1997; Sytch & Kim, 2021). Potential technological shifts and general market volatility similarly blanket nearly all market players in uncertainty (Gaba & Terlaak, 2013: 2; Ozmel, Reuer, & Wu, 2017: 2650).

One could probably advance a sweeping argument that companies today face high and rising uncertainty, regardless of its specific origins. Given the accelerating pace of technological change, worsening political polarizations, and the general interconnectivity of the economy, in which changes in one sector can cascade or create powerful interdependencies with others, such a broad argument would not be entirely untenable. Advancing this argument, however, is beyond the purview of this book. I focus instead on the source of uncertainty that is most germane to SID in professional services: the unknowingness related to the increasing abstractness and complexity of work in the knowledge-based economy.

Compared to the tangible raw goods and materials that dominated the manufacturing economy, the contemporary economy is defined by knowledge held by individual workers and organizations. Knowledge

---

4. Elsewhere, research has classically distinguished uncertainty from risk. In what is now often referred to as "Knightian" uncertainty, Frank Knight (1921) argued that risk corresponds to a context in which decision-makers *do not know* what an outcome to a decision might be yet *do know* of the possible outcomes of the decision, as well as the probabilities of each outcome occurring. Uncertainty, in contrast, encompasses a context in which decision-makers do not know the potential outcomes, nor their probabilities of occurring (see Ellsberg, 1961, for germane experimental designs). Scholars have also recognized that some of the knowledge and information needed to mitigate uncertainty is not knowable in principle, giving rise to aleatory uncertainty. The aleatory form of uncertainty has been subsequently contrasted with epistemic uncertainty, in which unknowingness is rectifiable in theory (Packard & Clark, 2020).

and skill inputs are largely intangible, and the concomitant labor outputs can be equally abstract (Treem, 2012). Commenting on this trend,
Staffan Canbäck (1998) observed that, while executive meetings dealt
with issues such as production costs in the mid-1900s, executive meetings in today's knowledge economy deal with complex and abstract
issues in strategy and finance. More broadly, the most recent evolution
of the economy has entailed "a move from the concrete (production) to
the abstract (finance), and a move from internal issues (production) to
external issues (markets for products and services), and on to even more
volatile external issues (capital markets)" (Armbrüster, 2006: 59; see also
Davis, 2011). The rising intangibility of work and the added complexity of digitization and globalization trends make knowledge-based work
more challenging to isolate, objectively evaluate, and reproduce.

Notably, the emergence of knowledge-based work is inseparable from
the degree of complex and specialized knowledge needed to carry out
this work. As an illustration, consider the field of strategic analysis,
which is illustrative of the forefront of knowledge-based work. Strategy formulation requires an organization to make difficult choices about
how to distribute limited organizational resources based on predictions
about the evolution of markets and consumer preferences, as well as
technological, regulatory, and competitive landscapes. It requires a company to decide what products and services it will offer; to whom, where,
and how it will sell them; with whom it will compete; and what will make
its offerings attractive compared to those of its competitors.

Imagine the levels of uncertainty that incumbent energy producers are now experiencing about how quickly people will be supplant-
ing fossil fuels with alternative energy sources, what the winning
alternatives will be, and how significantly the adoption rates will vary
across developed and developing economies. Or consider the automakers facing uncertainty in figuring out how quickly the world will embrace
autonomous vehicles, just how autonomous they will be, and how they
will be powered and regulated.

One could argue that such uncertainty has always existed as executives have perennially faced difficult strategic dilemmas. Possibly.
Different, however, is the growing interdependence of the modern

economy, wherein developments in one sector can critically alter the dynamics in another. Winning energy alternatives, which can in part come from technological breakthroughs on energy storage and use, are bound to shape automakers' decisions on the best ways to power vehicles. And developments in the broadly defined technology sector, including specific car-development efforts by non-auto companies, such as Apple and Google, will influentially shape the outlook for autonomous vehicles (Burns, 2018; Oh, 2022). Moreover, with its complex and rapidly changing regulatory landscape, consumer privacy considerations and supply chain robustness to social and economic shocks will also critically affect automakers' strategic choices (Roth, 2020; Sytch, Kim, & Page, 2022). And all these considerations are likely to be interconnected with companies' deliberate efforts to influence and shape laws and regulations in their favor, while simultaneously countering similar actions by competing interests.

These complications illustrate an ever-rising "dynamic complexity," which pertains to how different elements of a given decision can interact with one another in shaping outcomes (Townsend et al., 2018: 673). As a result of dynamic complexity, decision-making in organizations has become increasingly multidisciplinary (Shek, Chung, & Leung, 2015). Contemporary strategic analysis thus requires a sophisticated understanding of the interdependencies among the legal, regulatory, and competitive environments, including those in adjacent and emerging sectors of the economy. Assessing how achievable a given strategy is will involve, in turn, dissecting interdependencies among the company's financial and operational models, available internal and external capabilities, organizational design, and networks of relationships involving its employees and external partners (Capron & Mitchell, 2012; Greve, Rowley, & Shipilov, 2014; Puranam & Vanneste, 2016).

The increasing dynamic complexity in strategy is not a case of exception. On the contrary, rising dynamic complexity has become quotidian. Analysts observe that, as digitization and globalization disrupt traditional systems of production, the contemporary economy increasingly resembles a complex system, in which numerous economic sectors are mutually interdependent and thus are subject to one another's influence

(Bauer, Hämmerle, Schlund, & Vocke, 2015). For example, the retail prescription drug market, auto manufacturing, and financial services all developed competitive interdependencies with the rapidly evolving technology sector. Amazon wants to replace CVS and Walgreens as the purveyor of prescription drugs, Apple and Sony want to build cars, and X (formerly Twitter) dreams of becoming the next big bank (e.g., Browne, 2019; Farr, 2019; Higgins, 2023; Shah, 2022). Airlines and energy companies live and breathe financial trading, which is focused on hedging the price of fuel and trading energy, respectively (e.g., Jacobs, 2023; Merket & Swidan, 2019). All in all, in addition to monitoring commercial, financial, political, and cultural risks, organizations must now additionally address technological disruption (e.g., automation, digitization, machine learning, artificial intelligence), cyber security issues, globalized trade and production, social and environmental pressures, and "black swan" occurrences (Cavusgil, van der Vegt, Dakhli, De Farias et al., 2021). This creates an environment of unparalleled dynamic complexity.

Further differentiating the present-day knowledge-driven economy is the rapid rise in "detail complexity." This concept relates to the available knowledge, data, and analytical techniques that could be brought to bear on organizational issues (Townsend et al., 2018: 673). Strategic analysis was previously described pejoratively as "drawing curves" (Susskind & Susskind, 2016: 80). These days, however, it represents a highly complex endeavor that can require analyzing volumes of the company's, consumers', and competitors' data. Such ever-growing sophistication requires specialized knowledge to select relevant information, analyze it in the most appropriate way, and infer actionable insights from the analysis. Contemporary strategic analysis has thus evolved to incorporate scenario planning, game-theoretic analyses, and computational modeling, as well as mining volumes of data using natural language processing, network-analytic, and machine learning techniques.

Rising detail and dynamic complexity also define much of today's work in the legal, financial, and technology sectors. It characterizes work in engineering, design, and operations. All these factors—the growth of knowledge-based work, rapid environmental change, and the rise in dynamic and detail complexity—make it very difficult for organizations to house needed expertise internally. Consider, for example, how the nature of legal services has changed: "laws are more intricate and enigmatic, corporate clients are more geographically dispersed, and the stakes in outcomes have magnified. Servicing clients with new, sophisticated, large-scale, tight-deadline problems requires a greater mix of specialties, disciplines, and law-office locations" (Galanter & Palay, 1990: 796). Sometimes the required knowledge may not even be readily available. For example, as artificial intelligence is evolving rapidly, there is neither a legal precedent nor structure regarding how to conduct patent litigation for AI-made inventions (Villasenor, 2022).

Mirroring external complexity, organizations have comparably grown to be more complex internally. Simpler, verticalized, functional organizational structures have yielded to a significantly more complex matrix design, in which workflows scaffold multiple geographies, customer groupings, products, and functions (Galbraith, 1971, 1973; Sytch, Wohlegezogen, & Zajac, 2018). An average US publicly listed company now retains 35 related companies under its corporate umbrella, which further fuels the complexity of internal organizational design (EIU, 2018). For many companies, internal complexity is further magnified by their growing size and international presence (Faulconbridge & Muzio, 2016).

Concurrently, internal organizational decision-making has become more multidisciplinary and complex, often requiring collaboration across many internal functions and external partners. Reflecting in part the need to access increasingly diverse and distributed expertise, managers now spend more and more time in meetings, with the estimates reaching well over 20 hours per week for senior executives (Bain, 2014; Rogelberg, Scott, & Kello, 2007). Furthermore, executives face a deluge of information when having to make decisions. In the 1970s, workers received fewer than 1,000 communications per year on average; this number has skyrocketed to more than 30,000 in the 2010s (Bain, 2014).

Such high and ever-growing external and internal complexity can be daunting. Surveys indicate up to 80% of executives single out complexity in their work as their most critical challenge, with 40% identifying it as the most pressing issue they face (EIU, 2018; KPMG, 2022; Thomiak, 2017). When the requisite knowledge, information, and competence to navigate such complexity are not available or are difficult to acquire, unknowingness ensues, and uncertainty colors much of organizational life (Milliken, 1987: 137; Ozmel, Reuer, & Wu, 2017; Packard & Clark, 2020). As Furusten (2009: 272) observed, "organizations can naturally experience uncertainty for various reasons, but it often has to do with a lack of internal capacity to come to grips with the situation they are in, and what an organization like them should do in a situation like this." In other words, uncertainty permeates the identification of problems or opportunities, the choice of the appropriate actions to address them, as well as the understanding and evaluation of the outcomes of those actions.

Stated in conceptual terms, the high and ever-rising abstractness and complexity of work lead organizational decision-makers to face problem, action, and outcome uncertainties. *Problem uncertainty* involves the unknowingness of the problem or opportunity facing the organization, which typically arises from the complexity of the organization's internal and external environments and their impact on the firm. *Action uncertainty* describes the unknowingness of the appropriate actions to take or the inability to predict their consequences (cf. Milliken, 1987: 137; Packard, Clark, & Klein, 2017: 6; Sutton, Devine, Lamont, & Holmes, 2021).[5] And *outcome uncertainty* relates to unknowingness regarding how to evaluate the impact of potential actions on the organization.

Problem uncertainty, for example, can manifest in the lack of understanding of whether and to what extent the company should expand or

---

5. With respect to Frances J. Milliken's (1987) seminal uncertainty typology, *problem* uncertainty is akin to the combination of "state" and "effect" uncertainty, whereas *action* uncertainty most closely corresponds to "response" uncertainty. There is some correspondence between action uncertainty and Mark D. Packard, Brent B. Clark, and Peter G. Klein's (2017: 6) "creative uncertainty." According to Packard and colleagues (2017: 6) creative uncertainty may be conceived of as an individual or a firm having to decide whether to spend resources to resolve the issue, bearing the weight of the uncertainty and not knowing "what, when, or how events will play out, how any specific course of action might alter those outcomes, whether superior strategies or solutions may exist, or whether specific solutions are even truly viable."

shrink its footprint in a particular market or what products and services it should or should not sell. Action uncertainty can engender vacillations regarding whether the company should acquire or divest assets, form partnerships with other firms, raise funds for organic growth, develop or enforce its intellectual property, or espouse a different organizational design. And outcome uncertainty may entail a lack of clarity regarding whether the undertaken actions were, in fact, successful. Coping with uncertainty thus becomes inseparable from dealing with complexity.

UNCERTAINTY AND EXPERTS' ADVICE

It is well established in the social sciences that uncertainty does not bring people comfort. Indeed, under uncertainty, people tend to experience anxiety, discomfort, and a loss of control (Cyert & March, 1963; Galbraith, 1973; Janis & Mann, 1977; Kakkar & Sivanathan, 2017). In fact, uncertainty can be so unsettling that it activates the amygdala, a part of the human brain that is associated with responses to threats and fear (Whalen, 1998). Uncertainty, therefore, creates a powerful impetus for action. When limited knowledge and information are to blame for uncertainty—such as when dealing with detail and dynamic complexity—people naturally try to fill in that missing knowledge and information.

In searching for needed information, people are known to delay decisions, hoping that additional information will become available to them at a later time (Hirst & Schweitzer, 1990). When objective information is not available, people desperately cling to illusory patterns in random events (Whitson & Galinsky, 2008). More generally, uncertainty opens the door for influence, which can mean heeding others' advice and actions. For example, under uncertainty, people and organizations tend to imitate the actions of others, in part because they assume that the others have access to better or more complete information (Cialdini, 1993; Haunschild & Miner, 1997; Rao, Greve, & Davis, 2001).

Relatedly, in what is known as the social amplification effect, the state of unknowingness in uncertain situations leads people to be particularly attuned to the significance of social indicators surrounding decisions. These could include social affiliations, status, reputations, charisma, and even the trappings of others offering advice, endorsements, or engaging in specific behaviors (Collins & Evans, 2007; Haunschild & Miner, 1997; Jacquart & Antonakis, 2015; Pfeffer, Salancik, & Leblebici, 1976). Put differently, when there is insufficient "physical reality" (Festinger, 1950: 273) to make decisions or validate beliefs, we tend to supplant it with proxies that help us reduce anxiety and restore a sense of control.

It is therefore understandable that a salient strategy to deal with uncertainty involves soliciting help and advice from experts (Lipshitz & Strauss, 1997; Saint-Charles & Mongeau, 2009). We turn to experts for the things we do not know or understand. In addition to offering substantive advice, experts bring a plethora of social standing along with it. Recent breakthroughs in neuroscience and functional magnetic resonance imaging (fMRI) allow us to peer inside the human brain and understand why we might seek expert assistance when faced with uncertainty. It turns out that receiving advice from experts triggers the modulation of activity coming from a caudate nucleus, a paired, C-shaped subcortical structure deep inside the brain (Klucharev, Smidts, & Fernández, 2008). Such caudate activity has been linked to both increased intentions to trust and reduced levels of ambiguity in choices (Hsu, Bhatt, Adolphs, Tranel et al., 2005; King-Casas, Tomlin, Anen, Camerer et al., 2005; Klucharev, Smidts, & Fernández, 2008). Thus, advice coming from experts evokes feelings of trust and compensates for the lack of additional information, both of which become powerful remedies for uncertainty.

Advice from experts is not only sought but also heeded. Studies show that the same information, when received from experts rather than non-experts, more strongly activates the regions of the brain that are responsible for logic and associative reasoning (Klucharev, Smidts, & Fernández, 2008). Experts' advice similarly triggered stronger neural activity and blood oxygenation in the medial prefrontal cortex, which is linked to the cognitive processes of evaluation, self-reference, and sensitivity to rewards (Falk, Berkman, Mann, Harrison et al., 2010; Meshi, Biele, Korn, & Heekeren, 2012). For example, the same brain areas that respond to value and the expectation of rewards when receiving money or valuable objects are also activated when individuals find out they will be getting expert advice.

PROFESSIONALS AS MEDIATORS (AND INDUCERS) OF UNCERTAINTY

Thus, under uncertainty, clients seek professional service firms—as prominent and visible experts—to help make sense of situations and decide on a course of action. The increased complexity of economic and professional management systems and the resultant unknowingness have escalated the real and perceived need for professional expertise (Groß & Kieser, 2006: 90). And nearly half of executives surveyed are inclined to respond by delegating decision-making to outside providers (Grossmann, 2022; KPMG International, 2011). Professional service firms, in turn, proactively step in to mitigate such uncertainty by soliciting business. They do it because, at some level, professionals' "effective contact with the disorderly" is the cornerstone of their status and survival (Abbott, 1981: 829).

Promotional materials of professional service firms are replete with references to the unique expertise needed to navigate the complex problems and institutional environments that companies face. Consider, for example, the following excerpt from the promotional materials of a leading financial institution:

> We are advocates in a world marked by complexity and uncertainty. Our expert insights and smart strategies help companies grow, improve cash flow and invest for the future. Our state-of-the-art technology eases day-to-day management and increases efficiencies. We encourage invention and have more patents and applications than any other bank. (Bank of America, 2022)

or this equivalent from a leading consulting company:

> ... because of the more complex regulatory environment, rapid globalisation, and the diversity of legal regimes across the world, we see

that legal departments face a wider range of risks . . . This is result-
ing in increased complexity and demand from the business which
is creating an unsustainable workload for existing in-house legal
departments. (Deloitte Legal, 2020: 0, 5)

According to the "professional purity" hypothesis (Abbott, 1981), one
could expect the gravitational pull of occupational prestige to draw professional service firms toward more complex and abstract work, rather
than away from it. Under this hypothesis, work that is closer to the core
of the profession's abstract knowledge is more professionally pure and
prestigious.[6] Thus, one could conceive that the evolution of professional
service offerings could magnify the complexity of the work and bring it
to the forefront of economic exchange. Due to professionals' superior
niche and recombinant expertise, as well as the professional service
firms' carefully cultivated image of elite expertise, clients perceive professional services as a good match to rising levels of detail and dynamic
complexity.

   Clients thus utilize professional service firms as instruments to regain their sense of control that may otherwise dwindle in uncertain
market environments. In other words, clients hire professionals to fight
the "cognitive chaos" (Suchman & Cahill, 1996: 681). Overall, due to
the confluence of structural pull and agentic push, professional service
firms have ascended to play the vital role of uncertainty mitigators for
their clients.

   The ensuing alleviation of uncertainty can take the form of substantive or symbolic action. Substantively, lawyers, for example, can execute
complex transactions, reducing uncertainty by providing insight into

---

6. As such, professionals with the lowest status are those characterized by human complexity
or those from which the dimension of human complexity cannot be removed (Abbott, 1981:
823–824). These professionals generally serve as "front-line" professionals, as they work in
fields in which their professional knowledge must be balanced with the client's actions and
reality (Abbott, 1988). In the legal industry, this translates to securities, tax, and antitrust
law maintaining the highest professional status, followed by commercial, civil rights, and
criminal law, which are then followed by debtor, tenant–landlord, and divorce law. Similar
hierarchies have been observed in the medical field, in which specialty surgeons maintain the
highest status, followed by general surgery, internal medicine, general practice, dermatology,
and psychiatry (Abbott, 1981: 820, 822).

regulatory constraints, liabilities, and strategic objectives. They are also widely credited for "community structuration" in specific communities, such as Silicon Valley. These processes involve lawyers working with various stakeholder groups, such as investors, entrepreneurs, and nonprofit organizations, to construct a system of norms and relations in a regional community (Suchman, 2000; Suchman & Cahill, 1996). For example, lawyers educate new entrepreneurs on the informal practices of Silicon Valley's venture capital market. Moreover, lawyers leverage their social structures among key market participants to facilitate a culture of mutual concessions in business negotiations. Thus, by establishing and maintaining distinct normative structures underpinning the high-risk market, lawyers can "absorb and control some of the central uncertainties of encounters between venture capitalists and entrepreneurs, facilitating what might otherwise be prohibitively costly, complex, and unpredictable transactions" (Suchman & Cahill, 1996: 683).

Lawyers, like other professionals, can also mitigate uncertainty symbolically. Examples of such activities can entail putting their opinions in writing in more or less direct terms or merely embodying a mediating presence in negotiations of a financing deal (Suchman & Cahill, 1996). The symbolic reduction of uncertainty becomes particularly important because knowledge and information asymmetries make the exact nature of professionals' work and output difficult to assess. In lieu of material reality, professionals' work is often procured and assessed based on signals (Wittreich, 1966). Such signals can involve esteemed personnel, in which a potential client buys on faith the reputation of the professionals; the method, wherein professionals emphasize how the data is obtained or the analysis conducted; or the prominent success stories from similar clients, which selectively showcase prior successes. Under uncertainty, many of these signals act as powerful touchpoints of social amplification that further help experts reduce clients' uncertainty.

Because signals often substitute for materiality in mitigating uncertainty, professional service firms invest to carefully cultivate their reputations and actively project them in the marketplace. Social approval of the service provider becomes the uncertainty mitigation tool (Pfarrer, Pollock, & Rindova, 2010: 1133–1134; Rindova, Williamson,

Petkova, & Sever, 2005: 1035). And because managers are judged in part based on how they handle situations of uncertainty, hiring consultants is often perceived to be a sign of "good management." Thus, "good management" is equated with identifying the best consultants and buying their expertise. In such cases, organizational reputation is not just the proxy of perceived service quality, as is traditionally stipulated in economics research. Rather, reputation also reflects an organization's prominence, which captures the organization's significance and recognition in the collective public attention and memory. The latter may reflect the general media buzz about professional service firms, their involvement in high-profile projects, or their high placements in various industry rankings (Rindova, Pollock, & Hayward, 2006; Rindova, Williamson, & Petkova, 2010; Rindova et al., 2005).

Professional service firms' established reputations can instill confidence in their clients regarding how professionals make sense of the complex world, the problems and opportunities they identify, and the actions they recommend. Writing as a university professor, I would be remiss if I did not draw a parallel here to higher education. As in the case of professional services, the quality of higher education is difficult to observe and assess. As a result, students' and parents' decisions are routinely shaped by the litany of educational institutions' reputational signals, including rankings, the prestige of faculty members' degrees, or media coverage of the school (Rindova et al., 2005).

Buyers' pursuit of professional services for social approval in the face of problem and action uncertainty can take extreme forms. In some cases, companies retain a professional service firm to project an image of being institutionally correct (Furusten, 2009). My fieldwork yielded many variants of the same account, in which professionals were hired because this is how similar situations—such as declining organizational performance—were handled at peer companies. Organizational theorists will instantly recognize this as a classic case of organizational imitation, in which legitimacy is secured through compliance with the prevailing norms and expectations of the environment rather than by addressing the technical needs of the work (DiMaggio & Powell, 1983).

My interviews also revealed that when companies imitate others in retaining professional service firms, these imitations are frequently accompanied by a healthy degree of executives' conscious deliberation, rather than a blind herd mentality. One executive, for example, analogized conformity in retaining professional service firms with "swimming with the school of fish." Failing while departing from the school of fish can result in much more severe consequences to executives' careers compared to failing while staying with the metaphorical school.

When uncertainty blurs a promising course of action, or tough organizational decisions are necessary, companies may strategically retain professional service firms to distance their leaders from possible failures or employee resentment. In this case, my interviewees revealed that clients bring in professionals as a "stamp of approval" for potentially controversial managerial actions. Examples of such actions include selling a part of the company, outsourcing decisions, reorganizations, personnel reductions, or compensation changes.

It is important to recognize that all these buyers' behaviors—engendered by uncertainty—can open the door to SID. They create opportunities to sell professional services where there could be none. Uncertainty can thus enable SID by originating professional services when they might not be necessary. It also opens the door for influence regarding the degree to which professional services are necessary, as exemplified by the routine "more-is-better-than-less" approach (Eddy, 1984).

In legal contexts, this often translates into lawyers spending more time in the discovery phase, collecting potentially irrelevant information while increasing the hours billed to the client (Wistrich & Rachlinski, 2013). Note here, too, that even in such a seemingly simple scenario, professionals may find themselves between a rock and a hard place. Uncertainty blurs the exact amount of work needed for thorough discovery in a lawsuit or due diligence in a merger transaction. Thus, overdoing discovery brings the risk of being accused of over-discovery. Not doing enough work can incite the client's wrath and even pose the risk of litigation for inadequate discovery.

More broadly, it is important to recognize that professional service firms are not immune to uncertainty. They, just like their clients, can struggle with defining a problem and devising the optimal organizational response. The knowledge advantage professional service firms hold over their clients is just that—an advantage. It is no panacea to uncertainty. Dubbed the professional uncertainty hypothesis (Wennberg, Barnes, & Zubkoff, 1982), this view highlights that professionals frequently diverge widely from one another in their diagnosis of the same situation. Additionally, they may struggle to ascertain the value that their clients attribute to a particular course of action. This latter point speaks to the fact that the clients' and professionals' attitudes toward risks, costs, and rewards may differ, and that the professionals may find it difficult to uncover the clients' true preferences.

When professionals encounter high degrees of uncertainty, SID can arise because professionals reflexively follow the actions and policies of their own peers (Watts, Shiner, Klauss, & Weeks, 2011). Such mimicry of fellow professionals under high uncertainty—and the concomitant undifferentiated offerings to clients—has been raised in research on SID in healthcare economics. Indeed, a physician who comfortably imitates his or her peers is "safe from criticism, free from having to explain his or her actions, and defended by the concurrence of colleagues" (Eddy, 1984: 86). In other words, professionals may be swimming, too, with their own school fish. Chapters 6–8 further expound upon the genesis of SID under uncertainty, which can be attributed to a series of professionals' biases, shaped by the evolving institutional dynamics of the professional services domain.

Intriguingly, the work of professional service firms can counterintuitively *heighten* the same uncertainty it wants to tame. Experts are hired regularly to come in and help make sense of a situation in which the company finds itself (Armbrüster, 2006; Furusten, 2009). Such work often involves finding external, environmental "problems" or "threats" for clients, whether substantive or perceived. The constructed environment can effectively heighten or even generate uncertainty in the eyes of the clients, affecting their sense of losing control. A chief legal counsel I interviewed for this project likened this to "scaremongering":

They'll [external legal counsel] come to you and they say, did you know that the Foreign Corrupt Practices Act requires you to have this policy and have that procedure and to ensure you're auditing this thing and checking that thing? And "look at this case," which is, of course, some outlier case, and the facts are very specific. See, look, you need to be worried about this. And when you have a fancy lawyer from a fancy outside firm telling you [that] you need to be worried about this, a federal prosecutor who has moved to Asia, who's in touch with the FBI office there who investigates American companies for Foreign Corrupt Practices Act violations. Yeah, you kind of take notice.

It is, in part, such induction of uncertainty and its subsequent legitimization that often justify the need for professional service work (McDonald, 2014). These dynamics led some scholars to describe professionals as simultaneously acting as "agents of anxiety" and "providers of managerial control" (Ernst & Kieser, 2002). Imagine you are a manager, trying to navigate the choppy waters of the business world. You are bombarded with phrases like "the war for talent" and "extreme competition," which make you feel like you are constantly on the brink of disaster. It is enough to make you feel like you are drowning in a sea of uncertainty. This is when professionals come in, offering expert diagnoses and solutions to the issues, empowering you to regain control. The problem is that these professionals may also create a sense of deeper uncertainty. As they are constantly coming up with new management concepts and fashions, threats, and opportunities, and you cannot possibly implement or address them all at once. You are left wondering what you are missing. It is a vicious cycle, which is also psychological in nature. Managers, just like any of us, crave the positive feelings that come with solving problems and recovering control. And so, they keep turning to professionals, even as they become more and more dependent on them (Boussebaa & Faulconbridge, 2018; Ernst & Kieser, 2002; Kieser, 2001).

Professional service firms do not just directly influence their clients; their actions can have far-reaching effects throughout markets. This is largely due to their privileged network positions, granting them access to extensive market segments. Through these connections, professional service firms can unintentionally amplify uncertainty by promoting management trends and portraying the environment as complex, dynamic, or hostile. Such depictions of the business landscape can breed uncertainty, leading to undue pressure on client organizations to act. Scholars have raised concerns about this, and rightly so. When professional service firms emphasize "complexity" or "hostility," it can create a sense of urgency for their clients to act, even when there's no clear understanding of the appropriate course of action (Groß & Kieser, 2006: 70).

* * *

CHAPTER SUMMARY

The modern knowledge-based economy, characterized by increasing abstraction and complexity, breeds a palpable sense of uncertainty. This uncertainty manifests in various forms, such as problem, action, and outcome uncertainty. Consequently, organizations grapple with understanding the situation, determining the optimal course of action, and evaluating potential outcomes. In response, professional service firms have emerged as elite experts adept at navigating this uncertainty. Consequently, companies often delegate complex decision-making to these firms, regarding them as knowledgeable and reputable experts. However, this reliance also exposes organizations to the influence of professional service firms, potentially leading to supplier-induced demand. Moreover, professional service firms may unintentionally exacerbate the uncertainty their clients face, further solidifying their clients' dependence on external expertise. These dynamics highlight uncertainty as one of the primary enablers of supplier-induced demand.

CHAPTER 4

The Power of Professional Service Firms

THE EXPERT ADVANTAGE

Discourse about the preconditions of supplier-induced demand (SID) cannot occur without addressing professional service firms' power. In this case, *power* can be seen as the potential to control others' actions and outcomes, while *influence* is the actual dynamics of affecting the attitudes, behaviors, and outcomes of others (Emerson, 1962; French & Raven, 1959; Pfeffer & Salancik, 1978). Professional service firms' power over their clients and the ability to influence them stems from several bases. One of the main bases is the knowledge and information asymmetries between professional service firms and their clients. In the words of John R. P. French and Bertram H. Raven (1959: 163), the strength of an individual's expert power over another varies based on the extent of knowledge (or the perceived knowledge) that the latter attributes to the former in a particular domain. Certainly, the distinctive and widely acclaimed expertise of a professional service firm serves as a crucial resource that buyers seek to utilize (Emerson, 1962; Gulati & Sytch, 2007; Pfeffer & Salancik, 1978), while also bolstering the perception of authority and expertise, thereby acting as a powerful tool of influence (Cialdini, 1993; Milgram, 1963).

To understand professional service firms' expertise advantage, it is useful to examine the nature of their work. Professional service firms can assist with clients' capacity constraints. In the words of one in-house counsel, "*Sometimes there are bandwidth concerns. So it's just too much work, we don't have enough people in-house, we'll use local law firms to help us with extra capacity.*" Another senior leader echoed the sentiment with respect to external strategy consultants, "*apparently, we do have a strategy team. We have a chief strategist, strategy officer, and a couple of guys, but the amount of data that needed to be reviewed and analyzed and the result that [consultants] brought to the table was hundreds of slides with tons of data. So it was something we couldn't tackle so quickly in house. So it seems we didn't we didn't have the strength, the muscle. Some brain power we did have but not to that scale.*"

A chief financial officer (CFO) of a large manufacturing company similarly described recruiting a professional service firm to help with routine financial transactions. Routine work may occasionally come in surges, such as following a significant transaction or toward the end of reporting cycles. In addition to punctuated changes in the demand for routine work, organizations may face drastic changes in the supply of internal labor, such as following an aggressive downsizing or high levels of attrition. Professional service firms are also enlisted when the work stakes are particularly high, and clients need an extra pair of eyes and validation for the work performed. These types of engagements notwithstanding, the major reason companies retain professional service firms is to access their *unique* and *specialized* expertise.

The very rise of professional service firms is explained principally by the increasing division of labor and specialization in the contemporary economy (Abbott, 1988; Sharma, 1997; Treem, 2012). Even definitionally, professions are viewed as occupations tethered to the applications of "abstract" (Abbott, 1988: 8), "esoteric" (Larson, 1977: x), and "specialized" (Sharma, 1997: 758, 769) knowledge. In practice, most companies do not have the in-house expertise to perform investment banking services, litigation, or strategy formulation work, to name just a few such specialized areas. An in-house counsel for a large commercial real estate company echoed this sentiment, "*We have mortgage regulatory work and mortgage-like corporate work. And that's very specialized. And we send that to law firms that have that specific expertise. So that's one main reason we would send something out to outside counsel, we need very specialized expertise that we don't have in-house.*" An associate in-house counsel for a healthcare company offered a similar sentiment, *"So for example, in the healthcare space, you have a highly regulated climate, and you have Stark Law and anti-kickback law,*[1] *and Stark Law alone contains 40 different exceptions. So it becomes incredibly difficult to be a niche specialist and a niche expert in those areas when you're in house and you handle large volumes of legal projects."*

A highly pertinent sidebar here concerns the decision to outsource services to professional service firms. In my fieldwork, executives cited irregular and unpredictable demand for these services that did not justify employing highly specialized experts internally. Reflections from the buyers of professional services also frequently referenced the disparity in compensation between the employees of professional service firms and those of their corporate clients. In other words, even if corporate buyers chose to bring expertise in-house, they claim they could not afford the labor market premia paid by professional service firms.

Moreover, desirable specialized expertise can be difficult to develop and maintain inside a prototypical corporate client. Consider patent infringement litigation as a notable illustration. Patent infringement litigation is an immensely complex form of legal conflict. Each case is a unique fusion of patent law and the technology in question, requiring specialized knowledge of both. Accordingly, patent lawsuits involve large numbers of expert witnesses and generate hundreds of thousands of documents (Hewitt, 2005). With their complexity, patent cases require lawyers to possess exceptional knowledge of the technology itself, litigation procedures, and courtroom dynamics. At the same time, lawyers need to synthesize and communicate that knowledge to a jury or judge who lacks a technical background. Thus, although corporate clients were once content to be represented in intellectual property cases by lawyers distinguished by extensive scientific or engineering backgrounds, they increasingly prefer lawyers with both high technical

---

1. Stark Law, also known as the Physician Self-Referral Law, is a US federal law that prohibits physicians from referring Medicare or Medicaid patient to entities in which they or their family members have a financial interest. The Anti-Kickback Statute is another US federal law that prohibits healthcare providers from accepting or offering bribes or kickbacks in exchange for Medicare or Medicaid patient referrals.

expertise and extensive trial experience. This combination is difficult for in-house counsel to develop.

Due to their unique knowledge, skillset, and experience, external intellectual property counsel typically holds a significant knowledge advantage over in-house counsel and company executives. External lawyers are more familiar with the intricacies of patent infringement litigation and are consulted for their expert judgment regarding the strength of the patent, the scope of the patent claims, or the likely efficacy of legal action. This expertise advantage is compounded by information asymmetries, which can take the form of legal constraints on the in-house counsel's ability to access key information pertinent to the dispute. In some cases, protective orders—driven by the litigating parties' desire to safeguard competitive information—may prevent clients from seeing key documents during various phases of the dispute.

A partner of a large intellectual property litigation firm elaborated on the role that restricted information disclosure plays in many disputes:

> You're looking at confidential information [from] the other side, [which] is a competitor, and so there's constantly a protective order in every one of these cases put in place as to who can see what levels of information. And, typically, much of the key evidence with regard to the merits of the case... is kept at a confidential level for outside counsel's eyes only... Pfizer does not want Merck to see their NDA [New Drug Application], the way they're set up, the way they negotiate them, and the way they correspond. That's all highly trade-secret-protected and confidential information.

In-house counsel may be limited even further in their involvement due to potential conflicts of interest, such as when a company's in-house lawyers become witnesses in the legal proceedings.

Similarly, in mergers and acquisitions consulting work, consultants and lawyers gain privileged access to sensitive information from both the acquirer and the target companies. Such information is often redacted from the purview of the merging parties themselves, generally because it can compromise their competitive advantage in areas unrelated to the merger or if the merger does not materialize.

The consultants I interviewed recalled sitting in dark and musty rooms, behind closed doors, going over hundreds and hundreds of pages of sensitive documents with black markers. One consultant described it as the least gratifying work he had ever done: as he put it, there is no reward if you get it right, but a single mistake—typically in the form of a sensitive piece of information left unredacted—can cost him the job. This experience illustrates that, paradoxically, agents can have broader access to the information on a given transaction than the principals they represent.[2]

Knowledge and information asymmetries between external service providers and their corporate buyers persist throughout the entire cycle of service engagement: before work starts, during, and after it is completed. Regarding legal services, particularly in small- and medium-sized companies, in-house counsel has general expertise and carries out fairly general responsibilities. It would attend to areas of law such as contracts, tax, securities, labor and employment relations, and privacy matters. In the words of one in-house counsel, *"they [external counsel] have deeper expertise. As in-house counsel, we go wider, outside counsel, they go deeper, and they know that and so they know they can provide expertise that we don't have in house, and that we're always trying to get that kind of expertise."* Similarly, few companies have the luxury of specialized units working exclusively on digital business strategies or mergers or divestitures.

As transactions unfold, knowledge and information asymmetries persist and exacerbate. For example, in-house lawyers typically attend

2. This discussion illustrates the importance of attending to both knowledge *and* information asymmetries in understanding the power advantage of professional service firms. While information asymmetries concern different degrees of access to information regarding a specific case (e.g., a legal or consulting case), knowledge asymmetries refer to different levels of expertise or stocks of insight in a particular field (e.g., the years of training and experience in litigation or management consulting). As described, even seemingly commoditized information (Eisenhardt, 1989) can be asymmetrically distributed between professional service firms and their clients due to legal constraints. Knowledge, of course, differs from information because it necessitates the actors' reflection and interpretation (Powell, 1998: 236). Developing and applying knowledge entails a complex set of cognitive processes involving its acquisition, retention, retrieval, and synthesis, all of which can be shaped profoundly by the social actors' skills, past experiences, and the surrounding social networks (Hargadon & Sutton, 1997; Maroulis, Sytch, & Cifuentes, 2024; Reagans & McEvily, 2003). A lot of that knowledge is tacit, or not easily codifiable, and thus not easily transferrable between organizations, which serves to sustain professional service firms' expert knowledge advantage.

big-picture strategy meetings in intellectual property litigation. However, they are rarely involved in accessing documentation, determining the boundaries of evidence, and taking depositions, all of which may be conducted by external legal counsel. By the same token, strategy consultants and investment bankers typically select, analyze, and present data germane to setting a new strategy or assessing the potential of an asset sale or purchase. Therefore, an expert's knowledge of the area, coupled with the undivided focus on the transaction itself, further feeds knowledge and information asymmetries. One experienced intellectual property litigator reflected on this issue from his experience: *"You always feel that you know the case ten times better than [the in-house legal counsel]. Because that is all I do."*

To be clear, not all professional services entail high levels of knowledge and information asymmetries between buyers and sellers. As mentioned, some of the work professional service firms deliver is unremarkable to their buyers. Despite this, extant research and my own fieldwork point to the presence of such asymmetries in an array of services offered by professional service firms, including intellectual property litigation and regulatory work in privacy, foreign corrupt practices, and commercial real estate, as well as specialized insurance and financial transactions, strategy consulting, and investment banking in merger and acquisition transactions (Anagol, Cole, & Sarkar, 2017; Brown & Minor, 2012; Cai, Li, & Zhou, 2021; Mullainathan, Noeth, & Schoar, 2012). Furthermore, recent years have seen an increased emphasis on professional service firms performing non-routine work, further exacerbating the knowledge asymmetries in question.

The outsourcing of specialized work to professional service firms creates a recursive cycle that intensifies the expertise asymmetry between the firms and their clients. On one hand, it enables professional service firms to maintain an advantage in staying up to date with cutting-edge developments in their fields. On the other hand, it leads to a decline in clients' capabilities in those same areas because they fail to internalize them and develop them in-house. This asymmetry can make clients even more reliant on the professional service firms, perpetuating the outsourcing of specialized work and their expert advantage.

DEEPENING NICHE AND RECOMBINANT EXPERTISE

Andrew Abbott (1988) emphasized the importance of viewing professions through the evolving landscape of interconnected "jurisdictions" or areas of practice. Jurisdictions link an occupation and its work, creating a system, or ecology, in which changes in one jurisdiction affect other jurisdictions. As such, professions develop through jurisdictional conflicts that incentivize the creation of new practice areas or the abolishment of old ones. This creates an interlinked history in which different professions are inherently interdependent. It is important to recognize that jurisdictional expansions and conflicts, including those that corporate clients trigger, have profoundly shaped, and continue to shape, professional service firms' expert advantage.

The confluence of three mutually reinforcing trends created a series of jurisdictional conflicts that have pushed professional services to become even more specialized, venture into new practice areas, create new areas, and expand their production of new professional concepts (Malhotra, Morris, & Hinings, 2006). First, together with the rise of professional service firms, many mirroring functions in corporate clients have also grown. For example, in parallel with big law firm growth, companies observed a significant rise of in-house counsel. In-house corporate law departments increased in budget, size, authority, and function. As a result, corporations conduct significantly more of their routine legal work in-house, which has cut into law firms' historical streams of income and shifted relationships with outside law firms to become even more specialized (Baker & Parkin, 2006; Nelson & Nielson, 2000; Replogle, 2017; Wald, 2020).

Second, the growing size and scope of corporations and their complicated managerial structure—all due partly to globalization—have led clients to expect additional services from specialized providers, such as non-audit services from their accountancy firms (Malhotra, Morris, & Hinings, 2006). Finally, competitive pressures on service providers reinforced the trend of offering complex bundles of services. A partner at an audit firm illustrated: *"Most people could not hack mainstream audit work for prolonged periods. They get their kicks out of value-added business advisory work. The fee rates are higher for non-audit work. Their objective is always to boost this element of their work*" (Morris & Empson, 1998: 618).

These trends work together to reinforce and amplify professional service firms' expert advantage by leading them to discover new areas of expertise or recombine established areas into novel service offerings. Professionals thus become *niche experts*, who possess deep expertise in a given domain, and *recombinant experts*, whose expertise lies in identifying and synthesizing relevant knowledge across domains. These two types of expertise often go hand in hand in deepening the specialization of professional service firms.

In the words of Abbott (1988: 102), "Many occupations fight for turf, but only professions expand their cognitive domain by using abstract knowledge to annex new areas, to define them as their own proper work." Claims over new jurisdictions frequently involve deepening niche expertise in new domains. As Daniel Susskind and Richard Susskind (2016: 136–137) observed, "as disciplines evolve and become increasingly populated, professionals seem driven or attracted to ever more esoteric and often arcane corners of their world." At traditional strategy-consulting firms, the share of work that is classic strategy has been decreasing steadily and is now about 20%, down from 60% to 70% about 30 years ago. Strategy work is complemented by the relatively newer areas of digital consulting, which leverages sophisticated machine learning, artificial intelligence, and big data analytics; and behavioral consulting, which applies insights from social psychology, anthropology, and experimental research (Christensen, Wang, & van Bever, 2013; Susskind & Susskind, 2016: 80–81, 114).

When asked about what qualities are needed to be promoted to manager at a top consulting firm, a senior partner reflected on the importance of newly developed expertise:

First, you need to have sales, or at least show the potential to do so ... you need to be known for something, like, anything related to what we believe is important for our success. So these days, if you're highly skilled in some technology or strategy thing from 15 years ago, you can better pack your bags. If you happen to be the super expert on

The Power of Professional Service Firms   75

artificial intelligence, you're on the hotspot, our whole compensation is based around that, we even have hot-skill bonuses. So, if you're talented in a certain area, you're in a good place.

Another example of deepening niche and recombinant expertise through jurisdictional expansion is Deloitte's new practice of legal management consulting (LMC). It is a practice area spanning the legal and consulting domains, which Deloitte actively positions as a new jurisdiction: "[LMC] is a *new approach* and a *new discipline*, developed for lawyers by lawyers and other experts. It builds on mainstream management consultancy, risk advisory services, as well as tax management consulting. LMC is a collection of models, frameworks, and systems to help in-house lawyers run their departments more efficiently and comprehensively meet their business needs" (Deloitte Legal, 2020).

The deepening of professional expertise—both niche and recombinant—is similarly visible in the infusion of industrial design and reliability engineering in offering new management and operations consulting services. As Nathan Simon and Michael Taylor (2016) summarized:

Consultants are launching new offerings, including ongoing managed services such as Deloitte's Supply Chain Managed Services, a form of outsourcing for high value-add activities such as pricing and demand forecasting, "as a service" assets such as the McKinsey Solutions portfolio that allow clients to license the tools consultants have perfected in the course of their engagements, and capability and skills development programs such as the Boston Consulting Group's Client Enablement programs.

Similar trends persist in investment banking, in which new jurisdictions and the concomitant niche expertise—such as those in agtech (agricultural technology) and regtech (regulatory technology)—are emerging at an increasing rate. Some of the new jurisdictions, such as cryptocurrencies, are described as "new, uncharted territory" even for investment banks, let alone their clients (Pitchbook, 2018).

Professional service firms' expansion into new jurisdictions creates endogenous jurisdictional conflicts, which pressures peers to deepen and differentiate their expert advantage. An ensuing response often involves deepening recombinant expertise, wherein professional service firms position themselves as expert integrators of numerous expert areas. In illustrative trends, the Big Four accounting firms have moved toward providing a portfolio of professional services, aiming to mirror "total service providers," such as IBM or Accenture. Deloitte's consulting sector has grown significantly faster than its core accounting sector in the last decade, leading Deloitte to become an elite consulting firm (Christensen, Wang, & van Bever, 2013). Similarly, KPMG is now marketed as an "advisory firm," reflecting a growing emphasis on the firm's broad category of advisory services (Brock, 2006: 164). And traditional accounting firms now even attempt to use their expertise in project management and technology to gain a foothold in the legal services market (Wilkins & Ferrer, 2018).

To keep the expertise edge over their clients as a signal of value, professional service firms identify and absorb new expertise quickly, often through acquisitions or strategic partnerships. For example, to set up their legal management consulting service, Deloitte acquired ATD Legal in 2014, a Canadian document-review service provider. And, in 2016, it acquired Conduit Law Professional, a well-recognized provider of outsourced legal services and formed an alliance with Kira Systems, a provider of artificial intelligence services (Wilkins & Ferrer, 2018: 1006–1007). A partner of another leading consulting firm shared with me that his organization spends billions of dollars yearly acquiring companies with cutting-edge technical expertise. The goal of the firm, in his words, is *always to be a step ahead of the client.* He elaborated, *"So what you see is that a lot of our clients are building up those capabilities. But they are either starting, or they've done so in the last ten years, but they're nowhere in terms of maturity, like what we do. We just have a lot more experience."*

The rapid acquisition of new expertise is also reflected in the changing patterns of personnel development. Historically, professional service firms hired associates at the entry level and recruited partners from their associate pools. Beginning in the 1970s, however, lateral hirings in professional service firms increased appreciably and evolved into a systematic method of enhancing a firm's specialties and means of attracting new business. In legal services, firm- or department-wide defections and mergers similarly increased in occurrence, allowing firms to establish new departments and offer new services. In fact, professional service firms have become so good at bringing in new expertise and new people quickly that many of them now aim to sell onboarding and training services to their clients' employees.

The deepening niche and recombinant expertise of professional service firms, coupled with the dizzying speed of acquiring new knowledge, reinforces and exacerbates knowledge asymmetries with their clients and provides a strong structure for power and influence. A senior corporate executive buying professional services reflected on how such a pace of expertise acquisition can affect interactions with consulting firms, *"And the challenge is that if you go into the new space, you may not have internally that capability or that expertise to even know, what are the smart questions to ask in order to demonstrate to them [consultants] that they need to do a better job."* This observation speaks in part to the classic concerns agency theory raises, which involve the principals' difficulty in monitoring the expert agents' behaviors and evaluating their output (Fama & Jensen, 1983; Jensen & Meckling, 1976). Such concerns are particularly acute in the knowledge-intensive work of professional service firms, whose inputs and outputs are inherently not easily measurable. For avid followers of the agency theory, I will again ask for patience in not leaping from such breakdowns in principals' (i.e., clients') control over agents (i.e., professionals') to the agents' opportunistic pursuits. We will turn to the issue of motivation in Chapters 6 and 7.

THE VISIBILITY OF THE EXPERT ADVANTAGE

Professional service firms' expertise advantages over clients are foundational to securing an enduring level of occupational prestige (Abbott, 1988). It is therefore not surprising that professional service firms make a concerted effort not only to sustain and grow such an advantage, but also to prominently showcase it. "*I always tell my clients that over 90% of our employees have college degrees,*" shared a consulting practice leader in one my interviews. An in-house counsel of a multi-billion-dollar manufacturing firm, who previously had experience at a leading law firm, was even blunter in his assessment: "*If you go and you do an analysis of the qualifications of general counsel of Fortune 500 companies versus qualifications of partners in the top, I don't know, 100 law firms of the United States. Simply look at where they went to undergrad and where they went to law school. That's it. I suspect you will find a big gap.*"

It is indeed widely known that professional service firms favor prestigious educational institutions in their hiring practices (Rider, 2014). For example, at the Big Four accountancy firms in the UK, only 30% of new graduate trainees obtained their education from a non-selective state school in the UK, compared to around 90% of the population (Ashley & Empson, 2016: 131–132). By the same token, McKinsey, a leading management consulting firm, publicly emphasizes that the firm picks only the best graduates from the top universities to create an elite workforce, whose skills and expertise are regularly appraised (Groß & Kieser, 2006). This "elite" workforce is thus widely touted as composed of the "best and brightest" minds with the capability to innovate, conceptualize new forms of knowledge, and develop solutions in dynamic, complex fields. This pattern of elite firms recruiting from elite institutions is facilitated by developing strong relationships with elite universities and the subsequent "milk round," in which elite professional service firms offer aspiring professionals help and advice such as mock interviews and coaching for psychometric tests (Ashley & Empson, 2016: 128–129).

In contrast, hiring highly qualified individuals from lower-tier institutions creates a perceived risk that the professional service firm itself might be viewed as a lower-tier organization. According to a partner at a leading law firm in the UK (Ashley & Empson, 2016: 130–131):

Where you sell knowledge . . . it's very hard to take the risk on that . . . I think the natural inclination, just as our clients would go to who they perceive to be the best law firms, to provide the best service for us when we're looking to recruit . . . you're going to try to get the best. That's business sense. So naturally you would go to your old stomping grounds, the established universities, people where you've recruited from before.

Furthermore, the subtle cultural matching dynamics in professional service firms—such as those based on surfacing common interests and leisure activities in the interview process—serve to powerfully reinforce the selection of graduates from elite educational institutions by professional service firms (Rivera, 2016).

The elite educational credentials of professionals are prominently on display in investment banks' "beauty books," as they are known in the industry. These are the project pitch books to clients that showcase the bankers' picture profiles and their key accomplishments. Professional firms' websites, promotional materials, and pitches are replete with phrases such as "leading," "cutting-edge," "precedent-setting," and "premier" experts who have a "distinctive reputation." These references are sometimes legitimized by the cottage industry of professional ranking agencies and media outlets, which routinely publish the regional and national lists of top specialists in a given practice area.

Senior leaders of professional service firms are both encouraged and incentivized to be known as an expert in a particular area through trade publications, conferences, and media appearances (Groß & Kieser, 2006: 92). In fact, in several consulting firms whose employees I interviewed, attaining such expert status is inextricably linked to securing and keeping a partner position. Showcasing one's expertise conveys that professional service firms are constantly producing new knowledge and innovative, best-practice solutions, thus working to reinforce the firms' and the individual employees' expert status (Mitchell & Harvey, 2015). Some of the pressure to innovate and constantly stay a step ahead of the clients emerges from the professional service firms' proposition of highly customized work, which cannot be easily resold to a new client

(Løwendahl, 2005: 41). Nearly all the professional service firms offer specialized training to their clients, often free of charge. A management consulting firm can offer training in strategic analysis, whereas an intellectual property law firm can focus on recent developments in trademark litigation. Such training further highlights the professionals' state-of-the-art expertise.

THE NETWORK BASE OF POWER

Aside from securing a knowledge edge over their clients, professional service firms have grown to occupy pivotal network positions in the economy. Their professional activities situate them at the intersection of many different industrial sectors, thereby enabling them to bridge the flows of resources, knowledge, and information among parts of the network that are otherwise only weakly connected. Professional service firms frequently service clients from multiple industrial sectors and geographies, and they span commercial, governmental, and nonprofit organizations.

Extant research has widely associated such positions of brokerage with enhanced power and influence (Burt, 1982, 1992; Sytch, Tatarynowicz, & Gulati, 2012). By bridging distinct domains of expertise across diverse pockets of the economy, professional service firms access knowledge and information that their clients cannot. Generally speaking, an expert's standing does not arise solely, or even mainly, from producing completely original creations. More likely, one can develop an expert's reputation by borrowing insights and wisdom in one part of the network and applying them in another. Such advantage of a locally renowned genius has been variously described as "export-import" (Burt, 2004: 388), "bridging and learning" (Hargadon, 2002: 71), "borrowing" (March & Simon, 1958: 188), or "cross-realm transposition" (Powell, Packalen, & Whittington, 2012: 449).

Professional services firms' unique, boundary-spanning network positions enable them to excel at such knowledge transfers, and much of professional services' expert stature stems precisely from this advantage (Hargadon & Sutton, 1997). Professional service firms acquire such privileged network positions not only through their unique cross-cutting workflows, but also through the strategic placement of their "alumni." Many employees exit every year in the up-or-out system that still describes the majority of professional services. The firms subsequently work hard to place their ex-employees in the best possible corporate positions, further reinforcing their network advantage. The placement often occurs organically through a "revolving door," in which working with a particular client while at a professional service firm may morph into a future full-time position with that client (Wald, 2020).

In fact, evaluating the workers' future potential *beyond* professional services has even permeated the professional service firms' hiring practices. For example, many evaluators in professional services perceived the prestige of a candidate's school as an indicator of the candidate's "potential for future influence, fame, and status in society more broadly" (Rivera, 2011: 80). Furthermore, roughly 25% of evaluators who used educational prestige as the core screening variable admitted doing so out of the belief that "individuals from super-elite schools were more likely to 'be somebody' later in life than individuals from 'lesser' institutions" (Rivera, 2011: 80).

For example, an attorney at a top law firm justified his selection of a Yale Law student despite his belief that the individual would likely not remain in the legal field for long nor enjoy it:

> She will probably quit in two years, but I want people from Yale Law to walk through our doors. They are highly unlikely to be failing at life, and she could potentially one day be a judge or a congresswoman, or a client, or a politician. And if she has a connection to our firm, it bodes well for us in the future. (Rivera, 2011: 80)

Subsequently, relationships with a firm's alumni are maintained deliberately through a series of seminars, workshops, and other types of recurring events the firm organizes. The resultant boundary-spanning status further contributes to the professional service firms' network base of power, allowing their expert reputations to be widely known.

IMPLICATIONS FOR POWER AND INFLUENCE

The intricate mix of the professions' substantive and symbolic elements—all extolling the professionals' unrivaled expertise—coupled with their unique network positions create a strong edifice for professional service firms' power and influence. In fact, the power advantage of professional service firms can be so substantial that it may even flip the evident advantage of the principals presumed in the classic formulations of the agency theory. In the words of Anurag Sharma (1997: 770):

> The power asymmetry assumed in agency theory is reversed in exchanges involving professional agents who have power over lay principals because they control relevant task-related knowledge and have the expert authority to influence greatly (if not drive) the standards of exchange.

A long range of studies, dating back to Stanley Milgram's (1963, 1965) infamous electric shock experiments, instruct us that people are strongly compliant with signs and signals of expertise. In Milgram's experiments, which were disguised as a memory game, he separated the participants into teachers and learners. Teachers were asked to initially read a list of word pairs to the student and then only read the first word of the pair along with four different pair options. The student was asked to indicate which of the four terms was the original pair of the word, signaling the answer by pressing a switch that lit up one of four numbered quadrants in an answer box.

If the learner made a mistake, the teacher was asked to administer an electric shock to the learner; while all participants perceived the shock generator to be real, the instrument was a simulated shock generator. With every mistake, the teachers were asked to increase the voltage of the shock. There were 30 switches in front of the teacher, which increased the voltage in 15-volt increments, all the way to 450 volts. Milgram asked how likely people were to administer the electric shock to others and go all the way to 450 volts, all because a scientist on the premises of the prestigious Yale University, wearing an authoritative lab coat, told them to continue.

Milgram polled 40 medical psychiatrists to estimate the results. They believed, on average, that 3.7% of the participants would administer 300 volts and only 0.1% would administer 450 volts (Milgram, 1965). In reality, in some variants of Milgram's experiments, not a single participant stopped before 300 volts, and as many as two-thirds administered the 450-volt shock twice before he told them to stop (Milgram, 1963, 1965).[3]

Certain dramatism permeates the classic studies of people's compliance with expertise and authority. The point of citing this research is not to equate professional service firms' power and influence with ethical transgressions. Not at all. In fact, it would be inaccurate to leap from the asymmetry in knowledge—as some scholars of agency do—to the motivations behind certain observable actions with almost inseparable references to opportunism. This work aims to illustrate that an expertise advantage is a potent precursor for influence, which can materialize through both conscious and unconscious cognitive processes.

Consider the elite status of professional service firms obtained in part through selecting graduates from elite educational institutions. Research is unambiguous that educational credentials are widely interpreted as signals of status, expertise, and authority, thus further perpetuating an expert advantage (Rider, 2014; Rivera, 2011; Spence,

---

3. A relatively unfamiliar background story behind these experiments by Stanley Milgram is that he was trying to explain the Nazi's atrocities during the Second World War by the German people's unusual authoritarian tendencies. He intended to use American participants as the control group. His expectation was to show non-compliance with authority ordering electric shocks in America and strong compliance in Germany, which would support his theory. However, Milgram never got around to studying Germans because the results on the Americans were so shocking (Abelson, Frey, & Gregg, 2014: 247). The conclusions that stemmed from his research, in contrast, indicated that because people were generally so compliant with expertise and authority, even democratic societies such as the United States "cannot be counted on to insulate its citizens from brutality and inhumane treatment at the direction of malevolent authority" (Milgram, 1965: 75).

1973). Educational affiliations are perceived as reflecting peoples' intellectual, social, and moral worth, as well as superior cognitive and noncognitive abilities (Rivera, 2011: 75). All these perceptions are known to powerfully shape people's compliance with experts. An in-house counsel offered observations on how this can play out in practice:

> *I went to Harvard, I went to the top, you know, I practiced at a top-tier law firm. I, from the beginning, have split my time with the business school, so I don't think I'm your typical lawyer in that regard . . . But for a lot of lawyers that I know and, especially if they don't have that top branding of law school, because law school is so—in the same way that business school is, I think—but even more because it's more academically focused. So it's kind of like that hangover of where you went to school implies something about how smart you are, which I don't think is true, necessarily, but I've seen other colleagues get intimidated by this, you know, fifty-year-old partner who comes in saying, "This is what has to happen," and then they just go, "Okay, I'll do that" . . . I don't do that. But I think it happens to other people.*

Considering, as described above, that professional service firms are indeed more likely than their clients to draw talent from elite higher education institutions, the dynamics the counsel referenced are likely to be present at scale.

Complementing the professionals' elite educational credentials in projecting authority and expertise is the selection and training of professionals on self-presentation. In general, people often conflate confidence with expertise. This means that people's communication skills could be interpreted as expertise, regardless of their ability to engage effectively in the focal task (Collins & Evans, 2007). This is especially true when concrete, task-relevant information is limited (Bottger, 1984; Littlepage, Schmidt, Whisler, & Frost, 1995), which is often the case in ambivalent knowledge-based work and which characterizes much of professional services. Acutely aware of such confidence bias, professionals are often pressured to project confidence, even when they are unsure.

Not surprisingly, professionals' internal training and development is focused on how to exude knowledge and confidence, which further buttresses their expert status in the eyes of the clients.

Structural work constraints on information flows can powerfully complement the professionals' expert standing. For example, once litigation begins, there is typically limited direct communication between the plaintiff and defendant, who do not want to inadvertently disclose injurious facts or otherwise weaken the case. The same dynamics can emerge between two companies entering a merger transaction. Executives may protect sensitive competitive information with respect to parts of the business beyond the transaction's scope or in the event the transaction does not close. As a result, external counsel, consultants, or investment bankers can effectively acquire the *tertius gaudens* (i.e., the "rejoicing third") position by serving as a third-party intermediating between the two alters who are not directly connected or may even be in tension (Simmel, 1955: 154). This structural position is known to engender power and influence (Burt, 1992; Fernandez & Gould, 1994).

It is, therefore, understandable that several studies in economics, psychology, and sociology have raised concerns about the degree of control that professionals can acquire over their clients due to asymmetries in knowledge and information (Arrow, 1963: 948, 951; Balafoutas & Kerschbamer, 2020; French & Raven, 1959: 267; Reed, 1996: 583–586). This power asymmetry is unique to professional–principal relations. It gives professionals distinct power over principals through their disproportionate influence on the standards of exchange as well as "by virtue of their expertise, functional indispensability, and intrinsic ambiguity associated with the services they provide" (Sharma, 1997: 768). As the perfect and imperfect agent can be perceived as two ends of a spectrum, Peter Zweifel and Willard G. Manning (2000) attributed the supplier's degree of decision-making authority as a key factor determining the nature of the agency relationship.

It is essential to note that such power and influence are *not* inherently detrimental to the clients. For example, Parsons (1968) emphasized that the ensuing control is essential for professional service firms to carry out their work. Indeed, professionals often come into their client organizations as outsiders who are tasked with changing entrenched processes and norms, implementing new practices, and driving other forms of structural and behavioral change. They must do so while being relatively unfamiliar with the nuances of the clients' work and lacking strong working relationships with them. In such circumstances, projecting the image of expertise and authority is indispensable for accomplishing any type of meaningful action. Notably, however, the very same power and influence that create a powerful edifice for professionals' ability to drive change can also result in SID.

As discussed thus far, professionals' advantageous network positions greatly enable their recombinant expertise and the ensuing power by allowing them to quickly tap into and synthesize insights across distinct knowledge domains. Such privileged network positions often allow professional service firms to control the structure of economic exchange. For example, lawyers can play a significant role in determining which clients interface with which investors, playing a critical "gatekeeper" role in investment transactions (Suchman & Cahill, 1996: 698).

In addition, such privileged network positions offer the added benefit of control over clients' reputations. One senior executive I interviewed mentioned that she frequently had to self-censor in criticizing professionals' work. "Why?," I asked in bewilderment, "You are paying for their services." "*Because they're present in the external market, and they have a very, very heavy weight on your image and reputation,*" was her response. The executive then elaborated on the possible implications of consultants' referrals in financial markets: "*You know, the senior partner of [leading consulting firm] is constantly with the same bankers and this and that, and he talks about the CEO of a particular company, 'oh that guy is fantastic, we work so well with him, you know, we just help them with this and this and this and that.'*" Another executive cited the key role professional service firms can play in providing referrals for new jobs. It is indeed often the case that companies searching to fill senior executive positions turn to financial services, consulting, and law firms for informal referrals regarding possible succession candidates.

Another senior executive reflected on the similarly powerful position occupied by major investment banks:

The core lead banks, Goldman, JP Morgan, you know, they just drive such a percentage of the market. I just have never seen anything come back on them negatively, ever, even if it's clear that they have botched an IPO and that company got screwed . . . They wield such power, especially over the IPO market. We would never say anything bad— I won't even tell you who it is right now, who I think was incredibly sketchy—we would never say anything bad about them because they are such a power player in the market, that it could never get out that we were saying bad stuff about them because if they tried to blackball us or say that we were bad for some reason in an analyst report about us that was bad. We're tanked. Companies have no recourse against the bankers. None.

All in all, the coalescence of professional service firms' unique and visible expertise coupled with their advantageous network positions endow them with a significant power and influence advantage over the buyers of their services. Such an advantage stands alongside uncertainty in being the second key enabler of SID.

CHAPTER SUMMARY

In addition to uncertainty, the second key enabling market condition of supplier-induced demand is the power advantage wielded by professional service firms over their buyers. This advantage is primarily rooted in the firms' superior expertise and access to information. At the core of professional service firms' strategic differentiation lies their proficiency in cutting-edge professional expertise. This often manifests as specialized knowledge within a given domain (niche expertise) or the capacity to integrate insights from various related fields (recombinant expertise). Integral to professional services are the mechanisms that render this expertise visible and compelling to clients, reinforced through personnel selection and training practices, such as recruiting from elite schools and aiding professionals in developing superior self-presentation skills. Additionally, professionals fortify their bases of power through their unique positions in market networks of economic and informational exchange. This arises from professional service firms' cultivation of networks that bridge otherwise unconnected clients or sectors of the economy. Consequently, professionals frequently wield power by controlling deal flows for companies or even influencing the personal outcomes of client executives in the labor market by shaping job referrals. These power advantages coalesce into a formidable influence, wherein clients are more inclined to adhere to the advice and recommendations of professional service firms both consciously and subconsciously.

CHAPTER 5

The Imperfect Agents

In conjunction with uncertainty of work and power advantage of professional service firms, an essential condition for the creation of supplier-induced demand (SID) is the imperfect agency of professional service providers. "Don't Ask the Barber Whether You Need a Haircut," the title of Daniel Greenberg's (1972) article, perfectly captures the agency relationship that characterizes contexts in which SID may occur. Discussing the notion of technology assessment, Greenberg (1972: 58) observed that "the creators of a technology constitute the worst possible source of advice as to whether it should be utilized." This is because, in the contexts conducive to SID, suppliers are "imperfect agents" (Mooney & Ryan, 1993). Not only do they take on the role of the consumer's agent—diagnosing their needs and supplying expert advice on how to fulfill such needs—but they simultaneously sell them the goods or services to do so. Put differently, markets for contemporary legal, consulting, financial, marketing, and other types of professional services often deviate significantly from the classic blueprints of competitive markets, in which buyers know what they want and then knowingly choose the best supplier to meet those needs. In contrast, in many types of professional services, suppliers play a critical agent role in determining the nature of the problem or opportunity that buyers face, as well as the course of action to address that opportunity (cf. Arrow, 1963; Kosnik & Shapiro, 1997).

Concerns about a problematic relationship between agents and principals are most famously raised in the context of the separation between corporate ownership and control. In what has become known as the agency theory, companies are viewed as collections of contracts between company managers (agents) and risk-bearing shareholders (principals) (Fama, 1980; Jensen & Meckling, 1976). The agents control the day-to-day operations of a company and may differ from their principals in both risk tolerance and individual aims. Because it is challenging for the principals to surveil the agents' daily activities, agency theory focused on recommendations that revolved around either (1) better monitoring of the agents' actions through enhanced monitoring mechanisms or (2) better alignment of the agents' and principals' objectives through outcome-based contracts. So, if you ever wondered what explains our collective fascination with independent directors on company boards or the exorbitant equity-based compensation handed out to senior executives, you now know what to blame.[1]

Later research has transcended this "positivist" application of agency theory to corporate control. It illuminated instead that agency concerns permeate a broad range of situations in which "a principal and an agent . . . are engaged in cooperative behavior, but have differing goals and differing attitudes toward risk" (Eisenhardt, 1989: 59). Relationships between clients and professional service firms have been found to exhibit key elements of agentic relationships and have subsequently been fruitfully analyzed through the lens of agency (Anagol, Cole, & Sarkar, 2017; Chen, Huang, Ma, & Yu, 2021; McLaughlin, 1996; Sharma, 1997; Uribe, Sytch, & Kim, 2020).

More important, relationships with professional service firms constitute a rather unusual form of agency that departs from the theory's foundational assumptions. Two of these departures appear consequential. First, as described in detail in the preceding chapter, in professional service contexts, the power advantage is often ascribed to the agent, rather than to the principal (Kosnik & Shapiro, 1997; Sharma, 1997). This is due to the deep asymmetries in knowledge and information

---

1. Note that much of the empirical research is skeptical about the effectiveness of agency theory's normative recommendations. For example, stacking boards of directors with independent directors is known to elicit powerful cooptation behaviors from senior managers that tend to overwhelm the directors' structural independence (Westphal & Park, 2020; Westphal, 1998). The alignment of outcomes with increasingly short-term-oriented owners can similarly lead to dubious outcomes for organizations (Ahuja, 2022).

between agents and principals, the limited control of principals over the agents, and the agents' advantageous network positions. Kosnik and Shapiro (1997: 8), for example, reflected on the ensuing power relationship in the context of investment banking:

> What actions can principal clients take to protect their interests from self-serving representatives? The traditional solution offered by agency theory is to design 'optimal contracts' that realign the interests of principals and agents. However, there is a caveat in this remedy. This rational prescription rests on the assumption that principals have the power to control their agents by overseeing the agents' behavior and assessing the quality of their representation. In the relationship between investment banks and prospective acquisition partners, this assumption may have limited validity.

The second difference concerns the fusion of the role of an agent and a seller that professional service firms play. Standard agency theory assumes the principal's and agent's utility functions are independent. In contrast, professional service contexts are described by interdependent agent and principal utility functions, convoluting the role of the seller and giving rise to the notion of an imperfect agent (Mooney & Ryan, 1993). Thus, whereas standard agency theory addresses problems related to the agent potentially shirking, professional service contexts may encompass explicit conflicts of interest and incentivize the agent to act in direct contrast with the principal's interests (Richardson & Peacock, 2006; Van Doorslaer & Geurts, 1987).

Unease about the role imperfect agents play famously surfaced in healthcare economics. On the one hand, physicians act as the patient's agent by undertaking the responsibility of medical care provision and assistance. On the other, they may simultaneously act as a service provider, wherein providing a particular medical service and the corresponding income and satisfaction can be related to the price and amount of the service rendered (Evans, 1974; Mooney & Ryan, 1993; Zweifel & Manning, 2000). Similarly, the problem of imperfect agency has been of increasing concern in professional service contexts, including real estate brokerage, investment banking, marketing, management consulting, and many others (Kosnik & Shapiro, 1997). As agents, professional service firms routinely help clients diagnose their needs and problems, identify promising opportunities, and consider the required spectrum of organizational interventions. In the words of Robert Dingwall (1983: 5), "not only do professions presume to tell the rest of their society what is good and right for it: they can also set the very terms of thinking about problems which fall in their domain. They exemplify in an extreme form the role trust plays in modern societies with an advanced division of labor." As sellers, though, professional service firms strive to sustain their own growth and drive profitability by touting the services they offer.

For example, acting as agents, investment banks advise on the scale and scope of commercial enterprises and proactively offer opportunities for asset acquisitions and divestitures.[2] The CFO of a startup company I interviewed described that an investment bank greatly influenced even such a foundational decision regarding whether to take his company public. "*You are ready, you are ready,*" was the incessant call to action from the investment bankers. As sellers, the same investment bankers are eager to collect the fee for taking the company public or closing a merger transaction. In legal services, law firms routinely approach potential clients with offers to initiate intellectual property litigation against potential infringers, which the law firms proactively identify. Their agent role in this respect encompasses a complex analysis of the scope of the client's patent claims, the features of the potentially infringing products, and the strategic considerations of choosing to enforce the company's intellectual property in court. The seller in them vies for the opportunity to amass billable hours in protracted litigation. In management consulting, an agent assesses whether the current organizational structure meets the needs of a company's strategy and its operating demands. As a seller, that same consultant could be keen on selling a consulting engagement to change the company's structure and its operating model.

2. By doing so, agents also significantly influence the market for corporate control, which ironically is believed to mitigate a class of agency problems (cf. Fama, 1980; Fama & Jensen, 1983).

The dual agent–seller role professional service firms play describes both the initiation of transactions and the decisions regarding their continuation. Corporate finance executives I interviewed reported how investment bankers get closely involved in conceiving the merger and actively take part in decisions as to whether the deal should continue once the process is underway. Likewise, once the formal complaint has been filed in a court of law, external legal counsel is ordinarily embroiled in decisions regarding whether to continue with litigation, settle out of court, or drop the case. And management consultants often help determine the scale of reorganization, the reach of a new operating model, and the degree to which employees need to be trained in the new ways of working.

MISALIGNED INCENTIVES AND CONFLICTS OF INTEREST

The most frequent link drawn from imperfect agency to SID is glaringly evident. It often arises inseparably from the motivations stemming from the conflict of interest and misaligned incentives inherent in imperfect agency. Imagine a doctor caught in the crosscurrents of conflicting interests. On one hand, there is the noble oath to prioritize patient well-being above all else. Yet, lurking in the shadows, there's also the temptation—a siren call, if you will—of financial gain tied to prescribing certain treatments or medications.

The agentic relationship between clients and professional service firms entails clients delegating decision-making authority to professionals. In turn, the imperfect agency and the accompanying incentives create a conflict of interest in which professionals' wealth maximization does not align well with the clients' long-term interests. As readers know, a significant body of agency theory is devoted to the elusive quest for the perfect contract, in which the principals can pay the agent in such a way to make her behave precisely in line with the principals' desires (e.g., Agrawal & Mandelker, 1987; Jensen & Meckling, 1976).

The heavy focus on economic incentives has led to the emergence of standalone theories explaining SID principally through this lens.

Among the most prominent of such theories is the target-income perspective, which suggests that professional service providers adjust their
workload to maintain desirable levels of income (Evans, 1974). Conceptually, Evans (1974) and subsequent research argued that suppliers
induce demand as long as the marginal disutility of inducement is small
enough (Grytten & Sørensen, 2001: 380). Pragmatically, a supplier will
induce demand until the supplier reaches an optimal income–leisure
tradeoff point, such that the losses of leisure equal the benefits from
increased income. Scholars have relied on the professionals' presumed
desire to maintain a certain income level to explain, for example, why
professionals induce demand for their services when they encounter an
increase in the volume of service providers and the supply of services
(Carmignani & Giacomelli, 2010; Richardson & Peacock, 2006).

   Associated empirical research has examined how changes in the economic incentives for service providers shaped the provision of specific
services. In one such illustration, existing studies in healthcare explored
the consequences of the fee-for-service systems (FFS), in which medical
professionals are compensated for each service they provide. The effects
of this compensation system are studied relative to those of the capitation payment systems, in which physicians receive a fixed compensation
per consumer per unit of time for the services delivered. The primary hypothesis of this work is that FFS systems incentivize service providers to
induce demand relative to capitation systems (van Dijk, van den Berg,
Verheij, Spreeuwenberg et al., 2013). In line with this hypothesis, Arnold
M. Epstein and colleagues (1986) found that physicians working under
FFS systems ordered 50% more electrocardiogram tests and 40% more
chest X-rays—both highly profitable tests in the FFS system—compared
to physicians working under capitation systems. Along similar lines,
pediatricians paid under the FFS system scheduled visits in excess of the
national pediatric care standards, compared to their salaried colleagues
(Hickson, Altemeier, & Perrin, 1987).

   In more recent work, scholars have similarly identified the effects of
remuneration changes on SID following the introduction of a new Dutch
health insurance act in 2006 and the corresponding changes in financial incentives (van Dijk et al., 2013). In more extreme cases of SID,

Hitoshi Shigeoka and Kiyohide Fushimi (2014) investigated how likely newborns were to be kept in the neonatal intensive care unit (NICU) following a change in the remuneration system that made NICU stays more lucrative for hospitals than regular hospital stays. They found that while the NICU stays for infants with low birth weight increased by more than 10%, the infants' total hospital stay did not change. This finding implied that infants could have stayed just as safely in regular hospital beds (Shigeoka & Fushimi, 2014: 169–175).

Even how babies get delivered—by natural birth or a cesarean section—which can result in different health risks for moms and babies, can be shaped by incentives. Lennart Bogg and colleagues (2016) analyzed two different programs the Indian government introduced to attract people to hospitals over home deliveries. In the Indian state of Madhya Pradesh, obstetricians were paid more for cesarean sections than for vaginal deliveries. By contrast, in the Indian state of Gujarat, obstetricians received a fixed amount for 100 deliveries, regardless of the type of delivery. Stunningly, the rate of cesarean deliveries in Madhya Pradesh—where obstetricians were incentivized to perform c-sections over vaginal deliveries—increased from 26% to 40.7% of all deliveries in just four years. By contrast, in Gujarat, where the incentives were procedure-agnostic, the rate of c-sections slightly declined.

The previously cited studies furnish evidence consistent with the notion that suppliers' incentives play a discernible role in stimulating demand in healthcare. Noteworthy is that recent investigations of incentives in healthcare have used natural experiments, which represent some of the most robust econometric research designs. A natural experiment occurs when a policy change permits scholars to compare behaviors or outcomes between groups affected by the policy alteration and those that are not, or between the behaviors and outcomes within the same group before and after the policy change. The rigor of such approaches, which relies on the pseudo-random assignment of territories or individuals to new policies, serves to mitigate the risk of erroneously classifying spurious correlations as causal effects.

However, this evidence does not always offer definitive insight into the ultimate impact of induced healthcare practices on patients. This uncertainty is a common challenge in research on SID in healthcare, leaving analysts to question whether patients are being "over-served" with induced demand or whether they were "under-served" before it, relative to their needs. For instance, does ordering more electrocardio-gram tests and chest X-rays aid in diagnosis and eventual treatment? Or does prolonging stays in the NICU enhance newborns' health outcomes?

Although hardly more disconcerting compared to how babies are born or treated, similar concerns about pernicious incentives have been raised regarding professional services. In legal services, especially in litigation, scholars contrasted the models of compensation based on (1) contingency fees, in which the lawyers share in the legal outcome; and (2) those based on work hours or legal acts (e.g., Bielen & Marneffe, 2018). If a lawyer is paid using a contingent fee structure, the lawyer usually receives a fraction of the settlement or trial awards but remains responsible for litigation-related costs. In the billable-hour or fee-per-legal-act models, the compensation is based on the time spent working on the case or on the number of legal acts executed (e.g., motions or witness requests), regardless of the outcome.

Neither compensation structure is perfect. Under the contingency structure, the lawyer may encourage an unattractive settlement, spend inadequate time working on the case, or lack the incentive to bring the case to court. In the billable-hour or fee-per-legal-act models, lawyers may be incentivized to spend more time working on the case than necessary, bring it to court even if that course of action is not in the client's best interest, reject a settlement despite it being the better op-tion for the client, or initiate unnecessary legal actions and submissions (Carmignani & Giacomelli, 2010; Polinsky & Rubinfeld, 2003). The non-contingency models of compensation in legal services routinely trigger concerns about SID: the billable-hour model has become nearly synonymous with overbilling, yet it remains prevalent in litigation.[3]

---

3. Many of the lawyers interviewed for this book commented that the billable-hours system has developed a "bad rep," and that some firms are trying to implement hybrid compen-sation systems, in which at least some remuneration is contingent on the legal outcome. However, the interviewees mentioned many constraints on implementing these systems in intellectual property litigation. For example, few patent lawsuits make it to the verdict phase, with the majority ending up in private settlements. This makes it difficult to develop clear

Similarly, when heeding a financial advisor's advice on which investments to choose, research instructs us to pay close attention to the personal commissions the advisor would get from those recommendations. One study documented how advisors—compensated based on the generated fees—sold actively managed funds with higher fees, even if the client started with a well-diversified, low-fee portfolio (Mullainathan, Noeth, & Schoar, 2012). Another study used data on reverse convertible bonds issued from 2008 to 2012, which included information regarding the commissions paid to financial brokers. The study documented that brokers influenced consumers to buy inferior, higher-fee products that entailed significant economic benefits for the brokers (Egan, 2019).

In investment banking, scholars and practitioners raised the alarm about the misaligned incentives in mergers and acquisitions (M&A). In M&A transactions, banks are usually compensated with a percentage of the total deal value. Yet they collect only a small percentage of their commission, or none at all, if the deal is not completed. Thus, banks are compensated based on making the deal happen, regardless of its long-term success (Kosnik & Shapiro, 1997). In this regard, an investment banker—compared to the owners of the firms themselves—is more strongly incentivized to initiate and push for the completion of M&As (Parvinen & Tikkanen, 2007: 768–772). Numerous studies, accordingly, have documented that engaging external financial advisors leads to a higher likelihood of deal completion (Chen et al., 2021; Ertugrul & Krishnan, 2014; Rau, 2000).

Disconcertingly, because the skewed incentives lead investment bankers to push for a greater number of M&As, such circumstances, in turn, may reduce the average quality of M&A transactions (Moeller, Schlingemann, & Stulz, 2005). In other words, under the fee-per-deal structure, completing *any* M&A transaction is better for the investment banker than completing none. Thus, professionals may both overestimate the benefits of an M&A and suggest acquisition targets that

outcome metrics. Even if the case makes it to a verdict, a similar challenge may persist because many parties bring several claims. Frequently, only some of the claims are supported, whereas others are not, which complicates the development of outcome metrics. All in all, alternative compensation systems have failed to spread in intellectual property law, and the billable-hours system continues to dominate intellectual property litigation.

align with personal strategic objectives rather than with their clients' goals (Kesner, Shapiro, & Sharma, 1994; Parvinen & Tikkanen, 2007).

My fieldwork reinforced this suspicion. One experienced senior executive reflected:

> So bankers are the most egregious actors in this regard, in my opinion. And they are also the most self-serving because they make the most money on it, because they're doing fee-based transactions. So they take a percentage cut of whatever the deal is. So they have huge motivation to move deals, and to move IPOs . . . and the main experience that I have with them is on IPOs and M&As. And so they are coming to us, at every company I've been at all the time, 'Let us run a search for you, let us get you IPO-ready.' And they will tell you whatever they think you want to hear in order to try and drive that business, even if it's not as accurate . . . There is no incentive for bankers to walk away, which is why they push, push, push.

Another senior executive echoed this sentiment:

> There definitely is misalignment with incentives, particularly with bankers, because they really want the deal to close . . . they want the IPO to launch, they're also not going to get paid if the IPO doesn't launch. So they have this very significant all-or-nothing incentive to make sure that deal closes, the IPO launches, and the transactions are consummated.

Consultants were similarly under intense scrutiny for the incentive conflict in their dual role of an advisor and a seller of services (Cain, Loewenstein, & Moore, 2005). Indeed, these incentives often stimulate the pursuit of reorganization programs, changes in operational models, or entry into new markets—or any other organizational activity—all of which entail more consulting work. In some cases, concerns over conflicts of interest stem from the assortment of services the same firm offers. For example, the combination of audit and consulting services provided by traditional public accounting firms has rightly made many observers uneasy (Demski, 2003; Drucker, 2022). Similarly, the UK Competition and Markets Authority (2019) expressed apprehension about investment consultants performing both advisory and fiduciary management services for company pension funds. This dual role makes it challenging for individual employees to adequately assess information about the fees and quality of investment products.[4]

In the most extreme cases, concerns about incentives have been elevated to fraud, in which the supplier has either an observed or presumed intent to deceive the buyer deliberately. "If a mechanic tells you that he has to replace a part in your car, don't forget to ask him to put the replaced part into the trunk of your car," is the fraud-averting advice from scholars of credence goods (Dulleck & Kerschbamer, 2006: 5). Like any other field, professional services are not entirely immune to the problem of deliberate deception. For example, the 1994–1995 survey conducted by the Cumberland School of Law in Alabama reported that 23% of participating lawyers had billed more than one client for the same hour of work and 66% were aware of specific cases of bill padding (Segal, 1998). Numerous lawyers have been charged, suspended, or disbarred for billing more than 24 hours a day (Rubino, 2022; Weiss, 2010).

In a similar fashion, several consulting firms, including some of the leading global brands such as McKinsey, have been mired in legal proceedings for deceptive billing practices and other forms of fraud (Department of Justice, 2021, 2022; Forsythe & Bogdanich, 2022; Raymond, 2016; Stempel, 2022; Voisin, 2022). In financial services, the

---

4. The issue of conflict of interest arising from dual roles has also been raised concerning governmental organizations. For instance, when the Central Intelligence Agency (CIA) was established in 1947 in the United States under the National Security Act (1947, Section 102), its structure diverged from similar setups. In contrast to the British model, where there was a clear separation between personnel analyzing intelligence and identifying actionable opportunities, and those executing covert operations in the field, the CIA amalgamated all these functions under one roof. This meant advising the President of the United States on situations and recommending specific operations, while simultaneously executing those actions. As one expert put it, "this naturally gave the incentive to present the world as if covert action was necessary everywhere" (Knappenberger, 2024).

incentives geared toward sustaining a flow of new deals were linked to misreporting and deliberately concealing credit risk, all of which contributed to the 2008–2009 US housing and financial crisis through various forms of fraud and deception (Griffin, 2021).

THE COUNTERFORCE OF EMBEDDEDNESS

Although there is a pervasive concern regarding the potential for opportunistic behavior in professional services, it is unlikely to be the underlying cause of SID. This is due to the counteracting effects of embeddedness. For strategic reasons, professional service firms have prioritized cultivating long-term, close relationships with their clients, moving away from purely transactional, arm's-length arrangements (Armbrüster, 2006; Broschak, 2015; Greenwood, Li, Prakash, & Deephouse, 2005; Sturdy, Kirkpatrick, Reguera, Blanco-Oliver et al., 2020).

Extant research has suggested that this trend toward long-term relationships is increasingly apparent. As Andrew J. Sturdy and colleagues (2020) indicated, a substantial proportion of consultants' revenue is derived from repeat business, with 50% to 70% of consultant projects being completed for past clients. While consulting projects in the 1960s–1980s were often transactional in nature, with consultants working on a single, self-contained project, consultants have increasingly established enduring relationships with client firms (Poulfelt & Olson, 2018). Bain is perceived to have pioneered the consulting–client long-term relationship model by exclusively serving a large client in a single industry, rejecting projects from other firms in the same industry. IT consulting firms have followed suit, frequently establishing offices within clients' facilities for multimillion-dollar projects and remaining with the client for five years or longer. Currently, the prevailing practice in numerous large consulting firms is to cultivate long-lasting relationships with clients, with around 60% of consulting revenue stemming from existing or prior clients (Poulfelt & Olson, 2018: 30).

Cultivating long-term, close relationships with clients, versus maintaining purely transactional arrangements, is not unique to the consulting industry. The shift toward strategic partnerships is increasingly apparent in professional services more broadly. A survey of 289 participants who had contracted a professional service firm over the previous 12 months, as reported by the *Financial Times*, found that 62% of respondents believed that their relationships with professional service firms had become more strategic and less transactional. Furthermore, an overwhelming majority of respondents (72%) agreed that they preferred to work with firms on a long-term, rather than on a project-by-project, basis (Financial Times, 2021). At an event for senior partners of a leading accounting firm I attended, many joked that they had managed their key clients for so many years—approaching 10 or 15 in some cases—that they knew the client firms better than the clients' own senior executives. Many professional service firms make a point of locating their employees near their clients. These client relationships often involve a range of services, leading to greater mutual dependence between clients and service providers. Over time, these repeated economic exchanges become embedded in social relationships characterized by trust, cohesion, fine-grained information sharing, and joint action (Granovetter, 1985; Gulati & Sytch, 2007, 2008; Uzzi, 1997; McEvily, Perrone, & Zaheer, 2003).

The development of social relationships is a hallmark of embedded economic exchanges, where business relationships evolve from being driven solely by economic imperatives to being influenced heavily by social considerations. This is largely due to the repeated nature of business transactions, which gives individuals the opportunity to get to know one another beyond their professional roles. In doing so, they gain insight into each other's preferences and interests outside of work, building a bond that extends beyond just instrumental value. As such relationships strengthen over time, uncertainty about exchange partners diminishes, leading to a shift from rigid formal contracts to more informal, oral agreements and mutual understanding. This is because transacting parties grow comfortable with one another and become less concerned about opportunism (Emerson, 1981; Gulati & Sytch, 2008; Mayer, Davis, & Schoorman, 1995; Molm & Cook, 1995). Specifically, Ranjay Gulati (1995) found that repeated exchanges between organizations were characterized by less formal contracts, reflecting the development of mutual understanding and trust. This encourages parties to rely more on oral agreements and remain confident that unexpected contingencies will be resolved fairly.

Embedded relationships in professional services are often driven by the mutuality of dependence, which occurs when parties conduct a larger share of their business with one another. To strengthen this dynamic further, professional service firms have increasingly engaged with clients on an entire portfolio of services, rather than just a single service. This strategic approach offers a range of benefits, such as reducing client search and marketing costs, increasing switching costs for clients, and creating unique offerings that are more difficult for competitors to imitate. However, a crucial byproduct is the increase in mutual dependence, which fosters more open joint collaboration characterized by fine-grained information transfers and high levels of joint action (Gulati & Sytch, 2007).

Scholars have similarly examined extensively the concept of "relational cohesion" and its role in fostering commitment in repeated exchange relationships. According to this body of work (Lawler, Thye, & Yoon, 2000; Lawler & Yoon, 1993, 1996, 1998), emotions that individuals experience during repeated exchanges can trigger a cognitive process that attributes some of these emotions to the relationship itself, effectively imbuing it with intrinsic value. Positive emotions that result from these exchanges can then enhance the level of cohesion and commitment among the involved parties. Empirical evidence has suggested that this can lead to more frequent unilateral contributions to the relationship and a willingness to remain committed to it, even in the presence of alluring alternatives (Lawler & Yoon, 1993, 1998).

Consider an illustration of how embedded economic exchanges could suppress opportunistic motives and pursuits. Do parties in a business relationship continue to collaborate when the endgame is known? Classic game theory says no. Once players know the end is near, they become self-interested and cooperative behavior is greatly diminished. But what if the players are embedded in social relationships? According to a study by Brian Uzzi (1997) on the New York City apparel industry, parties in embedded relationships can defy game theory and continue to cooperate even when the endgame is clear. A manufacturer in Uzzi's (1997) study was moving its entire production to Asia, signaling the beginning of the endgame for its contractors in New York City. In this situation, game theory suggests that the manufacturer should keep this information to itself, so contractors do not produce lower-quality goods or otherwise reduce their commitment to what is now a temporary relationship. But instead, the CEO personally notified his embedded ties, trusting they would continue to provide quality goods and services, even in the face of losing his business. Surprisingly, the notification of the loss of business only reaffirmed the commitment between the manufacturer and its suppliers, which the suppliers repaid by continuing to provide quality goods and services.

When examining the research on the negative impact of incentives, it becomes evident that many of the studies were conducted in contexts in which embedded relationships were lacking. For example, in research on biased financial advice, auditors posed as new customers meeting financial advisors for the first time (Mullainathan, Noeth, & Schoar, 2012). This scenario eliminated any pre-existing relational history or social foundation. Similarly, in medical settings where decisions were made about the delivery of babies, such as whether to opt for cesarean or natural birth, or how long infants should stay in neo-natal units, it is unlikely that long-term, embedded relationships existed between medical professionals and the mothers (Bogg, Diwan, Vora, & DeCosta, 2016; Shigeoka & Fushimi, 2014). For example, in the previously mentioned study on cesarean versus natural birth deliveries in Indian hospitals, different incentives aimed to influence patients to choose hospital deliveries over home deliveries, indicating patients' limited prior exposure to hospitals (Bogg et al., 2016).

This work on healthcare brings to mind a personal experience. Picture this: a large, flashy, and bustling dental office where patients come and go like subway trains. In such a frenzied environment, where you encounter a different dentist each visit, it is no surprise that patients might feel as if they were just another widget on a conveyor belt, with little personal attention or care. For me, the issue was much more serious than a mere lack of warmth or bedside manners. Every year, like clockwork, the dentists presented me with a treatment plan that was suspiciously designed to exhaust my insurance coverage. It did not matter which dentist I saw—each one had a knack for recommending new procedures that would conveniently be covered by my insurance. Whenever I questioned the need for such interventions, the response was always the same: "Don't worry, your insurance will cover it." But I did worry. I worried that I was being taken advantage of, that my health was being compromised for the sake of the dentist's bottom line. So, I did what any reasonable person would do: I found a new dentist and went for two and a half years without having a single major procedure.

However, the professional services context, characterized by embedded relationships, presents a significantly different landscape compared to many other service domains. Let us be clear: the imperfect agency of professionals—where they simultaneously offer advice on issues or opportunities and sell services—does indeed serve as a precursor to SID. However, the extensive embedded relationships within this sector should deter us from hastily attributing the derivative motivation of SID solely to incentives. Analyzing the phenomenon of SID in such settings must go beyond the narrow focus on incentives and resist the temptation to cast sweeping aspersions on the entire field. Being preoccupied with incentives alone risks overlooking a more intricate and multifaceted reality.

It is worth noting, of course, that not every client–provider relationship within professional services is deeply embedded. In scenarios where a provider pursues a singular transaction—think of an investment bank chasing after a specific initial public offering (IPO)—concerns about opportunistic behavior may indeed hold merit. Yet, as a general rule, professional service firms have placed a paramount emphasis on cultivating intimate ties with clients, fostering repeated interactions. In this domain, the notion of an unchecked pursuit of opportunistic gains as the primary impetus behind SID seems improbable.[5]

---

5. These arguments do not imply that embedded relationships are a universal panacea for more economically rewarding partnerships. There are clear downsides to relationships that are "over-embedded" in that they can completely subjugate economic imperatives to social

Take, for instance, the practices of banks like Goldman Sachs or Morgan Stanley. These institutions often extend their involvement beyond just the realm of investment banking during IPO discussions, roping in private wealth management advisors. These advisors are not the gatekeepers of the IPO; they hail from an entirely different division within the company, specializing in assisting individuals in managing and investing their savings. The banks recognize that senior figures within the IPOed company are poised to amass significant wealth, and thus, the banks offer supplementary services. Yet, entwined within this motive is an inherent commitment to cultivating lasting connections—a testament to the intrinsic value placed on embedded client relationships within the realm of professional services.

If it is not the overt pursuit of personal gain, then what exactly motivates SID? In the Chapter 6, we will delve into the transformative shifts that have swept through the professional services sector, reshaping its foundational institutional logics—those sets of practices, norms, and cognitive perspectives ingrained within us through our professional experiences (Friedland & Alford, 1991: 248). These changes have left an indelible mark on the nature of the work itself, altering how professionals perceive their roles, redefining their measures of success, and even reshaping the very meaning of being a professional. It is this seismic shift that has largely fueled SID.

CHAPTER SUMMARY

Complementing uncertainty and supplier power, a third and final precondition for the emergence of supplier-induced demand is a supplier's "imperfect agency." Imperfect agency arises when suppliers simultaneously act as agents and sellers. In their role as agents, professionals diagnose the needs, problems, and opportunities faced by consumers. However, as sellers, they offer goods or services to address these needs directly to the same consumers. The prevailing belief in both academic

ones (Sorenson & Waguespack, 2006; Uzzi, 1997). In such relationships, for example, inferior performance may be more challenging to spot, call out, and walk away from.

discourse and practice is that imperfect agency drives supplier-induced demand through conflicts of interest and misaligned incentives. This would imply professionals' deliberate pursuit of personal gain at the expense of the client. However, in this chapter, I caution against over-simplifying the role of incentive conflicts, particularly in professional services. Much of the work in professional services is grounded in embedded relationships between clients and service providers, characterized by reduced opportunism and increased trust. Therefore, while imperfect agency enables supplier-induced demand, it should not be conflated with the professionals' motivation for such behavior.

CHAPTER 6

The Arrival of the Commercial Institutional Logic

In the preceding chapters, three conditions emerged as key enablers of supplier-induced demand (SID) in professional services. They involved, first, the uncertainty regarding the buyer's needs and the best ways to meet those needs, which accompanies—and is reinforced by—the ever-growing complexity of the knowledge economy. Second, the power of professional service firms, arising from their expert advantage and superior position in interorganizational networks. And third, professional service firms' imperfect agency, which entails simultaneously being both an agent advising the firm on a particular course of action and a seller of specific products and services.

Taken together, these three conditions create fertile soil for SID to emerge. Yet, even in aggregate, they cannot explain what motivates supply-inducing behaviors. A natural starting point in this respect is the explanation that is blindingly obvious. It is likely that when we think of SID, our minds turn to a conspicuous culprit: the economic incentives and the resultant conflicts of interest for service providers. This is exactly what each of us may be thinking if we have doubts, for example, about overpaying for a car repair job or plumber's services. And the insinuations of greed and opportunism have, at various times, been made with respect to lawyers, bankers, and consultants, among other professions (Moeller, Schlingemann, & Stulz, 2005; Parvinen & Tikkanen, 2007). Moreover, the model of billable hours—which incentivizes provisions

of (any) services to clients in large volumes—has gotten the worst reputation that anyone could have ever imagined (Parker & Ruschena,
2011).

And yet, as the preceding chapter elucidates, when we attempt to apply this explanation to the realm of professional services, what appears
glaringly obvious is, in fact, misleading. The provision of professional
services has evolved into a landscape characterized by ongoing interactions and deeply entrenched, multifaceted relationships with clients—a
far cry from the one-off transactions often seen in other sectors (Poulfelt
& Olson, 2018; Financial Times, 2021; Sturdy, Kilpatrick, Reguear,
Blanco-Oliver et al., 2020; Broschak, 2015). These embedded relationships are steeped in a tapestry of trust, open information exchange,
and social obligation that transcends mere economic calculation. It is
an environment where opportunistic pursuits find themselves at odds
with the very fabric of these connections, rendering the rampant pursuit
of self-interest far less likely (Granovetter, 1985; Gulati & Sytch, 2007,
2008; Lawler & Yoon, 1996; Uzzi, 1997).

So, if it is not misaligned incentives, fraud, or malice that motivate
SID, then what does? The next few chapters begin to unveil the forces
that are far more insidious. Chapter 3 serves as a poignant reminder that
human behavior is best understood at the crossroads of structure and
agency, and SID is no exception. The motivation for SID stems from
the shift in the guiding institutional logic of professional services. Institutional logics are the practices, norms, and cognitive perspectives
into which we are socialized at work, and they are powerful organizing
principles of how we see and carry out our work (Friedland & Alford,
1991: 248).

Over recent decades, a seismic shift has rocked the foundations of
professional services, with the commercial institutional logic of sales,
growth, and profitability permeating every corner of the industry. Professional service firms have developed into flagship global corporations
fueled by the incessant quest for profitable expansion. As contemporary commercial logic has proliferated, it has largely supplanted the
traditional advisory institutional logic, in which professional service

firms were the bastions of independent advisory prowess, viewing themselves first and foremost as independent advisors and agents of their clients.

This shift in institutional logics has left no stone unturned, affecting every facet of professional services—from governance structures and promotional strategies to the very essence of professionals' identity. The following chapter unveils how this change in institutional logics, coupled with the professionals' internalization of this change, affected the professionals' cognition, decision-making, and behaviors in ways that support the proliferation of SID.

INSTITUTIONAL LOGICS

In organizational research, institutional logics are "socially constructed, historical patterns of material practices, assumptions, values, beliefs, and rules by which individuals produce and reproduce their material subsistence, organize time and space, and provide meaning to their social reality" (Thornton & Ocasio, 1999: 804). Institutional logics thus encompass frames of reference that influence actors' decision-making, behavior, and personal identity. The symbols, principles, and practices underlying institutional logics distinctly shape how individuals perceive, experience, and enact their surroundings.

At their core, institutional logics are both symbolic, involving ideals and meanings, and material, incorporating structures and practices. The symbolic and material elements are often closely intertwined in shaping actors' cognitions and behaviors (Friedland & Alford, 1991; Dacin, 1997; Pahnke, Katila, & Eisenhardt, 2015; Thornton, Ocasio, & Lounsbury, 2012). They thus establish formal and informal rules of behavior, action, and interpretation that influence how decision-makers view and carry out organizational tasks. Institutional logics simultaneously comprise an array of assumptions and values—generally implicit—regarding "how to interpret organizational reality, what constitutes appropriate behavior, and how to succeed" (Thornton & Ocasio,

1999: 804). Thus, institutional logics help understand how institutional forces can motivate individual behaviors. Namely, institutional logics motivate people to act in ways to secure legitimacy as individuals and professionals, including by complying with professional norms and cognitive frames of reference and interpretation (Vedula, York, Conger, & Embry, 2022).

In a classic application of the institutional logic perspective, Patricia H. Thornton and William Ocasio (1999) explained how the dominant institutional logic in the higher-education publishing industry shifted from an editorial to a market-based logic. Their research revealed that an editorial logic stewarded the US publishing industry in the 1950s and 1960s. Under this logic, owners of smaller publishing houses viewed publishing as both a profession and an art. Central leadership functions rested with founder-editors, whose legitimacy stemmed foremost from their editorial skills, the stature of their books, and their network in the editing industry. Publishers perceived an editor's role as principally cultivating the prestige and sales of the publishing house through organic growth and by hiring other editors with the highest editorial prowess and reputation.

During the 1970s, however, market-based logic overtook editorial logic, wherein publishing shifted from being viewed as a profession to being viewed as a business. Under the emergent market logic, the leadership laurels rested with the CEO, whose authority and legitimacy were based on the publishing house's market position, performance, and the shareholders' reception, and increasingly less on editorial functions. Key norms and values shifted from producing the highest quality material to increasing profit margins. As a result, publishing house leadership focused more on addressing resource competition by developing strategies such as growth by acquisitions and the cultivation of new market channels. The focus on the explicit marketing of books, in particular, stood in sharp contrast with the earlier editorial logic that claimed that books of high value would sell themselves. Overall, the traditional logic focused on producing the highest quality editorial work was supplanted by the focus on market expansion and profitability.

Many readers are sure to recognize similar transitions to commercial logics—albeit to varying degrees—in many other sectors of the economy that historically resisted the infusion of managerial capitalism. They range from higher education, medicine, and public health to journalism, media production, and even savings and loans associations (e.g., Haveman & Rao, 1997; Scott & Davis, 2007: 263–277). Many of these sectors underwent growth and aggregation, espoused management by commercial metrics, and couched their organizational rhetoric in terms of value maximization, efficiency, and profitability. The growing reach of Wall Street's influence and the financialization of the economy could be felt far and wide. Emerging as powerful enforcers of the commercial institutional logic are precisely the financial markets and the players that drive them (Davis, 2011; Wooten & Hoffman, 2017).

It is essential to recognize that such a transition in institutional logics has been particularly acute in professional services. Underpinning many observed trends in the sector, such as financialization, the dominant institutional logic has shifted from one of traditional professionalism to that of commercial success. In Kevin T. Leicht and Elizabeth C. W. Lyman's (2006: 17–18) words, "Many of the current challenges to professional authority are rooted in a broader intellectual crisis created by the turn toward markets as a normative principle for organizing social life."

THE SHIFT FROM ADVISORY TO COMMERCIAL LOGIC IN PROFESSIONAL SERVICES

Starting in about the 1980s, professional services have undergone a shift in managing and organizing, which scholars have characterized as a change in archetype from a "professional partnership" to a "managed professional business" (Cooper, Hinings, Greenwood, & Brown, 1996: 625). In contrast to a partnership structure of practicing professionals leading the firm, managed professional businesses increasingly have adopted corporate-style governance identified by the separation of professional and managerial tasks, a more sophisticated hierarchy, increased functional differentiation, strategic planning, implementing or bolstering firm marketing, formal performance control systems, and more sophisticated internal management systems (Lawrence, Malhotra, & Morris, 2012; Morris & Pinnington, 1998; Pinnington & Morris, 2003).

The increase in detail and dynamic complexity of professional services, described in Chapter 3, went hand in hand with the surge in professional service firms' size and internal complexity. Responding to competitive pressures, jurisdictional contestation, and client demands, professional service firms sought to deepen their expertise in established areas and to innovate, grow, and diversify into new and more profitable services (Gardner, Anand, & Morris, 2008). Consequently, professional service firms increased their specialization and structural complexity, formalizing functions such as finance, knowledge management, quality control, and human resources (Malhotra, Morris, & Hinings, 2006).

Alongside this trend, many professional service firms adopted complex, multidimensional matrix structures, rivaling the sophisticated organizational design of global corporations, such as Procter & Gamble or General Electric. One consulting leader I interviewed used an endearing term, "the cube," to describe her employer's three-dimensional matrix structure that spanned internal lines of authority by the types of service offerings as well as by the geography and industry of their clients. In such a structure, a consultant working on a project could potentially have three partners to whom she would report: one managing the type of service delivered (e.g., operations consulting), a second managing a particular territory (e.g., Northern Europe), and a third managing a sector of clients (e.g., telecommunications). Law firms, investment banks, and marketing agencies have adopted similar matrix designs, which depart from a clear vertical structure with a single line of authority. And while such elaborate structures can offer advantages for companies operating in complex and dynamic markets, they are notoriously difficult to manage and are rife with conflicts, power struggles, and coordination failures (Galbraith, 1973; Sytch, Wohlegezogen, & Zajac, 2018).

In another consequential development, many professional service firms have undergone significant changes regarding their ownership models. Traditionally, partners have owned professional service firms internally. However, many firms have shifted toward embracing external ownership. For example, reforms in Australia and the United Kingdom in 2001 and 2011, respectively, ended restrictions on non-lawyer ownership of law firms (Robinson, 2016: 8). Similarly, many states in America have relaxed non-lawyer ownership restrictions (Barnard & Underhill, 2021). The accounting sector has similarly undergone a shift in governance from internal professional ownership to increasing external ownership (Barry, 2018). The 1990s and early 2000s observed significant regulatory and legislative changes in numerous countries around the world that allowed the incorporation of accounting firms and their registration as limited liability partnerships in the United States (Hamilton, 1995). Subsequently, the United States experienced a strong trend toward public ownership of accounting firms. This shift has had a profound impact on the ownership structures of professional service firms; indeed, around half of the accounting firms in the top 100 globally in the early 2000s were structured as corporations rather than professional partnerships (Greenwood & Empson, 2003; Shafer, Lowe, & Fogarty, 2002).[1]

Anthony Pustorino and Allan Rabinowitz (1998: 13) wrote on this trend:

> For the many in this profession who remember when advertising by CPAs was an anathema; when solicitation of competitors' clients or employees was a compromise of standards; when taking commissions or contingent fees or giving investment advice to clients was unequivocally prohibited; when any attempt to limit professional liability was considered a violation of our public trust; for them, the current groundswell of non-CPA ownership of CPA

1. Despite the continued requirement for majority ownership by certified public accountants (CPAs) in most states, there has been a growing movement toward non-CPA ownership within the accounting industry (Pustorino & Rabinowitz, 1998). In fact, the American Institute of Certified Public Accountants and the National Association of State Boards of Accountancy jointly developed the first model bill in 1984, which came to be known as the Uniform Accountancy Act. This act stipulates that CPAs must hold a simple majority in accounting firms, as per Section 7(c)(1) and (2) (National Association of State Boards of Accountancy, 2018). Most states have adopted a version of the act that permits non-CPAs to own up to 49% of an accounting firm (Grumet, 2007).

firms seems like the final twist of the dagger into the heart of these 'archaic' professional values.

It is increasingly evident that the issue of non-CPA ownership has proceeded past the debate of whether it is good or bad for the public of the profession. It seems obvious that it is the juggernaut of economics that is propelling this inexorable march toward acceptance by firms, boards of accountancy, and state CPA societies. A comparison of the survey results (1997 and 1998) taken of boards of accountancy . . . and state CPA societies . . . indicates a trend toward acceptance of non-CPA ownership by the profession.

The aforementioned shift away from professional partnership structures and toward external ownership has not spared management consulting firms, advertising agencies, or investment banks. The majority of firms in these sectors are now structured as corporations rather than partnerships. Indeed, a study of the top 100 firms in the early 2000s found that only 17 management consulting firms, and none of the large advertising agencies, were professional partnerships (Greenwood & Empson, 2003). Another study documented that the proportion of management consulting firms with a partnership structure had already steadily decreased from approximately 50% in 1950 to 17% in 2002 (Greenwood, Li, & Deephouse, 2002). Furthermore, all of the major investment banks abandoned the traditional partnership structure and adopted a public ownership model following a New York Stock Exchange decision in 1970 to allow for publicly quoted members (Morrison & Wilhelm Jr., 2008).

The aforementioned changes in the professional service industry have resulted in a significant influx of external investors, who have become residual claimants of the firms' profits (Løwendahl, 2005; Robinson, 2016). In fact, many professional service firms have even gone so far as to become publicly listed corporations. Individual and institutional investors can now easily beef up their investment portfolios with the shares of consulting firms such as Accenture, Booz Allen Hamilton, or Tata Consultancy; investment banks, such as Morgan Stanley, Goldman

Sachs, or Jeffries; or law firms, such as the DFW Group, Slater and Gordon, or the Keystone Law Group. As a result, many professional service firms are now subject to the same investor pressures to maximize growth and profitability that keep corporate executives up at night. And with the enormous size of some professional service giants now vastly exceeding that of most publicly traded companies, their sophisticated internal management systems, and their reliance on external investors, professional service firms began to epitomize a prototypical corporation (Empson & Chapman, 2006).

While traditional advisory logic espoused a partner promotion system based on collegiality and seniority, partnerships under commercial logic depend instead on the partners' profit-generating or rainmaking capabilities. A senior leader of a consulting firm recounted a series of criteria for becoming a partner at her consulting firm, which included developing expertise in a specific domain of work, building the next generation of talent, and being able to deliver value to clients while having a proven track record of doing so. She commented that, "*All of them [criteria] relate to being a rainmaker. Because you have to know something about something, you have to be able to build a set of relationships. All those ingredients are needed for rainmakers to create opportunities. And in our world, you need all those things to create opportunities that make your professional program self-sustaining.*"

The rainmaking potential is also being rewarded with newly created incentive structures in legal services. One senior lawyer explained:

So most law firms give credit to the people bringing in the work, even if they don't do the work at all—the rainmakers that are just bringing in the work, and they're all trying to do that, they're all trying to build their book of business.

A senior executive procuring legal services elaborated:

So if Partner A signs the first deal with me, Partner A gets a cut forever of all the other partners' work. And those are called rainmaker partner deals. Where you have some partners who bring in a vast majority of the business, and they just passively make a ton of money based on what happens.

The status of being a rainmaker has become firmly entrenched in the hierarchy of professional service firms, such that partners who bring in new business sit at the pinnacle. Significantly, partners maintain their elevated status only as long as they continue to exhibit their rainmaking abilities (Allan, Faulconbridge, & Thomas, 2019; Bartlett, 2000).

Personnel development strategies have correspondingly shifted from the internal promotion of home-grown professionals to seeking external talent with rainmaking skills and specialist expertise. Consider that, until the mid-1990s, many law firms abided by informal agreements not to poach one another's employees (Malhotra, Morris, & Hinings, 2006: 186). Now, the dynamics of lateral hiring in the legal profession are so widespread that they have become a subject of numerous scholarly inquiries (Carnahan, Rabier, & Uribe, 2022; Rider & Tan, 2015). Accounting, consulting, and investment banking firms are likewise looking to attract lateral hires at the partner level (Groysberg, 2010; Groysberg, Lee, & Nanda, 2008; Koltin Consulting Group, 2013).

The notion of partnership has also changed drastically. My interviewees across professional service sectors noted that, back in the days of the advisory logic, partnership used to be like tenure in academia, a variant of lifetime achievement with nearly absolute job security. Under the commercial logic, which accompanied the rise of managed professional businesses, this is no longer the case. The partnership model of profit sharing based on seniority has been replaced largely by profit sharing based on individual performance. In this model, sustained or improved performance levels—such as the volume of billable hours generated in legal services or new business generated in banking and consulting—are required for partners to retain their positions. Underperforming partners are asked to leave the firm (e.g., Tadros, 2023).

A mid-1990s survey of 100 US-based managing partners in public accounting firms reported that partners were leaving their firms mainly because they could not generate sufficient new business and profit

(Addams, Davis, Mano, & Nycum, 1997). Even top equity partners have found no respite from the continuous pressure to generate profit, resulting in growing anxiety over job security (Allan, Faulconbridge, & Thomas, 2019). Across a range of professional services, new generations of partners are increasingly valued based on their ability to consistently obtain clients and generate profit, with their tenure conditional on performance (Law Firm Associates, 2021; Malhotra, Morris, & Hinings, 2006; Pinnington & Morris, 2003).

My interviews revealed that it is often somewhat surprising to newly promoted partners that their lives do not change noticeably after the promotion. They still must produce and face the same concerns about job security they faced before the promotion. In the words of one interviewee, "*I work just as hard, if not harder, as a partner. I just make more money.*" The increase in compensation is, however, by no means assured. The continued growth of firms, the subsequent dilution of partnership shares, and the implementation of varied partnership levels have altered the meaning of being a partner. As a result, many partners lament the lack of distinction from middle managers in compensation, power, and status (Brock, 2006; Carlson, 2004).

Often, concerns about generating revenue and job security become even more pronounced for partners. One senior investment banking executive I interviewed detailed a situation when a punctuated change occurs in the reference group to which newly promoted partners are compared: they are compared to other partners who secured their rank because of their exceptional skills in generating new business. He reflected on widespread situations in which an investment banker who had previously been ranked a superstar would drop to the bottom of the peer rankings—just one year after promotion—and the debilitating effect it could have on the individual.

As commercial logic took hold in professional service firms, the focus on performance permeated many facets of daily management. Scholars have described the transformation of law firms into "law factories," in which informal controls to manage employee behavior were overtaken by explicit performance indicators, such as partners' annual fee generation, billable hours, and the types of clients and tasks that should be given priority (Brivot, 2011; Dezalay, 1992: 18). Organizational performance was gauged in terms of profit- and earnings-per-equity partner (Griffiths, 2005). These changes have affected a broad range of professional services, including consulting, investment banking, technology integration services, accounting, and law (Leicht & Lyman, 2006).

Pointing to these shifts, some scholars have posited that professional services have entered an age of financialization, in which organizing is subjugated to financial tenets, principles, and technologies (Allan, Faulconbridge, & Thomas, 2019; Alvehus & Spicer, 2012). In the words of Gerald Davis (2011: xi), "If the Rouge [Ford Motor Company auto factory] was a map of American society in 1950, then Nasdaq was a representation of American society circa 2000."

The reach of the market-based logic became so widespread that even our relationships with friends and colleagues turned into [social] capital, and our employees became [human] capital. Indeed, financialization said that everything became an investment in a world where the efficient market hypothesis convinced us that the markets correctly value assets and future cash flows (Davis, 2011). In professional service firms, financialization led to the tightening of internal organizational controls, the formalization of business activities, and organizational structures wherein financial technologies and metrics were increasingly used to monitor firm and employee performance and guide managerial strategy. Much like in other sectors of the economy, financialization also led to the increased association between internal organizational activities and the financial markets, with the guiding imperative of maximizing shareholder wealth (Faulconbridge & Muzio, 2009).

Specifically, accounting metrics and technologies, such as activity-based consulting, were used to track and discipline "productive" activities in ways that increase shareholder value (Ezzamel, Willmott, & Worthington, 2008: 109). To investors and clients, the use of such metrics additionally served as assurances that professional service firms were committed to cutting costs and adding value in their daily operations. Again, the shift toward financialization in professional service firms largely mirrored those happening in the broader economy at that time. Professional service firms, in some cases, led these financialization trends by propagating the use of strict financial accountability and obsessive shareholder orientation in their work with clients. And in some cases, they merely followed the trend, yielding to the same Wall Street pressures as did the rest of the economy.

The proliferation of the commercial institutional logic was intertwined with the rise and legitimization of marketing in professional services. Traditionally, professionals did not see marketing as a relevant practice. In fact, "selling" was beneath the role of a professional (Reid, 2008: 377) and was widely viewed as counternormative. Today, though, lawyers, accountants, management consultants, architects, engineers, dentists, doctors, and other professionals must do extensive marketing to maintain and build their practices. As Paul Bloom (1984: 102) reflected, "not many years ago, professionals could count on their reputations and country club contacts to obtain a steady stream of clients or patients." Now, professional service firms routinely invest millions in promoting their services, working with some of the leading marketing agencies.

It may be surprising to learn that, back in the days of rotary phones and black-and-white television sets, law firms, for example, were restricted from advertising their services. Then, in 1976, John R. Bates and Van O'Steen, two particularly entrepreneurial Arizona lawyers, decided to stand out in the competitive Phoenix market by placing an advertisement in the local *Arizona Republic* newspaper. By current standards, the ad was exceedingly mundane. It was titled, "Do you need a lawyer?" and it advertised a range of "legal services at very reasonable prices." Nevertheless, the Arizona Bar promptly suspended the pair for violating attorney disciplinary rules that stated, "a lawyer shall not publicize himself . . . through newspaper or magazine advertisements . . . or other means of commercial publicity."[2] Their appeal made it all the way to the US Supreme Court, which, in a close five-to-four call, ruled that attorney advertising was a form of commercial speech protected by the

---

2. Disciplinary Rule 2-101(B), incorporated in Rule 29(a) of the Supreme Court of Arizona, 17A Ariz. Rev. Stat., p. 26.

First Amendment of the US Constitution (*Bates v. State Bar of Arizona*, 433 U.S. 350, 1977).[3]

This decision opened the floodgates and led to the institutionalization of marketing in the legal profession. The National Association of Law Firm Marketing Administrators—now the Legal Marketing Association—was established in 1985, prompting a variety of new opportunities for marketing legal services (Chieffallo, 2019). Leading legal publications advised lawyers to "think marketing at all times, even when writing briefs or taking depositions" (Margolick, 1993). In contrast to injury lawyers' highway billboard advertisements, corporate firms often find more subtle ways to advertise their services. As remarked by a senior lawyer during my fieldwork:

Well, for corporate law firms, it's a little unseemly. Now, what we've seen and like in sports, there are law firms that sponsor; so, like what a lot of teams do, they'll give you legal business, but they want you to sponsor the team. So they may take an ad out in your team magazine, or on your website, or there may be some other relationship with the law firm where some of the fees are written down based on this marketing arrangement.

In a parallel trend, many law firms had already hired a marketing administrator by the mid-1980s, a practice unheard of just in the prior decade (Galanter & Palay, 1990). Indeed, once contradictory to the meticulously cultivated image of professional service firms, explicit marketing has become widespread and serves as a key instrument for professional service firms (Groß & Kieser, 2006; Reid, 2008). Starting in the 1990s, large firms set up internal marketing departments. The most recent data suggest that 97% of large law firms have internal marketing staff, and about a quarter additionally hire external marketing consultants (Johs, 2020). For example, Orrick, Herrington, & Sutcliffe—a San Francisco-based firm—ran a "ubiquitous 'O' ad campaign in the early 2000s," which the firm's former chairperson, Ralph Baxter, argued

3. Justice Harry Andrew Blackmun, writing for the majority, stated that "the First Amendment protects an advertisement as commercial speech, unless the advertisement is false, deceptive, or misleading."

was a large piece of Orrick's expansion from a few hundred attorneys to more than 1,000 attorneys (Jones, 2017).

Such growing emphasis on marketing has become ubiquitous in professional services. These days, leading professional service firms spend millions of dollars annually promoting their services. For example, research noted a shift from conservative professionalism to aggressive marketing in the consulting industry, which involved setting up dedicated sales forces and explicit advertising. Adrian Wooldridge (1997: 16) cited Robert Duboff, then a senior leader of Mercer Management consulting firm, as saying, "Ten years ago, if I'd suggested we advertise, I'd have been shot; five years ago, I'd have been whipped." Wooldridge (1997: 16) proceeded to observe that "Now Mercer has started placing discreet advertisements in Forbes magazine." "Direct advertising, once a 'no-no,' is now fairly commonplace" (Poulfelt & Olson, 2018: 22).

In keeping pace with the evolution of the marketing sector, outreach by professional service firms occurs through a variety of means, including direct email, social media platforms, and strategic prioritization of media search results. The Twitter account of Cravath, Swaine, & Moore (2024)—a leading international law firm—explicitly says that "Content may include attorney advertising." Indirect marketing channels such as webinars and podcasts are growing in use, which 80% and 38% of law firms use, respectively (Alvarez, Vermeulen, & Zimmon, 2020).

Direct email outreach has also grown to be more sophisticated. A partner of a leading consulting firm described to me how his company employs a group of people who scrutinize potential clients' comments in publicly available print and video materials for the exact words and phrases they use. When subsequently reaching out to executives with email pitches, they use the exact same words and phrases in an influence technique known as linguistic mirroring (Sytch & Kim, 2020, 2021).

Partner meetings of professional service firms prominently feature training in business development with a clear emphasis on proactively bringing opportunities to clients. In one meeting I attended, a seasoned partner of a consulting firm advised his colleagues on business development. He laid out a list of nearly 130 organizational stakeholders whom he managed, mapped onto the client firm's organizational chart. The intention was to leverage these connections to identify opportunities for new business. As professional service firms place increasing emphasis on the role of the seller in the imperfect agency, the foundational calling to serve (Abbott, 1988) clashes with the imperative of doing business (Sharma, 1997). Or, as Marc Galanter and Thomas M. Palay (1990: 756) aptly observed in their analysis of rapidly scaling law firms, "the imperative of growth collides with notions of dignified passivity in obtaining business."

Underlying their observation is the theory of endogenous growth of professional service firms. Galanter and Palay (1990: 749) were puzzled by the inexplicably rapid growth of law firms in the United States: while only 38 US law firms had over 50 lawyers in the 1950s, over 500 firms had over 50 lawyers by 1985. They later argued that law firms built in an endogenous growth engine. This engine stems from (1) the partner-promotion tournament system, in which a certain percentage of employees are promoted to partner every year; and (2) using multiple associates to support the work of a given partner. Their theory postulates that firm size will increase exponentially if the percentage of promoted employees and the associate-to-partner ratios are constant. Given that the two foundational principles of this growth theory describe professional services rather broadly, the theory generalized well to investment banking, accounting, and consulting firms (Galanter & Palay, 1990; Lupu & Empson, 2015; Morris & Pinnington, 1998). Considering that the impetus for professional service firms' growth is endogenous—determined by the inner workings of the professional service firms rather than by market demands—reflecting on how, exactly, the seller role could be enacted to sustain that growth can give a moment of pause.

Intriguingly, the shift in institutional logics is often accompanied by a change in the socio-linguistic framing of the surrounding social context. In a riveting account of the diffusion of hostile takeovers in the United States in the second half of the 20th century, Paul M. Hirsch (1986) showed how the previously unacceptable practice of acquiring a company, despite management's refusal, gradually became normalized alongside an increasingly accommodating linguistic shift. The early pejorative vocabulary of "black nights" and "pariahs" that described hostile acquirers yielded to the illustriously positive framing of "white knights" rushing to rescue "sleeping beauties."

Analogously, alongside the shift to the commercial logic, the business language related to efficiency, profit, market share, and shareholder wealth maximization has been increasingly accepted and normalized in professional service firms (Brock, 2006). As Galanter and Palay (1990: 752) described, professional service firm leaders started to worry "about billable hours, profit centers, and marketing strategies." Indeed, the mantra "eat what you kill" has firmly entered the parlance of professionals and supplanted the prior reverence for seniority as a basis for profit distribution, power, and status. In Chapter 7, we will delve into how this shift in institutional logics has profoundly influenced the identity of professionals, fundamentally altering the very essence of what it means to embody the role of a professional.

CHAPTER SUMMARY

This chapter has begun to uncover the motivations behind supplier-induced demand, locating them at the intersection of structure and agency, stemming from the shift in institutional logics in professional services. Institutional logics delineate the practices, norms, and cognitive perspectives ingrained within our work environments, shaping our perceptions of the work itself. Since the 1980s, professional services have undergone a profound transformation from an advisory institutional logic to a commercial one. These changes have permeated virtually every aspect of professional services, giving rise to sophisticated managerial structures and previously counternormative practices such as external ownership, marketing one's services, linking partnership status to partners' ongoing productivity, recruiting rainmakers from rival firms, and embracing market-oriented principles in pursuit of growth and profitability. This shift in institutional logics has laid a powerful foundation for how professionals began to see their roles and work.

CHAPTER 7

The Change in Professionals' Identity

In a more insidious effect on professionals, the shift from a traditional advisory to a commercial institutional logic entailed a subtle form of professional regulation that has deeply affected the professionals' identity. The increasing dominance of the commercial institutional logic—manifested in the adoption of organizational structures and functions, professional norms, promotion and remuneration standards, and even particular language used in the workplace, all of which prioritized revenue and profits—has significantly influenced employees' perceptions of their work and what it means to be a valued professional. As a result, professionals' success and self-worth have become increasingly associated with actively delivering value to clients, driving change, solving problems, and disrupting the status quo. These, and many variants of similar behaviors, have become inextricably tied to selling more services. Much of the motivation behind supplier-induced demand emanates precisely from such a shift in professionals' identity. In this chapter, I elaborate this argument in detail.

THE BLURRING IDENTITY BETWEEN THE PROFESSION AND THE SELF

Let's start by considering how a changing institutional logic can impact one's professional identity and why this effect is particularly relevant in professional services. As humans, we have a natural tendency to categorize ourselves and others into distinct social groups, including groups based on organizational and professional affiliations. These social categorizations help us organize and make sense of the world. More crucially, social categorization can shape our self-identity and how we define ourselves (Ashforth & Mael, 1989; Turner, 1982, 1991). When people perceive themselves as similar to or belonging to a well-defined social group, such as a profession or a particular organization, they tend to define themselves in terms of the group's characteristics (Turner, Hogg, Oakes, Reicher et al., 1987). Consequently, what people do at work is often influenced by their beliefs about what it takes to be a valuable member of their professional or organizational group; in other words, their professional identity (Ashforth, Rogers, & Corley, 2011; Ramarajan, 2014).

Note, too, that people crave social identification with professional groups. Group membership helps us locate and define ourselves in the social milieu. Specifically, identifying with a professional category or an organization may advance our quest for meaning, empowerment, and connectedness. It can reveal the purpose in our work (Gulati, 2022). Put differently, our answers to questions such as "Who am I?," "What do I do?," and "Why do I do what I do?" stem in part from identifying with a profession and an employing organization. Identifying with a professional group or an organization can similarly quench our thirst for belonging and boost our self-esteem (Sanchez-Burks & Sytch, 2021). Importantly, employers are keen to support their employees' social identification with professional or organizational groups. The ensuing psychological bond between employees and their work and the organization enhances commitment, boosts discretionary effort, and reduces intentions to quit (e.g., Riketta, 2005).

The organizational pull and the employee push for social identification converge in a combustible combination in the professional services industry; so much so that professional and individual identities can coalesce, engendering a blurred line between the self and one's occupation. Such coalescence can powerfully steer professionals' behaviors (cf. Hall, Schneider, & Nygren, 1970; Mullin & Hogg, 1999). Consider the main three factors that augment professionals' identification with their occupations and organizations. The first is the prestige and exclusivity of professional services as a field and of individual professional service brands. Social identity theory is unambiguous: prestigious collectives constitute markedly potent centers of gravity with which people seek to identify. This is because the distinctiveness of the collective and its social standing are known to boost people's self-esteem particularly strongly (Ashforth & Mael, 1989; Mael, 1988). The carefully cultivated image of exclusivity, elitism, and intellectual leadership that describes professional services in general, and many individual companies in particular, has been on the rise since the 1980s (Ashley & Empson, 2016). It makes professionals especially prone to define and categorize themselves as occupational and organizational members.

Second, the draw of prestige toward identifying with the profession and the organization is buttressed by professional service firms' meticulous workforce selection and intense socialization (Løwendahl, 2005). Naturally, the selectivity of the recruiting process for professional service firms is essential to sustain the firms' image of intellectual leadership and expert advantage. In addition, thorough skills-based and cultural selection in professional service firms creates highly cohesive social groups. Employees are even more likely to identify with such groups and, by doing so, enhance their self-concept and self-definition more emphatically (Alvesson, Karreman, & Sullivan, 2015; Jetten, Hogg, & Mullin, 2000; Rivera, 2016).

Cultural selection in professional service firms is especially noteworthy in this respect. In a study of elite professional service firms, Lauren A. Rivera (2012) discovered that the firms' hiring decisions were influenced primarily by the cultural alignment of candidates with the employees' personalities and interests. This cultural matching manifests in employees favoring job candidates with similar leisure activities, experiences, self-presentation, and self-perception. Similarly, Louise Ashley and Laura Empson (2013) found that law firms tended to select and recruit lawyers who projected an "upmarket" image, conveying high social status and elite cultural resources (cf. Bourdieu, 1977's cultural capital), which is crucial for clients to validate the quality of the knowledge-based outputs professionals produce that is otherwise hard to assess.

Robust socialization processes further reinforce the impact of work-force selection on social identification, through which one comprehends the values, norms, and expectations of an organization and organizational role (Chatman & Cha, 2003: 27). Professional service firms have been known to emphasize integrating the company's values, norms, and brand into employees' everyday lives, which not only promotes favorable communication of the brand but also guides employees in situations where the reach of managerial authority is limited. To wit, professional service firms epitomize organizations with flatter hierarchies and geographically dispersed team-based work, in which selection and socialization become effective substitutes for direct managerial control. Consequently, managers in such firms prioritize organizational socialization as a means to shape new hires' self-perceptions and situational awareness. This, in turn, fosters work consistency, organizational commitment, and productivity.

Lastly, identifying with an occupation or organization can alleviate the fear and anxiety professionals may experience regarding their ability to keep up with their peers' performance, which is commonly observed in professional service firms (Allan, Faulconbridge, & Thomas, 2019; Alvesson, Karreman, & Sullivan, 2015). Some scholars have suggested that high anxiety levels are essential for driving superior organizational performance, leading professional service firms to either ignore or actively encourage worker anxiety (Alvesson, Karreman, & Sullivan, 2015). In fascinating fieldwork, Scott M. Allan, James Faulconbridge, and Pete Thomas (2019) demonstrated just how tangible employee anxiety can be within professional service firms. For example, a partner they interviewed reflected:

[Y]ou never know quite what is coming next . . . [Y]ou could be tapped on the shoulder and told: you are doing really well. Or you could be tapped on the shoulder and told: you are doing so badly that you are coming down the [lockstep]. And where is the next place going to be? That is a structure which [the chairman and managing partner] would say drives performance. It's fear that . . . drives performance . . . That's my reality. (Allan, Faulconbridge, & Thomas, 2019: 121)

Another partner, who was complimented for her business development skills, responded that she felt that constantly generating more business was essential to her career progress:

> *It's fear! It's the fear! I've been there, I've had no work . . . You might think I'm joking, I'm not! It's the fear. When I started at [firm X] I had no clients, I had no work. Necessity is the mother of invention.* (Allan, Faulconbridge, & Thomas, 2019: 121)

Even those making the numbers rarely feel a respite from the anxiety to perform:

> *I got an email [confirming performance against budget at year end] and I saw we had done really well. Rather than thinking, terrific, that's a great thing, I thought, shit! What's going to happen when I get back is that somebody is going to be saying we want you to do even more!* (Allan, Faulconbridge, & Thomas, 2019: 122)

What follows is a curious twist: when faced with anxiety, professionals often find solace not in distancing themselves from their work and colleagues, but in embracing them more tightly. In other words, professionals often deal with their anxiety by seeking a *stronger* social identification with their occupation, employers, and colleagues, rather than distancing themselves from those sources of their anxiety. Surprising, isn't it? Yet, delve into the realm of uncertainty–identity theory, and you will find a trove of studies revealing just that (Hogg, Adelman, & Blagg, 2010; Jetten, Hogg, & Mullin, 2000; Mullin & Hogg, 1999). By aligning themselves closely with their occupation, professionals attempt to ease their anxieties. It is as if joining a clearly defined social group offers a better map through the murky waters of uncertainty, providing clearer answers to why we act as we do and how others perceive us.

In this landscape, the anxiety-inducing work morphs into exhilarating opportunities, ripe for conquest. By strengthening their bonds with a group, professionals thus navigate toward a more coherent and predictable reality. For them, the pride of belonging to a respected and esteemed field serves as yet another shield against anxiety, elevating their sense of self-worth (Alvesson, Karreman, & Sullivan, 2015).

When individuals inhabit the rarefied air of an exclusive professional realm, ensconced within prestigious firms and surrounded by the crème de la crème of their field, the boundaries between self and occupation can blur to the point of indistinction. This phenomenon is only magnified when professional identity becomes the buffer against job-related stress. As a result, the ethos, customs, and worldviews of the profession meld seamlessly with those of the individual, to the extent that personal values and behaviors may well yield to the collective dictates. Social identity scholars term this intriguing blend "depersonalization" (Mullin & Hogg, 1999). In contrast to many other industries in which a job is often regarded primarily as a source of income and work identity is of relatively little importance to both the individual and the organization, professional work blurs the distinctions between the self and the professional identity. For professionals, work is not just what they do; it is often what they are.

THE COMMERCIAL LOGIC AND THE CHANGE IN PROFESSIONALS' IDENTITY

The Importance of Productivity

Individuals' strong professional identities make them particularly vulnerable to how the identity impacts their behaviors. In the case of professional services, the dominance of the commercial institutional logic has had a particularly significant impact on professionals' behavior, because it has redefined the very nature of what it means to be a professional.

The pervasive market rhetoric has penetrated even the most distant corners of the profession, redefining the meaning of work. A former consultant recounted a scathing performance review she received from a manager, in which the manager justified her assessment in part by saying, "*creating shareholder value does not make you tick.*" When prompted to clarify her statement, the manager explained that she herself derived work meaning from creating value for companies and enhancing their stock returns, which allowed employees and investors to retire comfortably. More crucially, the commercial logic has also affected the perception of what it means to be a good professional and professionals' view of self-worth:

> *I remember sitting in a performance review one year where my supervising partner attended with one sheet of paper-a printout of my billings for the year. At the end of a year of long hours and hard work, everything I had given to the firm was reduced to one sheet of numbers—if my time didn't directly result in money made by the firm, it was of no interest to them.* (Campbell & Charlesworth, 2012: 104-105)

> *When I started with the firm I was told hours weren't that important. Since I started, the only thing I ever hear about is how associates need to bill 2000 a year. No one has ever said, "we want quality."* (Fortney, 2000: 275)

A former employee of a large accounting firm shared with me:

> *So one of my primary memories is utilization targets. And when your utilization target requires direct billing of someone else, it's nearly impossible not to, in some way, always feel guilty, right? I had to have 92% utilization, which simply means that of my 2080 hours a year or whatever, because it was obviously expected to be more than that, 92% of those had to be charged to a client, that's how they evaluate utilization. So inherently, there was this expectation that you would find ways to bill that client, whatever you were working on.*[1]

1. Billable hour targets have increased significantly as the commercial logic took hold on professional services, averaging around 1,500 per year in 1960 and ranging between 1,800-2,400 in recent decades (Campbell & Charlesworth, 2012: 103-104; Fortney, 2000: 247), and have become a key characteristic of many professional service industries. For example, 86% of respondents in a 2010 survey of Queensland law firms reported having billable hours targets (Parker & Ruschena, 2011: 637). Moreover, billable hours have been described as "the lifeblood of consulting," serving not only to measure consultants' performance but also to "legitimate the value of consulting services by assigning uniform dollar

On the surface, such evaluative standards led professionals to feel like "two-legged cost and profit centers" and report that their primary function in the company was to generate fees (Blackburn, 2006: 39; Campbell & Charlesworth, 2012). However, as professionals' behaviors became increasingly entrenched in the commercial logic, which reflected the need to demonstrate their value in terms of selling services and generating revenue, their professional identity began to change. Indeed, the far-reaching implications of regulating one's behaviors are "not so much behavior or the measurement of output as it is how employees define themselves" (Alvesson, Karreman, & Sullivan, 2015: 408). The introduction of targets, quotas, and benchmarks in terms of work sold—spurred by commercial logic—has not just made the work more transparent and malleable, but *ascribed value* to the work in terms of these criteria. It has led professionals to equate prestige and success with their performance on a financial target, such as hours billed or revenue generated. As a result of reshaping individual subjectivity and perception into financial terms, professionals began to perceive generated revenue to be valuable not only in monetary terms but also in terms of what a "good employee" looks like (Alvehus & Spicer, 2012; Campbell & Charlesworth, 2012; Fortney, 2000).

For one, professional service employees started to view their work and behavior as a form of capital investment that requires active mobilization, investment, or trading to achieve a positive return (Alvehus & Spicer, 2012). In the up-or-out system of professional service firms, the pursuit of achieving partner status creates an "identity deficit" (Allan, Faulconbridge, & Thomas, 2019: 120), where each promotion fails to satisfy, and the next promotion becomes necessary to be recognized as a top performer and someone who has attained professional success. This

---

rates to the hours billed" (Yakura, 2001). However, as particular facets of professional work cannot be billed to a client, the notion of utilization becomes an important metric. Utilization refers to the amount of billable time divided by full-time working hours (Alvehus & Spicer, 2012: 501). As approximately one-third of total work hours is averaged to be non-billable, billable hours considerably understate the actual volume of work required by individuals (Fortney, 2000: 248). Using this metric, a professional would need to work 2,700 hours to bill 1,800 hours and 3,600 hours to bill 2,400 hours—breaking down to 50 and 70 hour weeks, respectively, year-round.

sends a powerful signal of the professional's value to clients and fellow partners and, even more critically, reinforces their sense of self-worth (Grey, 1994; Karreman & Alvesson, 2009).

In professional services, both self-perception and perceptions of colleagues have become inextricably linked to performance on financial metrics. As a result, the standards by which the value of work is measured, such as billable hours or the amount of business generated, began to influence the definition of what constitutes a valuable employee. As an illustration, employees have internalized the concept of productive work behavior, which compels them to evaluate the value of work based on its chargeability to clients. As a result, tasks that cannot be billed to clients are deemed as lacking value. A study of trainee accountants documented how their orientation to time changed. Initially, the trainees viewed their downtime between projects, also known as "time on the beach," as a valuable benefit. However, they soon realized that this non-chargeable time had to be minimized, and they likened available time to "the unemployment benefit principle of 'actively looking for work'" (Coffey, 1994: 953).

The cultural and systemic work pressures to constantly "be busy" and "look busy"—all of which entail charging more work to a client— in turn forge more implicit cultural norms related to professional work. If explicit targets are set, implicit norms often equate "hard work" with surpassing one's targets. Terms such as the "audit machine" (Pentland, 1993) praise employees who are able to work extremely long hours at high intensity, reinforcing the unspoken norm that a hard-working, valuable employee goes above and beyond expectations by maximizing their chargeable work to clients (Lupu & Empson, 2015). Even more insidiously, working long hours and overtime—while finding or generating more work—are internalized as a sign of professionals' commitment to the organization, the work itself, and the clients:

We value hardworking, tenacious people a lot. Actually, one of our main performance indicators is number of hours worked . . . . On one

side, you have people who never say no [to one more piece of work]
. . ., and on the other, . . . you are a manager or partner, so you can
do what you want with people. If I want someone to work till 4 a.m.,
they work till 4 a.m. (Lupu & Empson, 2015: 1324)

Research has further suggested that working longer hours and seeking and generating more work, even to the point of severe physical breakdown, is internalized by professionals as self-chosen, and that the impact of organizational metrics, formal rules, and informal practices in this regard may even bypass employees' minds and deliberate cognition (Lupu & Empson, 2015; Michel, 2011). In her study of investment bankers, Alexandra Michel (2011) highlighted how the infusion of the commercial logic through "embodied controls"—unobtrusive work controls, such as the architectural layout of the floor, the availability of food at work, or the informal emphasis on recruiting and rewarding "high-energy" workers—powerfully motivated the bankers' behaviors while creating an illusion of autonomy. Working long hours, seeking more work, and logging billable hours—even when not explicitly asked to do so by the organization—became part of their agentic self. The professionals ended up competing with themselves and their peers for the amount of work done, which symbolized doing good work, being a good professional, a loyal employee of the firm, and a faithful servant of the clients.

The Emphasis on Selling as a Way to Create Value for Clients

Exhibiting excellence in selling and storytelling techniques has become a desirable and celebrated virtue in professional services. Training events for leading professional service firms are routinely filled with workshops on storytelling and various selling techniques, on how to "earn meetings" with senior client executives, and how to manage relationships in the client organization to identify selling opportunities. A celebrated professional, the one who might be invited to role model at these events and share career insights, and the one who is typically conferred the highest status in professional service firms, is the one who has succeeded in selling services.

Please note that the argument advanced in this book does not invalidate the right of professionals to market their services and to make themselves known. After all, who doesn't do that? The argument instead centers on the relative emphasis that professionals' new identity places on selling. Even as far back as the 1960s, well before the commercial logic became so ubiquitous in professional services, Warren J. Wittreich (1966) differentiated between the "professional salesman" and the "professional who can also sell." The professional who can also sell identifies foremost as a professional, primarily focusing on content-related issues concerning their profession, while not being opposed to demonstrating their ability to clients. On the contrary, the professional salesperson views their primary role as that of selling services and perceives their value as intricately related to their ability to do so. Already at that time, Wittreich raised concerns that professionals were succumbing to increasing pressures to sell, appearing more and more like professional salespersons in the process. The concerns Wittreich (1966) raised have only been compounded in the intervening years.

Consider how Lynn Turner, the Chief Accountant at the US Securities and Exchange Commission during the late 1990s, referred to the top partners at Arthur Andersen: "At the end of the day, Grafton, Samek, and Berardino were all business-people as opposed to public accountants. Meaning that their focus was more on running the business than on concerns investors might have" (Gunz & Gunz, 2006: 272).

Job forums are filled with quotes from exasperated employees lamenting the emphasis on selling:

You will be a salesperson rather than actually delivering technical expertise to your client. You will always have to sell instead of actually consulting. (Senior Manager, Indeed, 2020b)

Used to be a great company; not anymore. Leadership keeps changing. Really focused on sell, sell, sell and not service, service, service. (Director, Indeed, 2012)

Gotta sell to be successful: You have to be able to sell the company's products for management to like you . . . So much pressure to bring business to the company. Doesn't matter how quantitative you are. (Risk Advisory Services Director, Indeed 2019b)

The culture has changed to sell, sell, sell. Managers are more worried about metrics than actually helping the employees build relationships. (Relationship Banker, Indeed 2020a)

If I am not consistently selling and expanding my network then I am not doing my job. (Mortgage Banker, Indeed 2013)

If you can't sell [you] don't work here for a long time. (Senior Tax Consultant, Indeed 2019a)

Importantly, the rhetoric and the implicit norms guided by the commercial logic invariably connect selling to delivering value to clients. Selling thus enters the professionals' identity as doing well and delivering value to clients. Such belief pillars become central to professionals' identity and are often institutionalized at the level of an occupation. For example, leading IP law firms celebrate being recognized as the most active players in trial and appeal work (Fish and Richardson, 2016, 2023; Lex Machina, 2023). In many professional service sectors, metrics of size—whether it is revenue or the number of employees—have become implicit criteria for judging firms' relative standing in the industry.

Professional service firms' reliance on quantitative performance metrics has also created cultures of social comparison and intra-firm competition, which can intensify the focus on selling work to clients. It is no secret that, in professional services, much of the desire to sell work to clients is driven by the desire to outcompete one's peers. Part of this stems from professional service firms consistently recruiting smart, ambitious, driven, and high-energy individuals. Another key is that these individuals are socialized into cultures of hard work and performance excellence, in which only some professionals make it to the top. The commercial logic has transformed hours billed, utilization, generated revenue, and other quantitative performance metrics into a cornerstone of social comparison and competition among coworkers. Because performance information is frequently circulated formally, through social networks, or at minimum inferred by employees, the intense pressure on those who are perceived as underachieving exacerbates the influence of status hierarchies (Fortney, 2000; Parker & Ruschena, 2011).

In professional services, where one's professional identity is such an important part of the self, the effects are especially far-reaching. As Christopher Grey (1994: 494) observed with respect to accounting professionals, "The successful development of an accountancy career entails that the individual's whole life . . . becomes an instrumental project which is to be managed and achieved." One professional reflected on her career in this respect:

> *I really became a robot. I thought it was normal. It shocked me when everyone around me, my husband, my parents, and friends asked me, "Are you crazy?" I replied, "No, it's normal." It's like brainwashing. You are in a kind of mental system where you are under increasing demands, and you say to yourself that it doesn't matter, that you will rest afterwards, but that moment never comes.* (Lupu & Empson, 2015: 1310)

CHAPTER SUMMARY

The ascendance of commercial logic in professional services has altered professionals' identities. It has tied the value of being a professional to a host of productivity metrics, bolstered by changes in hiring, development, and evaluation practices, as well as formal management and informal cultural practices. Not only did the commercial logic regulate behavior with financial metrics and targets, but it has also led professionals to equate feelings of success and value with strong performances on financial metrics and selling. In professional services, where professionals' work value and personal success are so closely intertwined, their professional and personal success thus became tethered to the quantity of work completed, utilization rates, generated business, or the caliber of clients brought into the firm. Notably, professionals' bringing in new business became equivalent to serving clients, disrupting the status quo, and improving organizations. Securing new work was no longer just a win for the professional and the firm but it was also celebrated as a triumph for the innovative and forward-thinking client. This insidious shift equated doing work for clients with creating value and doing more work with creating more value.

CHAPTER 8

The Emergence of
Supplier-Induced Demand

The professional identity, which reified being a valuable employee with selling, fell on the fertile soil of the enabling market conditions. Recall that the market for professional services features three distinctive characteristics that enable supplier-induced demand (SID): (1) the high levels of uncertainty surrounding the problem definition, action, and outcomes of knowledge-based work; (2) the power advantage of professionals, stemming from their expert knowledge and privileged network positions; and (3) the imperfect agency of the professionals, in which they act as both advisors to their clients on a particular course of action and sell services. The conjunction of the professionals' identity, which associates being a valuable employee with selling, and the markets' enabling conditions creates an almost ineludible imperative for SID. This imperative can be dissected through three key biases: the bias for action, the familiarity bias, and the agreement bias.

THE BIAS FOR ACTION

The imperative at hand is manifested in the professionals' *bias for action* when confronted with problem and action uncertainty. To elaborate, in situations of uncertainty, professionals tend to exhibit a disposition toward action as opposed to inaction (cf. Peters & Waterman, 1982; Posen & Levinthal, 2012). When creating value is internalized as doing work for clients, professionals are more likely to stand behind the disruption of the status quo, a market entry, pursuing an IPO, filing a lawsuit, or acquiring a company, even if the case for such actions is unclear. Conversely, recommendations advocating a state of inactivity, maintaining the current market position, retaining private status, refraining from litigation, or remaining with the present scale and scope of the business are significantly less likely to garner support as value-creating propositions.

If you are a buyer of professional services, how often have you heard professional service providers utter statements such as, "We can't help you at this time," or "Let's give it some time to see how the situation plays out," or any variant of a statement delaying or declining work? Now compare that to the frequency of offers of new services. If you are a professional, how often have you thought that inaction, rather than action, is the real path to delivering value for clients?

Most professionals have embraced a productivity-oriented mindset that prioritizes maximizing the amount of work completed for clients. Consequently, professionals have come to regard assertiveness in representing clients as a pivotal attribute that ultimately defines their value. Regrettably, this line of thinking has led to a form of rationalization and a belief that more is better, resulting, at times, in aggressive behavior. This conduct is perceived as advantageous not only for clients but also for the firm, leading to its promotion and normalization within many professional service firms (Suchman, 1998). For example, according to a senior legal services associate quoted in Mark C. Suchman (1998: 860): "Being perceived as being aggressive in defending the client's interest will get me ahead in the law firm, get me on the cases that I want to be on and in the position that I want to be in." In my interviews, consulting professionals frequently characterized their counterparts at client organizations as "complacent" for failing to take specific actions. This perspective is notable because it reinforces the belief that generating value entails taking action, rather than avoiding it.

Consequently, professionals have moved away from traditional advisory behaviors in which an advisor may not have all the answers, may not have a solution to a client's problem, may need to learn alongside the client to understand the situation, or may even withdraw from the situation altogether. In situations described by problem and action uncertainty, this inclination toward taking action frequently results in professionals endorsing marginal, weak, or even harmful courses of action, which may ultimately enter the client's consideration set.

THE FAMILIARITY BIAS

When faced with action uncertainty—not knowing the appropriate actions to take—professionals naturally resort to their comfort zone, which is the products and services they can sell. I call this the *familiarity bias*. This bias leads them to sell the expertise they have, the products and services they know, and more of them, even if they are not the right match for the client's problem. Scholars have raised related concerns in examining "marketing myopia" (Levitt, 2004) or "product-centric organizations" (Gulati, 2009), both of which relate to companies touting their existing products and services regardless of customer needs. Consider the reflection of a senior finance executive on his interactions with professional service firms in this respect:

> But even in my recent experiences, what you also realize is that there is no task too big, even though they say they would tell you, "No, I've never experienced it." Which is I've never experienced them saying, consulting firms in general, in my opinion, stating, "that's probably not a skill set that we have. I would request you go to a more specialized firm such as . . ." Never, in my entire career, have I experienced that.

The tendency for familiarity bias can be reinforced more instrumentally. At an event for the partners of a major professional service company I attended, the senior leader of the firm was proselytizing that, "*[the] worst thing that can happen to you is if your client asks you, 'hey Joe, do you know so and so at your firm who can help us with X,' and you cannot think of anyone. Because that value will go to someone else.*" The ensuing advice was to unfailingly say "yes" to such requests, and then thereafter determine what services one can render to the client with the resources, personnel, and competencies at hand.

It is comprehensible that bankers may lean toward recommending inorganic growth and acquiring external capability, while strategy consultants may be inclined to suggest a strategy overhaul, and lawyers may opt for legal action in court. This phenomenon creates a situation in which, in addition to the systemic misdiagnosis of situations toward action-oriented approaches, professionals operating under conditions of uncertainty are prone to frequently misaligning problems with their corresponding solutions.

THE AGREEMENT BIAS

To exacerbate matters further, even in instances in which professionals are uncertain about their analysis or solution offerings, it has become imperative that they exude confidence. Demonstrating unwavering self-assurance is fundamental to establishing the stature of a professional expert marketing an uncertain, knowledge-intensive commodity. Over time, clients have come to expect and, in some cases, even demand this level of assurance, thereby placing further strain on professionals. A senior lawyer reflected on this respect:

> So something that I learned really, really quickly is that I always need to sound like I know what I'm talking about, and that I have the definitive answer, even if I'm still figuring it out. Because as soon as you sound like you don't, that you're unsure, it all just crumbles. They [the clients] don't trust you . . . they [clients] don't trust that you know what you're doing.

In the realm of professional service firms, these convictions run deep. Meet Corey, a consultant at a public accounting firm, who shared a tale of navigating two consecutive projects. The first nestled comfortably within his expertise, while the second ventured into unfamiliar terrain. Amidst accolades showered upon the first project, the second yielded a far less dazzling evaluation, casting doubt on the pursuit of the promotion Corey had envisioned. But the true revelation came with feedback on the latter project, focusing sharply on Corey's perceived lack of confidence with clients. His manager relentlessly drew parallels to Corey's confident demeanor in the first project, leaving him puzzled and unsettled, given the stark differences in his expertise between the two endeavors. Etched in Corey's memory was a particular incident where his manager chastised him for uttering the phrase "I hope" during a dialogue with a client, a moment crystallizing the unyielding demand for confidence in their profession.

In Chapter 4 of my exploration into the dynamics of power and influence, I delve deeply into the imbalance of power, which is a theme woven intricately into the very fabric of the relationship between clients and professionals. It is a tale of esteem, networks, and control, where the professionals, buoyed by their esteemed status and expansive networks, hold sway over the outcomes that matter most to their clients. But what is perhaps most intriguing is the subtle dynamics of compliance that can emerge from this power play. It is not always overt; in fact, it often lurks in the shadows of unconscious deference.

Clients, knowingly or not, find themselves yielding to the aura of expertise exuded by confident professionals. It is a deference that can stifle dissent before it even has a chance to surface. In that chapter, I drew upon a wealth of scientific evidence to illuminate the intricate mechanisms that drive our unconscious compliance with symbols of authority and expertise. From the firing of neural pathways to the nuanced responses triggered by expert counsel, the evidence paints a vivid picture of our susceptibility to the influence wielded by those we perceive as experts.

When experts confidently present options about which they themselves are unsure, the ensuing dynamics may give rise to the agreement bias on questionable actions. This phenomenon occurs when both professionals and clients agree on a course of action that neither party genuinely endorses (Harvey, 1974).[1] And even when subtle compliance with confident authorities may not be particularly pronounced, the

1. It is also known as the Abilene paradox—which describes a situation in which a group agrees on a decision that none of the individual members favor—and is named after a story that Jerry Harvey (1974) used to illustrate the group dynamic. In that story, on a hot summer day, one family member suggested driving to Abilene, Texas. Others agreed. After enduring a tiring and unpleasant trip, the family discovered that each of them went because they felt others really wanted to make the trip. None of them did.

pervasive knowledge and information asymmetries between clients and professionals hinder the clients from constructively questioning professionals' advice and recommendations.

SUPPLIER-INDUCED DEMAND

Seeing prospects for action where they do not exist, coupled with unsuitable solutions, and carrying out actions under the guise of apparent mutual agreement expose professionals and clients to the hazard of SID. SID can manifest in numerous ways. On the less significant end of the spectrum (a weak form of SID), organizations frequently disburse funds on superfluous accounting checks, legal discovery, consulting research, or banking due diligence. Such weak forms of SID are associated with expending additional time and capital for no discernable benefit. The accountant who earlier reflected on the 92% utilization rate proceeded to elaborate how the emphasis on utilization affected his behaviors:

> On the personal side, because I'm a driven individual, I felt the need to never miss that utilization. So I always was driving to make sure that I accomplished that. What influenced me personally was one, perhaps extra hours contributed to the company. So there was no such thing as a 40-hour week, you could forget about that math, as it is very difficult to achieve your utilization with 40 hours. Second, whether implicitly or explicitly [it led me] to, in some way, fabricate hours. I'm not saying that that was the goal or the intended outcome, but as I've reflected on that, over time, it was impossible that I didn't. It was otherwise impossible for me personally with my goal of making sure I accomplish company goals to achieve company performance feedback, on my own volition. I know that there had to be times when I was, let's say, I was not providing 92% worth of value. So, it is just that almost inherent need to—even if you felt you were creating value—to, if you will, create work that may not have otherwise been necessary. So if I had 32 hours' worth of work and a 40-hour week, well, either you're stretching it out, or you're doing things that may not be value-adding, if you were working in your very own business, you would contribute the 8 hours somewhere else.

He subsequently illustrated such unnecessary work with specific examples:

> *Over diligence, over review, where you review, look at something time and time again, even though the net outcome of your initial effort was more than sufficient. So, I was in the advisory space of the internal audit; your output is work papers. And the majority of my time, I was reviewing other people's work, where you can review those work papers and be done. You could also review those work papers and suggest that any number of reviews creates a better output. It also creates more billable hours in the process.*

> *[Another example] is expanding your sample size. Say, your sample size is 30. There is a standard process that if you have X number of failures [in account reconciliations], you expand your sample size to do more. That's a requirement. However, there's nothing that prevents you from doing more samples anyway. So you could always expand the number of tests that you did and those types of things. I know it comes across as very intentional, and I believe that most people don't do it intentionally; I'm just saying that the system is ripe for those types of things. And there was no doubt that I had to engage in those as well.*

A senior in-house counsel made similar observations with respect to their work with the external legal counsel:

> *We had an executive, who had a medical event, . . . go out on leave. And there are some weird tax and employment law issues regarding how you pay that person while they're on an extended medical leave. And with stock and benefits and cash bonuses, it's a little bit complicated, but I asked two very specific questions, "What are the highest-risk things? You know, how do we need to withhold this thing in this?" I thought that that would generate one to two hours of work. And be like a "yes" or "no" answer. And I ended up getting a bill for $10,000 and like 12 hours of work going into "Well, in this state, it would be this, but in this state, it would be this, but federally, it could be this." And that's the lawyer being paranoid that they haven't given*

110% of the answer, when what I needed was like a gut check on my primary high risk: what is the state going to be mad about if I don't withhold properly?

At the more consequential end of the spectrum (a strong form of SID), companies can engage in mergers and acquisitions, lawsuits, and reorganizations that disrupt work, upend morale, and destroy value. In these situations, induced demand could be outright detrimental to the buyers. For example, in consulting, equating work sold to clients with value celebrates instances when the completion of one project translates into the sale of a new project. Consider the Fortune 500 company mentioned in the opening chapter, which underwent a challenging reorganization project led by a prominent consulting firm. This reorganization completely reshaped the company's structure, redefined numerous roles and responsibilities, and led to a large number of employee reassignments and significant personnel turnover. Implementing a series of major disruptive changes in quick succession had a devastating impact on employee morale and productivity, which is often unnoticed by outsiders. And yet, despite enduring such organizational trauma, company executives struggled to assess the true impact of these changes, as another equally radical transformation was already underway, spearheaded by the same consulting firm.

Similarly, in legal services, patent infringement litigation entails substantial direct legal costs that can easily soar into the millions, as well as indirect costs, such as when companies' top engineers or executives are obliged to spend countless hours in depositions, thereby disrupting normal business activity. Furthermore, a standard defense strategy in patent infringement cases involves contesting the validity or enforceability of the patent in question. As a result, in addition to incurring significant direct legal costs and the indirect costs of business disruption, companies that initiate litigation may find themselves forfeiting patent protection, thereby inviting a flood of competitors into the market.

Importantly, neither weak nor strong forms of SID require an ethical transgression. Rather, the aperture of professional identity leads professionals to see value where value is ambiguous or nonexistent.

As a result, it is essential to recognize that the standard safeguards of professional services against fraud or opportunistic pursuits—including professional norms and codes of conduct, embedded relationships with clients, or the fear of reputational reprisal—become powerless in the face of SID. Professionals do not cheat, engage in unethical behavior, or knowingly deceive their clients. Rather, they seek professional success and legitimacy under the game's rules laid out by the commercial institutional logic, live out their professional identity, and sell work, all while believing that doing so helps their clients.

Compounding the situation is the palpable pressure to sell in professional service firms. Comments on career forums underscore the gravity of such pressure in some organizations, as detailed in Table 8.1.

The main thesis of this book is that much of this pressure has become internalized to the professional's identity, serving as a means to provide value to clients and achieve personal success. While relational embeddedness may serve to protect the majority of professional service firms –client interactions from overtly opportunistic pursuits,[2] it is inevitable that ethical ambiguities will arise. In situations in which professionals encounter ethical gray areas when deciding whether to promote additional work to their clients, the identity that drives them can rationalize dubious practices to help clients make financially prudent decisions and enhance their overall value proposition. For example, a former consultant recounted a situation in which the consulting company was

---

2. Consider an alternative perspective that uncovers systematic deception in professional service firms. For example, as Susan Saab Fortney (2000: 279) revealed, the billable hours system "encourages lying," where individuals are compelled to deceive to meet unrealistic expectations. Notably, failure to comply with these expectations is viewed as a sign of indolence, despite one's actual workload. Similarly, Johan Alvehus and André Spicer (2012: 505) identified numerous instances of "game-playing," where the same billable hours were manipulated or charged to multiple clients. In my view, such evidence aligns more clearly with the research stream that highlights how unattainable, aggressive goals promote unethical behavior (Ordóñez, Schweitzer, Galinsky, & Bazerman, 2009). It is essential to note that this effect is not unique to professional services, and it is ubiquitous across all sectors of organizational life. For example, companies may fabricate financial results to meet steep expectations that financial markets set, academics may falsify research studies to meet impractical tenure requirements, and bankers may open accounts without customer consent to achieve unattainable targets for the number of products sold to the same customer (e.g., Bhattacharjee, 2013; Eisen, 2022; Michaels & Gryta, 2020).

Table 8.1 THE PRESSURE TO SELL IN PROFESSIONAL SERVICE FIRMS

Quote	Reference
"The primary focus is to milk the customer for as much money as possible while expending as little effort (from a manager's point of view) as possible."	(Cyber Threat Management Intern, Indeed, 2018a)
"Overall the culture has deteriorated. Doesn't care much about client service, instead about the billing."	(Performance and Program Management Manager, Indeed, 2017a)
"You will be a salesperson rather than actually delivering technical expertise to your client. You will always have to sell instead of actually consulting."	(Senior Manager, Indeed, 2020b)
"Used to be a great company; not anymore. Leadership keeps changing. Really focused on sell, sell, sell and not service, service, service."	(Director, Indeed, 2012)
"If you're not ready to sell to get promoted to senior levels within the firm, this is not the place for you. You could make manager without selling, but as soon as business declines you'll be the first let go."	(Senior Associate, Indeed, 2019d)
"Gotta sell to be successful: You have to be able to sell the company's products for management to like you. So much pressure to bring business to the company. Doesn't matter how quantitative you are."	(Risk Advisory Services Director, Indeed, 2019b)
"Pressure to sell hours to my clients even if they didn't need them."	(Senior Tax Manager, Indeed, 2019b)

(Continued)

Table 8.1 (CONTINUED)

Quote	Reference
"If you can't sell, don't work here for a long time."	(Senior Tax Consultant, Indeed, 2019c)
"Be prepared to sell or else they will fire you. Getting assignments is particularly challenging for someone joining as an experienced hire who has not earned a lot of capital within the firm."	(Advisory Services Director, Indeed, 2018c)
"The firm is heavily focused on business development. If you are from the industry and looking to go into consulting, make sure that salesmanship is in your DNA. At [a Leading Advisory Firm], you will be rated on your work but more heavily on your business development IQ. Some services within the firm are not established, and the Partners are all about selling. For example, Partners will try to sell service A without having a procedure or process established to deliver it. They will talk up service A to the client and once the client signs the contract, the Partners will turn to the Directors and ask them to deliver it. The firm has a Car Salesman mentality."	(Director, Indeed, 2019a)
"the expectation that you have to sell additional services is not to my taste and that you are expected to maximize your billing hours sucks, but that's life in consulting."	(JD Edwards Functional Support, Indeed, 2016)

Quote	Reference
"Sell, sell, sell whether they have the expertise or not. Company fills engagements with warm bodies not necessarily the skill set needed to get the job done . . . Performance is judged against others in your group who have been there for years who bring in clients."	(Manager, Indeed, 2017b)
"Management forces brokers to sell in-house product. The brokers are fired if they don't sell product."	(Branch Manager, Indeed, 2021)
"The culture has changed to sell, sell, sell. Managers are more worried about metrics than actually helping the employees build relationships."	(Relationship Banker, Indeed, 2020a)
"The bankers are driven by incentives, so it really doesn't pay if you don't sell."	(Small Business Specialist, Indeed, 2018b)
"Management forces you to harass people and sell them things they really don't need."	(Former Employee, Indeed, 2013a)
"If I am not consistently selling and expanding my network, then I am not doing my job."	(Mortgage Banker, Indeed, 2013b)
"Upper management needs work, and they pressure you to sell products not needed to the customers."	(Personal Banker, Indeed, 2022)

persuading a client to enter a new market. When the consulting team's research produced a modest estimate of the market's potential size, the partner insisted, *"Find me a 100 million,"* claiming that he knew what it takes to convince the client to proceed with market entry. The partner's underlying belief in this exchange was that disrupting the status quo by new market entry is what the client needed.

William Ross (1996) provided insight into the ethics surrounding attorneys' time-billing and made an analogous observation. He notes that professionals often deceive themselves regarding their clients' needs and justify their behavior by believing that providing more services is inherently beneficial for the client. Consequently, this justification becomes deeply ingrained in the professional's perception of their role, worth, and self-concept. As Ross (1996: 261) posited, "Perhaps the greatest danger is that some attorneys have become so accustomed to rationalizing their liberal time recordation techniques or their decisions to perform endless services for their clients regardless of cost that they may not even recognize that their actions are ethically questionable."

Consider also what the identity of value-equals-selling does when professionals are brought into organizations for no pressing reason. One senior executive who regularly procures professional services was open in saying that much of the challenge in working with professional service firms lies "in our [the buyer's] inability to manage them properly." A recurrent theme in my interviews is that professional service firms are often brought in for symbolic reasons. Senior executives reflected that they often had a solution worked out but could not get through to their company's board until the solution came from a professional service firm. In this instance, seeking a rubber stamp of excellence from expert professionals, and creating a thicker paper trail in case the solution does not work out, may be the reason for bringing in a professional service firm. In other cases, the organizational solution was risky or unfavorably viewed by employees, and some of the company's leaders wanted to distance themselves from it by associating it instead with a professional service firm.

During my fieldwork, it was common to observe instances where clients retained professional service firms due to industry convention, with the prevailing rationale being that "swimming with the school of fish" offered a less perilous and more guaranteed course of action. In these and similar scenarios, uncertainty serves as a pivotal enabling factor of mimetic isomorphism, a phenomenon in which organizations conform to established norms and practices simply because they are prevalent in their field (Davis, 1991; DiMaggio & Powell, 1983; Westphal, Gulati, & Shortell, 1997). One senior executive reflected:

We came off with a pretty poor year, from a performance perspective relative to expectations, and relative to committed performance. And there's no denying that. And the board and the CEO, and all senior leadership felt that pressure of failure to perform. And it was very clear that the edict was we would acquire professional consultancy to help us . . . And more than anything, [we were instructed to choose] a brand so that we can communicate to our investors that they are helping management so management doesn't look like they're going at it alone to give some investor assurance.

In light of the increasingly abbreviated tenures of CEOs, with the median CEO tenure in the S&P presently hovering around a mere five years (Marcec, 2018), executives are frequently under pressure to leave a mark, which often takes the form of disrupting established practices and breaking with convention. In such instances, engaging the services of professional service firms is often viewed as a viable strategy for driving change. This, in turn, reinforces the professional service firms' inherent bias for action, which is readily apparent when new client leadership assumes the reins, even in cases of planned succession rather than a turnaround. Under these circumstances, change—rather than continuity—becomes the default, with executives seeking to project an image of boldness and innovative thinking by advocating for unconventional, potentially drastic measures. One executive commented on this with respect to engaging professional service firms, "*I think there is this constant comment of, you know, we got to be bold, and it's a way to suggest that you're being bold, something outside the box and moving something, you know, in a relatively drastic way.*"

Another senior leader elaborated the same theme with respect to soliciting the help of professional service firms, "*an organization feels the need to suggest that, in challenging times, they can prove that they're doing something very different. And even in non-challenging times that a leader has left their mark, and I'm no different in that I want to leave a mark on the organization, I want to do that."*

In reality, such engagements with professional service firms are rarely thought through carefully from an economic standpoint and may entail, in fact, adverse repercussions for the procuring organizations. These could include direct and indirect expenses, disruptions to business continuity, decreased morale, and personnel attrition. Moreover, it does not require much imagination to predict what could happen when the professionals' "selling-equals-value" mindset enters organizational premises and comes into regular contact with senior executives. The same executive whose company was coming off a less-than-a-stellar year reflected how the engagement with a professional service firm played out:

> *We engaged [name of the consulting firm]. And it started with relatively basic org reviews, zero-based budgeting work, how can we help, those type of things. And one of the key ways—and this is also a recent experience that I have—they got into that work was look, "we won't charge you unless you save money." This is a very common model now . . . Now let's jump to the end result. The end result is we outsourced a whole bunch of shared services to them.*

I do not present the aforementioned example as evidence of SID, a service that suppliers impose on their clients, adding no real value. Instead, I employ it as an illustration of the tendency of professional service firms to perceive their surroundings through their commercial identity, which can prompt them to actively pursue sales. In turn, the inclinations toward action, familiarity, and agreement, which are buttressed by enabling market conditions, put both professionals and clients at risk of SID.

THE ROLE OF GEOGRAPHICALLY PROXIMATE PROFESSIONAL SERVICE FIRMS

SID denotes the influence that suppliers exert over their clients. Central to this concept is the question of what factors enhance the effectiveness of this influence. *My contention is that professional service providers who are in close geographical proximity to their clients are the primary purveyors of SID.* As I illustrate below, research has consistently shown that spatial proximity is a highly influential predictor of the frequency and ease of face-to-face interactions. Such proximity creates an environment in which regular contact, which can lead to the formation of social relationships between professionals and clients, paves the way for enhanced influence. In addition, close physical proximity allows clients seeking professional advice to initiate more frequent consultations and for professionals to actively offer their services. It is important to note that clients are more likely to adhere to advice delivered through face-to-face communication. The convergence of these factors ultimately results in an increased likelihood of SID.

A wealth of empirical research offers compelling evidence that physical proximity is a powerful predictor of social contact and the formation of social relationships. James H. S. Bossard (1932) conducted one of the earliest studies on this topic by examining whether living near a potential marriage partner predicted the likelihood of marrying that person. He analyzed 5,000 marriage licenses in which at least one of the applicants resided in Philadelphia and calculated the distance between the applicants' homes in city blocks. James H. S. Bossard (1932) found that one-quarter of the couples lived within two blocks of each other, one-third lived within five blocks of each other, and the percentage of marriages decreased significantly as the distance between the applicants' homes increased. Subsequent research has confirmed that physical proximity plays a significant role in shaping social contact and can lead to the formation of friendships (Festinger, Schachter, & Back, 1950), scientific collaborations (Kabo, Hwang, Levenstein, & Owen-Smith, 2015), and partnerships (Balland, Belso-Martínez, & Morrison, 2016; Saxenian, 1994) among individuals and organizations in close physical proximity. Related research has suggested that our social networks, for the most part, are geographically bound and are not easily transportable across physical distances (Stuart & Sorenson, 2003). These findings underscore the importance of physical proximity in shaping social interactions and suggest that the benefits of such interactions may be more challenging to achieve when individuals and organizations are geographically distant.

These findings can be attributed to two fundamental and interconnected mechanisms. First, physical proximity heightens the likelihood of
both an initial interaction between two individuals and subsequent contact (Blau, 1977). In the physical realm, social life is organized around
social foci or locations that facilitate social gatherings. People tend to
meet and engage with one another in the context of shared activities
or social venues, such as community centers, places of worship, work-
places, parks, or parent–teacher organizations. Such shared social foci
are often responsible for establishing interpersonal ties and networks
(Feld, 1981; Small & Adler, 2019). Second, face-to-face interactions with
physically proximate others serve to mitigate the personal costs of contact. By reducing the time and effort spent commuting to meet with
others, individuals can engage in more frequent and meaningful interactions with those in their immediate vicinity (Funk, Sytch, & Nahm, 2023;
Zipf, 1949). Harald Bathelt, Anders Malmberg, and Peter Maskell (2004:
38–39) elegantly summarized these arguments: "Co-presence within the
same economic and social context generates manifold opportunities for
personal meetings and communication. These meetings can be planned
or occur spontaneously. They can be nondesigned, nontargeted, and
more or less accidental."

It is important to recognize that, in the context of interactions among
professional service firms and their clients, such interactions are buttressed heavily by a slew of professional venues. Let me take the case
of intellectual property (IP) litigation in biotechnology and pharmaceuticals, a professional service context in which I test my arguments
empirically (see Chapter 9). In addition to facilitating initial encounters
and subsequent interactions in social venues, proximity can enable IP
lawyers and biopharmaceutical company executives to maintain formal
and informal contact through locally connecting institutions (Marquis,
2003). For example, IP trial lawyers often participate in the Network of
Trial Lawyers, the Licensing Executives Society (LES), or the American
Intellectual Property Law Association (AIPLA). These are national organizations with multiple local chapters. Typically, cities also have vibrant
local organizations for IP professionals. Boston, for example, is home to
the Boston Patent Law Association (BPLA), while Chicago boasts the
Intellectual Property Law Association of Chicago (IPLAC) with about

a thousand members. Similar local associations for IP professionals are found in Detroit, Houston, New York, Philadelphia, and San Diego, as well as in smaller cities, such as Austin, Texas; Rochester, New York; and Toledo, Ohio, among others.

Opportunities for frequent contact among lawyers and potential clients are often woven into these organizations' membership and leadership structures. In LES, for example, corporate members constitute about 30% of its membership and law firms another 20%. Corporate members include executives representing the company's in-house legal counsel, which carries the primary responsibility for the company's legal strategy, as well as executives from licensing, business development, and science and technology functions, all of whom can be consulted on litigation. In BPLA, the leadership roles at one time were shared between the Boston-based associate senior counsel for the pharmaceutical company Eisai, Inc. and a partner from the Boston office of McCarter and English, LLP, a New Jersey-based law firm that represents Eisai in much of its patent infringement litigation.

The local chapters of national organizations and regional societies are also active in bringing corporate executives and lawyers together through activities such as seminars, speaker series, luncheons, educational programs, golf outings, and judges' banquets. One lawyer commented on the activities of the LES local chapter: *"we have monthly meetings, or so, so you could volunteer to hold a seminar, have a 45-minute luncheon here, something like that, just to inform the members of something that's interesting through our business."*

Notable, too, is that these venues do not just support random encounters. Rather, many lawyers actively use these venues to build relationships with new clients and maintain contact with current clients. As one experienced trial lawyer commented, *"We participate in the same seminars, we try to meet the in-house legal counsel, we wine and dine our clients."* Clearly, legal professionals are cognizant of how geographic proximity can help develop and maintain personal contact. Another lawyer confided:

There's no substitute for the personal relationship, I am totally convinced. No matter how much the Internet takes over and how fast the world is, to clients and me as a customer, . . . for some reason that's almost human nature, you want somebody close to you that you see on a regular business basis through, I don't know, local meetings, associations or whatever, or that you can have come over to your place or you can drop by without having somebody fly and go through all that stuff at the airport and whatever.

A company's enhanced contact and personal acquaintance with lawyers in proximate IP law firms may lead to SID in litigation for two reasons. First, the company's executives are more likely to seek counsel actively and openly on possible litigation issues. Essential to emphasize is that involving external legal counsel in patent infringement disputes is not only inevitable, but also occurs early—typically well before communicating with the alleged infringer. As one lawyer observed, *"In the beginning, if someone anticipates a dispute, they will call outside counsel for an opinion as to the strength of the patent and the application of the patent for that particular product, whether they infringe or not, is the patent valid or not. They want a feel for that."* The IP litigation firm serves as an important advisor at this early stage, helping delineate the boundaries of relevant claims and assessing the likelihood of proving infringement.

In interviews, executives repeatedly noted that it was easier to invite to lunch or call a law firm employee if they knew the employee personally. Working through personal contacts is decidedly different than engaging a law firm formally, which might require the company to use only official communication channels and exercise more thorough due diligence from the outset. Thus, a company whose executives have personal contacts in IP litigation firms might seek legal advice earlier, when perhaps only the suspicion of a dispute exists. As such, the executive might be more likely to solicit advice on a larger number of opportunities.

Second, geographic proximity can increase litigation levels through enhanced formal and informal contact, because lawyers can informally communicate opportunities for legal action to a company directly and thus exercise influence in a more overt way. Because product and patent information are both public, one lawyer observed that this could happen simply *"because you have an entrepreneurial law firm."* Another noted:

There's been a chime going on over, oh, the better part of several decades, to bring litigation possibilities to the client by helping them [with], for lack of a better term, what's called mining the portfolio. Basically, it's an exercise where you review the portfolio of IP, and you look at the competitors out there, making, selling products, and services that may be infringing these patents. And you can make recommendations to the company to enforce those patents.

The increased social contact that geographic proximity affords likely allows lawyers to present a greater number of patent enforcement opportunities to the client. Consistent with these observations, existing work has highlighted that lawyers' direct, personal contact with clients is an absolutely critical factor in engendering the growth of law firms (McEvily, Jaffee, & Tortoriello, 2012).

The context of intellectual property litigation is not merely an outlier case but rather a powerful illustration of the importance of geographic proximity for professional service firms. During a leadership summit at an accounting firm, a senior partner underscored this point to his colleagues, emphasizing the strategic advantages of being physically close to one's clients. To drive home his message, he shared a personal anecdote about a client whose leadership had recently changed, leaving him uncertain about how to approach the new CEO. When a colleague invited him to a gala, the partner's immediate response was, "Is the new CEO going to be there?" Upon learning that the CEO would indeed be present, the partner seized the opportunity, quipping, "Try to stop me." At the gala, he deftly sought out the CEO and delivered a well-prepared and rehearsed pitch that highlighted his firm's recent accomplishments with the client and ongoing joint projects.

Senior partners in the consulting industry that I interviewed reiterated the value of common social venues in building and maintaining relationships with client executives. One senior partner emphasized that many junior partners fail to realize that success in this field often requires them "to open up their wallets." When I asked him to elaborate, he shared an anecdote about his use of charity events to cultivate relationships with current clients and generate new business. In one memorable instance, he found himself at a fundraiser with a client

organization's CEO and his spouse, unsure whether to bid on a particular item. It was then that the CEO's wife leaned over and offered to
go in on the bid with him, prompting him to ultimately make the purchase. "At that point, I had to bid," he laughingly reflected. The broader
point he made was the importance of actively seeking out social venues
to maintain existing client relationships and build new ones.

At a training session for consulting firms that I attended, consultants
were given explicit instructions on how to make the most out of their
time at client sites. This included spending free time in areas with high
foot traffic, such as cafeterias, to meet new clients and cultivate relationships that could be leveraged for future business. A skeptic might
say there is nothing inherently wrong with this, as it is pure marketing. Not quite. My contention is that when such interactions take place
within an environment steeped in the commercial institutional logic and
conducive to SID, the frequent contact and social relationships between
professionals and their clients heighten the risk of SID.

Note the irony in which the same social mechanisms—the formation of embedded relationships—that can mitigate blunt opportunistic
pursuits are powerless in the face of professionals living out their new
institutional logic and professional identity. Worse yet, such close personal relationships can actually exacerbate the work of these antecedents
in stimulating SID. Importantly, extant research has suggested that
physical proximity represents one of the major determinants of effective
social influence (Latane, 1981). Studies hint at a variety of psychological
mechanisms that can stimulate increased compliance in close spaces.
Such mechanisms include the greater likelihood of remembering and
recalling interactions as significant (Latane, Liu, Nowak, Bonevento
et al., 1995); the feeling of liking, which arises from the increased anticipation of future personal contact (Darley & Berscheid, 1967; Latane
et al., 1995); and greater perceptions of intimacy (Argyle & Dean, 1965;
Patterson, 1976). Face-to-face encounters also create powerful opportunities for social influence through touch and gaze (Bull & Robinson,
1981; Goldman, Kiyohara, & Pfannensteil, 1984). Consider also that,
due to both selection and career progression demands, professionals
are particularly adept at social influence compared to representatives

of other occupations (Stern & Westphal, 2010). As such, professionals may be especially likely to capitalize on the levers of social influence that geographic proximity affords.

At this point, it is reasonable to wonder whether the suggested effects of geographic proximity still hold true in a post-pandemic world. After all, the COVID-19 pandemic compelled many organizations to embrace virtual work, which at the time seemed to neutralize much of the impact that geographic proximity had on building relationships with clients. However, it is now evident that most organizations are returning to some level of in-person work much sooner than anticipated (Kelly, 2022; Consulting Report, 2023; Walsman, 2022), and fully remote work is likely to remain an uncommon occurrence (Nguyen & Nishant, 2023).

Furthermore, despite the challenges presented by the pandemic, professional service firms have been leading the way in returning to in-person work, likely due to their understanding of its significance in generating business. For example, an examination of the consulting industry by Matthew C. Walsman (2022) revealed a noticeable shift back to in-person work immediately shortly after the pandemic. Specifically, the study found that, in 2022, 20% of consultants spent one to two days working in their corporate offices, compared to just 6% during the early stages of the pandemic. Additionally, the research concluded that although there is a general return to in-person work, consulting firms are adopting hybrid models wherein routine tasks are suitable for remote engagement, while non-routine tasks necessitate colocation (Walsman, 2022: 210).

Similarly, investment banks have taken the lead in reinstating a return-to-work policy. Justifying the cessation of remote work for senior bankers, JPMorgan's CEO stated in a recent memo: "They [bankers] have to be visible on the floor, they must meet with clients, they need to teach and advise, and they should always be accessible for immediate feedback and impromptu meetings" (Nguyen & Nishant, 2023). Crucially, even in instances where work temporarily shifted to remote settings, professionals actively sought out clients for in-person interactions in non-work venues. As a result, a majority of clients I interviewed post-pandemic reported extensive face-to-face interactions with professional service firms, underscoring the enduring relevance of geographic proximity in cultivating robust client relationships.

CHAPTER SUMMARY

The fusion of the commercial institutional logic and the resulting internalized professional identity leads to supplier-induced demand through three key biases. The first bias is the bias for action, in which professionals tend to lean toward taking action rather than remaining inactive in situations of uncertainty. The second bias is the familiarity bias, which prompts professionals to promote the expertise, products, and services they are familiar with, even if they may not be the best solution for the client's problem. The final bias is the agreement bias, wherein professionals and clients agree on a course of action that neither genuinely supports.

This resulting supplier-induced demand can manifest in a weak form, such as clients spending funds on unnecessary accounting checks, legal discovery, consulting research, or banking due diligence. In its strong form, supplier-induced demand can lead professional service firms to influence clients into engaging in disruptive activities like mergers and acquisitions, lawsuits, and reorganizations, which can harm productivity and morale, and destroy value. In these scenarios, induced demand can be outright detrimental to the clients.

Frequent social interactions and embedded relationships between buyers and suppliers, often facilitated by geographical proximity, make proximate professional service providers the most likely sources of supplier-induced demand. Under enabling market conditions and the prevailing commercial institutional logic, geographically proximate relationships become potent channels for social influence toward supplier-induced demand.

CHAPTER 9

Evidence From Intellectual Property Litigation

Most civil cases are settled before trial but not until years of legal wrangling have tied up the courts and run up large fees and expenses. Cases aren't settled sooner because lawyers, who benefit most from litigation, are in control—not the clients who pay the bill.

Whitney North Seymour (1992: A15)

The empirical evidence for the argument laid out in the preceding chapters comes from the market for legal services. Specifically, I studied the demand for legal services, as measured by the frequency and duration of legal disputes between organizations over patent infringement. With its heavy cognitive, emotional, and economic burdens, legal conflict is generally considered undesirable and is typically avoided. In addition to immense costs, the complexity and mutability of the legal system generate significant uncertainty regarding litigation outcomes (see, e.g., D'Amato, 1993; Moore, 2000). In patent infringement litigation, this uncertainty affects the defendant, who faces injunctions and punitive damages, as well as the plaintiff, whose patents may be ruled invalid or unenforceable and thus open the floodgates for competition. Many parties, therefore, try to work out disagreements through private settlements or mediation and avoid escalating legal action (e.g., Macaulay, 1963). When lawsuits are nevertheless initiated, the severity of these legal engagements suggests that it was the plaintiff's considerations, rather than the lawyers' influence, that drove the decision to litigate.

By contrast, this chapter offers an account of supplier-induced demand (SID), one in which lawyers do not just follow the demand for legal services, but also help generate that demand and therefore raise companies' levels of litigation. Specifically, I zone in on the role played by the increased opportunities for formal and informal contact among proximate lawyers and potential plaintiffs (Blau, 1977). This contact is expected to augment the demand for legal services, as evidenced by the frequency and duration of lawsuits under enabling market conditions of imperfect agency, power asymmetry, and uncertainty, as well as the commercial institutional logic governing the market for intellectual property (IP) litigation services. Notably, such increased litigiousness is unlikely to be accompanied by legal success.

The empirical findings presented in this chapter reveal that—even after adjusting for endogenous choices in law firm location, which are likely linked to areas of high legal and economic activity—companies situated near IP litigation firms initiate legal action more frequently. Moreover, the findings suggest that companies seeking legal counsel from IP law firms in closer proximity tend to become embroiled in lengthier legal disputes. However, although the involvement of nearby lawyers increases both the likelihood and duration of litigation, it simultaneously reduces the probability of the company achieving a favorable outcome in court. Consequently, the demand generated by local lawyers can impose a financial burden on producers by escalating legal costs while diminishing legal benefits. I find that these effects are significantly influenced by the characteristics of the local institutional environment. The findings qualify my initial expectations, documenting that the impact of SID is *not* uniform across all proximate IP service providers. These effects materialize only in circumstances of heightened action uncertainty, in which it is difficult to predict the outcomes of a given action. In such scenarios, IP lawyers wield significant expert control owing to their ability to mitigate legal uncertainty.

THE CONTEXT OF PATENT INFRINGEMENT LITIGATION

To begin, I provide some detail on the empirical context of patent infringement litigation in biotechnology and pharmaceuticals and what
makes this context attractive for testing the theory of SID. Legally,
patent infringement is defined in the United States as making, using,
offering to sell, selling within, or importing into the United States a
patented invention without authority during the term of the patent
(35 U.S.C. ∫271(a)).[1] A patent infringement dispute typically revolves
around claims of infringement by the patent owner, who can demand
an injunction or economic and punitive damages; and the counterclaims by the alleged infringer, who usually demands that the patent
be ruled invalid or unenforceable. The outcomes of such disputes can
determine the viability of the entire enterprise. In the words of one interviewed executive, "*Even as a $500 million biotechnology company, a
patent infringement lawsuit can take you out [of business].*"[2] Such legal disputes therefore represent some of the longest, fiercest, and most

1. To be patentable, an innovation must meet the legal requirements regarding (1) patentable
subject matter, (2) utility, (3) novelty, and (4) nonobviousness. Whereas early guidelines
for patentable inventions covered machines, multi-substance compositions, manufactured
products, and manufacturing processes, the 1980 US Supreme Court ruling that upheld a
patent for a genetically engineered bacterium that eats oil slicks (*Diamond v. Chakrabarty*,
443 U.S. 303 [1980]) triggered an influx of patents for life forms. This spurred the proliferation of patented inventions in biotechnology. Patented innovations in pharmaceuticals and
biotechnology now cover a wide spectrum of items, ranging from chemically synthesized
small molecules, active drug compounds, approved medical uses or indications for a drug,
and the formulation of a drug agent coupled with stabilizers or preservatives to recombinant products, genetic material, proteins, monoclonal antibodies, nucleic acids, and DNA
sequences. Patents can also cover the methods of manufacturing and using these items.

2. For example, in January 2001, when Transkaryotic Therapies (TKT) was found to have
infringed Amgen's patent covering Epogen (an anemia drug for patients undergoing kidney dialysis and chemotherapy), TKT's stock plunged 17%. In the 2002 patent infringement
case between Chiron and Genentech over Genentech's breast cancer drug Herceptin, Chiron
sought as much as $300 million in royalties from Genentech, albeit in vain. Note, too, that
patent infringement litigation in biotechnology and pharmaceuticals is typically substantive
and meaningful. Customarily, biopharmaceutical patents are tied closely to manufacturing
a set of related products and devices. This restricts the participation of entities, commonly
known as patent trolls (Cohen, Gurun, & Kominers, 2016), that simply amass patent portfolios and subsequently use litigation to extract royalties. These circumstances similarly limit
using patent litigation as an active strategy to build and develop IP portfolios, which is more
common in other industries.

consequential interorganizational confrontations in biotechnology and pharmaceuticals (see, e.g., Hewitt, 2005).

The principal attraction of this setting for testing the arguments about SID is twofold. The first advantage arises from the fact that both the enabling conditions and commercial institutional logic are well-represented in this setting. It is important to consider that the markets for legal services, litigation in particular, resemble numerous other professional service domains, as well as markets for healthcare in deviating substantially from the conditions of competitive markets (Arrow, 1963: 948, 951). This is due to several factors, including the imperfect agency in which lawyers simultaneously act as advisors on enforcement opportunities and sellers of their legal services; the lawyers' (sellers) significant expertise and information advantages over the clients (buyers); and the uncertain quality of the product being exchanged. Paraphrasing Kenneth J. Arrow (1963: 951), one can state that recovery in lawsuits is as unpredictable as their incidence. The preceding chapters of the book furnish copious qualitative evidence to demonstrate how the market for patent infringement litigation epitomizes these characteristics. Much like other legal services, the pervasive force of commercial institutional logic has made inroads into IP, permeating the organizational structures, culture, processes, and incentives of IP litigation firms. As discussed earlier, these factors are pivotal in engendering SID because they establish both the propitious conditions and the impetus for professionals to shape their clients' appetite for their services.

Another advantage of the litigation context is the analyst's ability to measure the value of professional services to clients in large samples with a relatively high degree of precision. This sets legal services apart from other fields, such as healthcare or management consulting, where determining whether patients or clients were underserved or overserved can be more challenging. In healthcare, for instance, SID has been associated with increased physician concentration and healthcare consumption. However, it remains uncertain whether patients have received necessary care or excessive services due to challenges in collecting data on patient mortality and health outcomes. Similarly, evaluating the outcomes of management consulting projects is often challenging, even in large samples, leading many studies to rely on vignettes rather than systematic empirical analysis (Guttman & Willner, 1976; Mazzucato & Collington, 2023). In contrast, the implications of demand for legal services can be evaluated more concretely through the outcomes of legal proceedings. Large-sample analyses enable the analyst to control for various lawsuit- and buyer-specific characteristics that could affect litigation outcomes, facilitating a more accurate assessment of the impact of SID on buyers.

TESTING THE THEORY OF SUPPLIER-INDUCED DEMAND

Early influential work attributed the demand for litigation services to entrepreneurial actors' relatively frictionless pursuit of self-interest. Such actors collectively contributed to the public utility of sustaining coordination in a complex society (Durkheim, 1949). The gradual endorsement of this perspective in both organization studies (Cartwright & Schwartz, 1973; Edelman & Suchman, 1997; Nelson, 1988) and economics (for a review, see Spier, 2005) has relegated, in turn, the role of lawyers to the periphery of scholarly analysis related to the emergence and continuation of litigation. By the same token, in economics, some of the most influential models of litigation are devoid of lawyers and focus instead only on the interests and behaviors of the plaintiffs and defendants (Bebchuk, 1984; Priest & Klein, 1984). The rare empirical inquiries of litigation assume lawyers take a rather limited role, which entails formalizing the dispute by referencing previously decided cases (Cartwright & Shwartz, 1973). Thus, the growing number of law firms and litigators has often been interpreted as an *indicator* of an increasingly litigious population (Edelman & Suchman, 1997: 485; Nelson, 1988). Alongside the perspective of lawyers playing a limited role in shaping demand for litigation, studies of regional clusters sometimes praise the lawyers' role in facilitating business exchange. Although these arguments are typically circumscribed to unique geographical areas, lawyers have been credited with helping reduce uncertainty in complex business transactions and with enforcing and transmitting norms of collaborative exchange (Buhr & Owen-Smith, 2011; Suchman & Cahill, 1996).

The theory of SID offers an alternative view of the role lawyers play, however. It suggests that lawyers can actively induce demand for their services, even to the potential detriment of the buyers. Importantly, the argument presented in Chapter 8 suggests that SID is concentrated in the efforts of lawyers who operate in geographic proximity to their clients. It allows them to enjoy frequent, spontaneous, and deliberate face-to-face contact with their clients, which becomes an edifice for the demand-inducing influence.

Empirically, I subject the theory of SID to the following tests. First, I anticipate that companies located in geographic proximity to IP lit-igation law firms will be more likely to initiate a greater number of patent infringement lawsuits. As described previously, clients often con-sult nearby lawyers regarding whether they should pursue legal action. Moreover, because both patent and product spaces are public, law firms actively analyze them for potential overlaps and present litigation op-tions to their clients. If empirical evidence supports this hypothesis while accounting for the endogenous placement of lawyers, it would be consistent with SID, indicating a link between increased consumption of legal services and the influence of nearby service providers.

Second, I examine whether companies collaborating with a nearby IP litigation law firm on a specific patent infringement case will spend more time litigating that case. Evidence supporting this prediction would once again link increased consumption of legal services to the influence of nearby service providers, this time at the level of a lawsuit. Such findings would be consistent with the presence of SID. While multiple nearby lawyers may be involved in identifying potential patent disputes suit-able for litigation, once the company elevates a dispute to a legal case, it engages a particular external legal counsel to represent it in that lawsuit. This external legal counsel assists in drafting the court complaint (which initiates the legal case) and works closely with the client during discov-ery to analyze relevant patents, their prosecution histories, and related inventions. As the case approaches trial, the chosen counsel formulates a theory of infringement, collaborates with the client on legal strategy, helps identify and prepare expert witnesses, and conducts mock trials.

As the lawsuit unfolds, geographic proximity gives the lawyers significantly more effective social influence due to more frequent face-to-face contact with the client. With a geographically distant legal counsel, whose transportation to the company's site requires taking a flight, face-to-face contact is less frequent and more sporadic. Typically, such contact is marked by key milestones in the litigation process, such as discovery or preparing witnesses for cross-examination or expert witness testimony. In contrast, my interviews revealed that in-person contact with a more geographically proximate legal counsel is significantly less constrained and is therefore more frequent and regular. As the lawsuit progresses, key discussions focus on whether the company should continue to escalate legal action or seek an out-of-court settlement. In line with the previously advanced argument, legal advice and lawyers' influence are likely to be skewed toward continuing litigation.

Third, the perspective of SID suggests that the increased frequency and duration of litigation will not result in legal success. In a "weak form" of SID, the presence of proximate lawyers may increase the frequency and duration of litigation but will not affect the companies' legal success. In this scenario, lawyer-induced demand may reduce the odds of relative success, meaning positive legal outcomes relative to the number of lawsuits filed or the amount of time spent in litigation. On the other hand, in a "strong form" of SID, the presence of proximate lawyers and retaining a proximate legal counsel may actually reduce the likelihood of legal success for the companies initiating litigation. This proposition assumes that lawyers may be influencing companies to initiate and prolong litigation that is of particularly low quality, as more attractive opportunities become exhausted or more difficult to identify.

If, by contrast, the presence of proximate lawyers and retaining a proximate external legal counsel lead to an increase in companies' legal success, this evidence would contradict SID. In fact, one can take this alternative view further by suggesting that proximity to suppliers could allow companies to leverage regional networks and local competition to select the most competent and credible purveyors of legal services and thus identify a larger number of promising legal opportunities. The book's arguments suggest that this alternative view is significantly more viable in situations where the markets lack the enabling conditions and where the commercial institutional logic is not as dominant as it is in professional services.

Finally, if the arguments concerning SID hold true, heightened levels of uncertainty should exacerbate these dynamics. As previously posited, uncertain environments may foster the development of particularistic theories of infringement, as objective standards become less applicable. In addition, heightened uncertainty may render in-house decision-makers even more reliant on expert suppliers to navigate the uncertainty and thus more likely to heed their professional advice. In more uncertain environments, the experts themselves may be uncertain regarding how best to proceed. It is precisely in such environments that action, familiarity, and agreement biases may be most potent, enabling the pursuit of less promising litigation opportunities and resulting in suboptimal legal outcomes. Accordingly, I anticipate that the levels of legal services consumed, as indicated by the frequency and duration of litigation, will rise under conditions of uncertainty without a corresponding increase in legal success.

In summary, SID suggests a shift in the locus of control regarding the initiation and perpetuation of demand, transitioning from the buyers to the geographically proximate suppliers. In my analysis, I therefore anticipate that, even after accounting for the endogenous placement of lawyers, companies surrounded by legal professionals in close physical proximity will initiate a greater number of lawsuits. Additionally, companies retaining more proximate legal counsel for a given lawsuit are likely to experience more prolonged litigation. Within this framework, geographic proximity fosters ongoing interaction between buyers and suppliers, thereby amplifying the suppliers' influence toward increased demand.

Furthermore, elevated levels of induced demand may not align with enhanced buyer outcomes. In the book's empirical context, therefore, heightened consumption of legal services, manifested through increased frequency and duration of litigation, may not necessarily correspond with improved legal success; rather, it could precipitate heightened legal losses. These dynamics of SID are anticipated to be especially pronounced in situations characterized by heightened uncertainty with respect to predicting outcomes of considered organizational actions. In such contexts, buyers are increasingly reliant on the counsel and expertise proffered by their expert suppliers. Empirically, I employ the variable unpredictability of legal outcomes as a means to scrutinize this proposition.

DATA

The sampling frame for this study included the complete 1998 Bioscan listing of biotechnology and pharmaceutical companies. To control for variations in regulatory and legal regimes and to ensure data availability, I retained all domestic, independent, dedicated biotechnology and pharmaceutical firms, which resulted in a sample of 405 companies. At the beginning of the observation period, 258 companies were publicly owned and 18 others went public at some point during the study's timeframe. I compiled all the companies' divisions and subsidiaries along with each unit's founding year, subsequently treating the firm and its corporate units as a single entity. I tracked the evolution of each company from 1998 to 2006, eliminating any company from the sample if it was acquired or if it went out of business (from the year of the event onward). Overall, 145 companies were removed from the sample at some point during the observation period, leaving 2,616 company-years out of a possible 3,248. After listwise deletion of observations with missing data, the effective sample was 1,439 company-years.[3]

3. The reduction of the sample was systematic, emerging from firm-year observations that characterized smaller, privately owned companies that had smaller patent portfolios and fewer collaborators and that were significantly less litigious. To explore the effect of the nonsystematic sample truncation in estimation, I eliminated control variables, thus avoiding dropping observations with missing data, then I reran all models on the full sample of 2,616 observations. Results were identical to those reported here and are available on request.

A patent infringement dispute is registered and becomes public when a complaint is filed in a US federal district court. I obtained patent infringement records from the Public Access to Court Electronic Records (PACER) database, the Federal Judiciary's center for electronic access to US district court records (e.g., Haslem, 2005; Lowry & Shu, 2002). To ensure the accuracy and completeness of these records, I verified them further using Westlaw and LexisNexis Law records. For each lawsuit record, I obtained the dates the lawsuit was filed and terminated and the list of participating parties. To mitigate left-censoring concerns in tracking the litigation histories of companies, the search was conducted from 1990 to 2006; it returned 1,103 lawsuits whose average duration was about 2.2 years.

Dependent Variables

Frequency and Duration of Litigation. The dependent variable for firm-level analyses consists of the number of unique lawsuits a plaintiff initiated in a given year, representing a count outcome. In lawsuit-level analyses, the dependent variable represents the number of days the focal principal spent litigating a given case, also a count outcome. The count of litigation days starts with the day the lawsuit was filed and continues to the day of settlement or adjudication by the district or the appellate court.

Legal outcomes. My fieldwork revealed the following key outcomes in IP litigation: (1) wins in summary judgment, (2) permanent injunctions granted, (3) verdicts won, and (4) monetary awards. Summary judgment typically represents a judgment entered without a full trial. A company ordinarily moves for a summary judgment to avoid the expense of the full trial when the outcome is clear. Permanent injunctions, in turn, force the infringer to refrain from making and selling a given product or device. In my interviews, lawyers often singled out permanent injunctions as one of the clearest and most consequential victories for the plaintiff. Not only does a permanent injunction shut out the focal infringer from the market, but it also sends a powerful deterrence signal to aspiring market entrants. With respect to verdicts, I operationalized a victory if at least one of the plaintiff's claims was supported in the verdict. Finally, monetary awards represent the combined amount of compensatory and punitive damages awarded to the plaintiff. Data on the outcomes of the lawsuits was collected from the PACER and Lex Machina databases.

To test my predictions, I use both firm-level and lawsuit-level analyses. In firm-level analyses, I use the count of wins in summary judgment, verdicts, and permanent injunctions granted to a firm in a given year, as well as the sum of monetary awards (a continuous measure) the firm obtained in that year. In lawsuit-level analyses, I use a series of binary outcomes that take on 1 if a firm wins a summary judgment, verdict, or is granted a permanent injunction in the focal lawsuit, and 0 if otherwise. The continuous measure of monetary awards, in turn, reflects the combined compensatory and punitive damages awarded to the plaintiff in the focal lawsuit.

For all dependent variables, I isolate lawsuits that the focal principal entered as a plaintiff. This allowed me to capture the principal's agency and hence minimize the variance emanating from others' decisions to initiate litigation against the principal. In the effective regression sample, the distribution of plaintiffs' filings in a given year was skewed toward zero, with about 89% of the firm-year observations overall. About 6% of the sample registered one lawsuit a year; 1.6%—two lawsuits; 1.1%—three lawsuits; another 1%—four or five lawsuits per year, with the remaining 1.2% registering more than five lawsuits a year. The average number of lawsuits a firm filed in a given year was 0.308.

Independent Variables

To calculate measures of geographic proximity between biopharmaceutical companies and IP litigation firms, I first identified the population of IP litigation firms. Using the counsel records for all the lawsuits in the study and the *Law360 Litigation Almanac* registry of IP litigation firms,

I identified 365 unique IP litigation firms. The operations of a typical law firm are dispersed geographically through multiple offices: less than one-third of the firms can be categorized as single-office organizations during the study period. Furthermore, individual regional offices typically exercise a large degree of autonomy in taking on and handling legal cases. I therefore used the *Martindale-Hubbell Law Directory* (e.g., McEvily, Jaffee, & Tortoriello, 2012) to extract the addresses for all 2,255 US offices of firms that were active at any point from 1998 to 2005.

After compiling the above information, I used the Martindale-Hubbell yearly listings and direct contact with relevant law firms to establish the founding year and (when applicable) the closing year of each office. This ensured that a given office entered the risk set only after its founding year and, correspondingly, exited the data the year it was terminated. The risk set of law firms' active offices ranged from 1,197 to 1,431 offices in any given year. Coupled with the instrumental-variable estimation technique described later in this chapter, this approach helps avoid the reverse causality argument that IP litigation firms establish offices in areas of high litigation activity, which in turn drives down the average distance between principals and IP litigation firms.

I used this risk set to test the argument regarding companies becoming more litigious when they are proximate to IP litigation firms. Specifically, I operationalized geographic proximity among biopharmaceutical companies and IP litigation firms using the *Number of Proximate Law Firm Offices (LFOs)* as the number of IP law firm offices within a 100-mile radius of each company's headquarters. It is a company-level measure. The choice of the 100-mile threshold is based on prior research that established 100 miles as the interval with the most prominent effect of distance on the formation of interorganizational relationships (Marquis, 2003; Sorenson & Stuart, 2001). For these calculations, I used the spherical distance formula, which corrects for the Earth's curvature (Sorenson & Stuart, 2001). For every pair of points (A, B), distance can be formalized as: $D(A, B)=3,437.8*[arcos(sin(lat_a)*sin(lat_b)+cos(lat_a)*cos(lat_b)*cos(|long_a-long_b|))]$, where *lat* measures latitude and *long* reflects longitude in radians. I obtained latitudes and longitudes based on information available from the US Postal

Service, which provides latitudes and longitudes for the center point of every ZIP code. The constant, 3,437.8, converts the distance, D, into mile units. The concentration measure was logged to correct for its skewed distributions and to account for the probable diminishing marginal returns of concentration.[4]

To test the argument that retaining a proximate IP litigation counsel prolongs litigation, I operationalized a dyadic distance measure between the company and the retained legal counsel. I did so to arrive at (1) a natural logarithm of the spherical distance between the company's headquarters and the office of the retained legal counsel (*Ln Distance to Legal Counsel*); and (2) a binary variable (*Distance to Legal Counsel>100 mi*), which takes on the value of 1 if the distance between the company's headquarters and the office of the retained legal counsel is greater than 100 miles and 0 otherwise.

Lastly, to test arguments about the varying levels of uncertainty, I use data from the US Chamber of Commerce Survey of State Liability Systems from 2002 to 2006, representing all the years for which the survey data overlapped with the study's observation timeline (1998–2006). This annual survey collects responses from in-house general counsel, senior corporate litigators or attorneys, and other senior executives who are knowledgeable about corporate litigation related to various dimensions of the legal systems in a given state. Attorney respondents, who averaged nearly 20 years of relevant legal experience, are drawn from a representative sample of companies with at least $100 million in revenue. Within the five waves of the survey data I use for the present study, the average number of respondents in a given year is 1,209, varying from 824 in 2002 to 1,456 in 2006. Respondents were asked to evaluate the predictability of juries in the states with which they were familiar using a 5-point grading scale from A to F. Because federal district courts naturally draw on locally available jury pools, these data are particularly applicable as a

---

4. In alternative tests, I relaxed the assumption of geographic equivalency of law firm offices in the 100-mile radius around the company's headquarters. To do so, I created a measure of proximity that captures the (inverse) distance to all offices in the 100-mile radius. Formally, $Proximity_i = \sum [1/(1+d_{ij})]$, where d_{ij} is the natural logarithm of the geographic distance from company i to law firm office j. This variable correlated with the baseline *Number of Proximate LFOs* measure at nearly 0.9 and produced identical results in estimation.

proxy of legal uncertainty for this study. The US Chamber of Commerce then created a numerical conversion scale, assigning 4 to A, 3 to B, 2 to C, 1 to D, and 0 to F. (In 2006, the Chamber increased the values by 1 for each grade, thus assigning 5 to A and 1 to F.) Scores were then averaged across all responses for a particular state (Hans & Eisenberg, 2011).

Given that the survey's timeline overlapped only partially with the study's observation period, I isolated the states that scored below the median on certainty in each of the five years for which the survey timeline overlapped with the timeline. I subsequently created a temporally fixed binary variable, *Uncertain Legal Environment*, which took the value of 1 if the state in which a company was located was below the median, and 0 otherwise. This approach enabled me to mitigate the risk of sampling variability across years (Eisenberg, 2009). More importantly, it allowed me to isolate the set of states with consistently unpredictable juries and hence significant levels of perceived uncertainty regarding legal outcomes.[5] Overall, 17 states comprised the group of states with an uncertain legal environment. In my empirical tests of the role uncertainty played, I interacted *Number of Proximate Law Firm Offices (LFOs)* and *Distance to Legal Counsel* with *Uncertain Legal Environment*.

Control Variables

To ensure robust estimation, I controlled for a comprehensive set of company-level characteristics (see Table 9.1). These characteristics can drive the company's inclination and ability to enter into and sustain lawsuits and can conceivably correlate with the concentration of proximate law firms. These control variables can be classified into six groups. First, I controlled for the traditional indicators of a company's size, age, and

5. Important to note is that some scholars have lamented that the perceived indicators of a legal environment by one audience may not always accurately reflect the actual (i.e., "objective") state of the legal system (Eisenberg, 2009). Although addressing the question of objectivity is beyond the scope of this study, the crucial value of these subjectively reported indicators lies precisely in capturing the legal uncertainty as *perceived* by the key audience of corporate decision-makers. These decision-makers are expected to be among the key targets of influence by the IP lawyers, and it is their perceptions of task-specific uncertainty (Milliken, 1987) that are likely to be most closely correlated with opportunities for social influence.

Table 9.1 CONTROL VARIABLES

Firm-Level Controls		
Variable	**Operationalization**	**Source**
1. SIZE, AGE, AND ACCOUNTING INDICATORS		
Headcount	Logged count of the company's employees in year t-1.	Bioscan, Compustat
Organizational Age	Number of years since the company's founding year.	
R&D Expenses	Company's research and development expenses in year t-1 (in millions).	
Profit Margin	Company's ratio of profit to sales in year t-1.	
Quick Ratio	Company's ratio of current assets to current liabilities in year t-1.	
2. FIRM'S DEGREE OF INTEGRATION INTO COLLABORATIVE SOCIAL STRUCTURE		
Collaboration Centrality	Number of R&D, co-manufacturing, co-marketing partnerships (contractual or equity) the company entered into from year t-1 to year t-5.	Recap, Factiva, Bioscan
3. FIRM'S TECHNOLOGICAL CHARACTERISTICS		
Biotechnology	Fraction of the company's patents that contained one or more of the three-digit classes assigned by USPTO to biotechnology (424, 435, 436, 514, 530, 536, 800, and 930).	USPTO
Patent Portfolio	Number of patents granted to the company from year t-1 to year t-5.	
Technological Overlap	For a given pair of companies, this measure can be defined as $TO_{ij}=(C_{ip}C_{jp})/\Sigma(C_{ip}+C_{jp})$, where the numerator reflects the number of citations made by companies i and j's patents to common patents, while the denominator reflects the sum of patent citations for both companies.	

(Continued)

Table 9.1 (CONTINUED)

Firm-Level Controls		
Variable	**Operationalization**	**Source**
	The measure is averaged across all dyads in the study and multiplied by 10^4.	
Patent Heterogeneity	Captures the level of heterogeneity of a company's patent portfolio; formally, $[1-\Sigma pc_i^2]$ where pc_i reflects the proportion of a company's patents falling into a given 3-digit US patent class. Higher values reflect a company that is more diversified in the technological space.[a]	
Product Portfolio	Number of product niches in which the company was active in year t-1. Product niches were determined based on the Bioscan's time-variant coverage of companies' participation in 166 product niches.	Bioscan
4. FIRM'S BASELINE PROPENSITY TO LITIGATE		
Infringement Rate	Likelihood of a company's products infringing on other organizations' IP (see Appendix 1 for details).	Bioscan, PACER
Susceptibility Rate	Likelihood of a company's patent portfolio being infringed upon by other organization (see Appendix 1 for details).	USPTO, PACER
5. FIRM'S CURRENT LITIGATION BURDEN		
Number of Adversaries	Number of unique adversaries opposing the company in its ongoing patent infringement lawsuits.	PACER
Number of Allies	Number of co-plaintiffs and co-defendants in the company's ongoing patent infringement lawsuits.	PACER

Lawsuit-Level Controls		
Variable	Operationalization	Source

6. REPUTATION OF LEGAL COUNSEL RETAINED

Top IP Law Firm	Binary measure that takes on the value of 1 if the retained legal counsel belonged to the top 30 IP law firm rankings in terms of patent case load as captured by IPLaw360 (and 0 if otherwise).[b]	*IPLaw360 Litigation Almanac*

7. FAMILIARITY WITH LAW FIRM

Familiarity with Law Firm	Number of unique lawsuits in which the focal law firm represented the company in patent infringement litigation from 1990 to t-1.	PACER

8. CONSEQUENTIALITY OF LAWSUIT

Number of Plaintiffs	Number of plaintiffs in a focal lawsuit.	PACER
Number of Defendants	Number of defendants in a focal lawsuit.	PACER
Media Cvg. of Focal Lawsuit	Number of unique articles covering the lawsuit from the day of filing to five days after.	Factiva

9. RELATIONAL DISTANCE BETWEEN PLAINTIFF AND DEFENDANT

Prior Partnership b/w Plaintiff and Defendant	Binary variable that takes on the value of 1 if the plaintiff and the defendant formed an interorganizational partnership at any point from year t-1 to year t-5 (and 0 if otherwise).	Recap, Factiva

[a]To allow for the highest levels of granularity in assessing the heterogeneity of a company's patent portfolio, the measure reflects a weighted heterogeneity index, in which the contribution of each patent class is weighted by the total number of times it appears in the company's patents.

[b]These sampling criteria resulted in the subsample of 56 top IP litigation firms and their 706 domestic offices. The rankings data are limited to 2005 and 2006, because these are the only years for which records are available in a systematic form. These firms were jointly responsible for handling more than 40% of the patent cases filed in US federal district courts over that period. Focusing on this period ensures a substantial degree of retrospective consistency, as many of these firms (e.g., Fish and Richardson, Jones Day, Kirkland and Ellis) are well-established and have held leading positions in patent infringement litigation for decades.

performance. Second, I controlled for the firm's degree of integration into the collaborative social structure. Third, I accounted for a comprehensive set of each company's technological characteristics, as they may present a set of unobservables driving both the recruitment of counsel and the propensity to litigate. Fourth, because patent infringement lawsuits admittedly represent only a fraction of all patent disputes occurring in an industry, and the selection of disputes to legal cases may be systematic (Priest & Klein, 1984), I controlled for the company's baseline propensity to enter into patent infringement lawsuits. Given that the entire universe of disputes is unobserved, I controlled for a firm's *baseline likelihood* of entering into a legal dispute (see Appendix 1 for details on these measures). Fifth, I accounted for the company's current litigation burden by counting the number of its current legal adversaries (parties against which it litigates) and allies (parties with which it litigates). Finally, in addition to these company-level controls, in models at the lawsuit level, I controlled for the reputation of the legal counsel retained, the number of prior interactions with a given law firm, the consequentiality of the lawsuit, and the relational distance between the plaintiff and the defendant in the lawsuit. In all models, standard errors were clustered by Metropolitan Statistical Areas (MSAs).[6]

METHOD

To estimate the count of lawsuits a company initiates in a given year, I used a Poisson regression, which is unbiased in the presence of autocorrelation, distributional misspecification, and outliers. Empirical

6. To also account for possible between-state variation in litigation in my estimation, in alternative firm-level models I accounted for the following state-level fixed effects: California, New Jersey, New York, Maryland, Massachusetts, and Washington. Taken together, these states accounted for more than 70% of the sample. The state-level fixed effects were insignificant, and the estimates remained consistent with those reported in this chapter. Furthermore, I reran all models while clustering observations at the state level and thus adjusting standard errors for state-level nonindependence of observations. Here too, the effects remained identical to those reported in the main tables. Finally, additional analyses revealed that companies located in California and Massachusetts were younger and smaller on average than other companies in the sample. These differences in organizational age and size, however, did not provide additional exploratory power on the rate of litigation relative to the effects of state clusters.

analyses revealed that Poisson nearly perfectly predicted the observed count of filed lawsuits. Supplementary tests using a negative binomial and zero-inflated negative binomial produced similar results.

To account for possible endogeneity in the location choice of IP law firm offices, I used a three-pronged approach. First, I estimated the effects of the concentration of proximate law firm offices on two distinct outcomes: the number of lawsuits a firm files as a plaintiff and the number in which it participates as a defendant. The argument presented here, which is premised on the pro-litigation influence of lawyers, suggests that the effect of proximate lawyers should increase the number of lawsuits companies file as plaintiffs, but not the number of lawsuits companies enter as defendants. Because the agency of initiating and continuing litigation lies with the plaintiffs, registering the effect of proximate lawyers on the frequency and duration of litigation for plaintiffs alone would significantly strengthen the argument for supplier-induced influence. Second, I employed a nearest-neighbor propensity score matching technique (with replacement), understanding the effect of being located in areas with a high density of local lawyers for the number of lawsuits filed as a plaintiff and as a defendant. Again, the expectation is that the effect of SID theorized here should manifest for plaintiffs but not for defendants.

Third, I estimated the models using a GMM instrumental-variable Poisson (IV Poisson) estimation (Mullahy, 1997) on the original count dependent variable. I used the number of top-tier law schools located within a 100-mile radius around the company's headquarters as an instrument. Top-tier law schools in a given year were defined using the top 50 law schools in the annual rankings of *U.S. News & World Report*. This measure represents a viable instrument for several reasons. First, the establishment of elite law schools pre-dates the establishment of most IP law firms. It is also reasonable to argue that the establishment of law schools was not related to the local dynamics of patent infringement litigation. For example, the locations of many law schools were essentially determined by the land-granting statutes of the federal government in the 19th century. The relevance criterion is rather straightforward: IP law firms are frequently founded by the graduates of local law schools, and law firms consider the local supply of law school graduates in making location choices. The focus on elite law schools is driven by the fact that IP practices are typically staffed with recruits from the most prestigious law schools. Model 1 in Appendix 2 documents a strong effect of the number of local, top-tier law schools on the density of local law firm offices. Following standard econometric conventions (Stock & Yogo, 2002), I evaluated the relevance requirement using the minimum eigenvalue of the Cragg-Donald (1993) statistic. In the case of a single endogenous predictor, as it is in the present analyses, the minimum eigenvalue of the Cragg-Donald statistic is the F-statistic, which tests the null hypothesis that the instrument does *not* enter the first-stage regression. The test for the significance of the instrument in the first stage returned an F-statistic (F=18.63) that exceeded the recommended threshold at 5% of OLS bias.

Finally, because external legal counsel typically manages IP litigation, it is conceivable to argue that the effect of local law schools on companies' patent infringement litigation is channeled through local law firms (see Model 2 in Appendix 2). That said, it is virtually impossible to conclusively establish the exclusion restriction. The main validation approach used in extant research is to check whether the instrument captures omitted variation in other factors that can affect the frequency of litigation (e.g., Fahlenbrach, Low, & Stulz, 2010; Knyazeva, Knyazeva, & Masulis, 2013; Rauch, 2006). To test this condition, I included economically plausible determinants of a firm's litigation that varied by geographic location but had no connection to the number of local law schools. This was done to assess whether their inclusion makes the effect of local law schools become statistically insignificant in the first stage. The instrument displayed a significant effect on the endogenous predictor, even after I controlled for the number of patent infringement lawsuits filed in the company's corresponding district court over the preceding five years (data obtained from Lex Machina IPLC and PACER), the number of organizations targeted for venture capital investments in the preceding year (data obtained from Zephyr), and the number of newly founded biotechnology and pharmaceutical companies over the preceding five years within the 100-mile radius around the company's headquarters (data obtained from ORBIS).

To estimate the duration of a given lawsuit in days, I used the Poisson regression; notably, OLS estimation on a log-transformed dependent variable produced similar effects. This estimation included company-level fixed effects, which helps account for a set of unobservable characteristics that may explain plaintiffs' varying lawsuit durations. In tests that required estimation of the fixed effects of state-level legal uncertainty, a company-level fixed-effects estimation was not appropriate.

To estimate legal outcomes incurring at the firm level, I used a series of Poisson models to estimate the effect of proximate law firm offices on the number of the firm's wins in summary judgments, verdicts, and permanent injunctions in a given year. I also used an OLS regression to estimate the aggregate amount of compensatory and punitive damages awarded to the firm in a given year. To estimate legal outcomes at the level of a lawsuit, I ran a series of logit models estimating the effect of retaining a proximate legal counsel on the odds of a firm winning a summary judgment, a verdict, or being awarded a permanent injunction in that lawsuit. Again, I used an OLS regression to estimate the amount of compensatory and punitive damages awarded to the firm in a given lawsuit.

RESULTS

Proximity to IP Litigation Firms and Litigiousness

Throughout the estimation procedure, the condition indices remained low, suggesting that multicollinearity should not pose a serious statistical issue. The theory of SID leads us to expect that a company's geographic proximity to IP litigation firms is likely to increase the company's propensity to file patent infringement lawsuits. Models 1 (Poisson) and 3 (IV Poisson) in Table 9.2 report a strong positive effect of the *Number of Proximate LFOs* on the number of lawsuits a company

Table 9.2 EFFECTS OF PROXIMATE LAW FIRMS ON A COMPANY'S FREQUENCY AND OUTCOMES OF LITIGATION

	(1)	(2)	(3)	(4)	(5)	(6)	(7)	(8)	(9)	(10)	(11)	(12)	(13)
	Number of lawsuits a company filed in a year as					A company's legal outcomes (success) in a given year as a plaintiff							
	Plaintiff	Defendant	Plaintiff	Defendant	Plaintiff	Sum. Judgm.	Perm. Injunct.	Verdicts	Monetary Awards	Sum. Judgm.	Perm. Injunct.	Verdicts	Monetary Awards
	Poisson	Poisson	Poisson IV	Poisson IV	Poisson	Poisson	Poisson	Poisson	OLS	Poisson	Poisson	Poisson	OLS
Headcount	0.578*	−0.273	0.577**	−0.271	0.578**	−0.651**	−0.620	−0.275	0.018	−0.738**	−0.621	−0.286	0.019
	(0.307)	(0.146)	(0.227)	(0.190)	(0.225)	(0.299)	(0.429)	(0.226)	(0.037)	(0.307)	(0.394)	(0.242)	(0.036)
Org. Age	0.014***	0.015***	0.014***	0.015***	0.012***	0.020**	−0.051*	0.012	0.009	0.022*	−0.042**	0.009	0.008
	(0.002)	(0.003)	(0.002)	(0.004)	(0.002)	(0.010)	(0.027)	(0.008)	(0.005)	(0.012)	(0.018)	(0.008)	(0.006)
R&D Expenses	−0.000	−0.000	−0.000	−0.000	−0.000	−0.001***	−0.000	−0.000	−0.001***	−0.001***	−0.000	−0.000*	−0.001***
	(0.000)	(0.000)	(0.000)	(0.000)	(0.000)	(0.000)	(0.000)	(0.000)	(0.000)	(0.000)	(0.000)	(0.000)	(0.000)
Profit Margin	0.001	0.002	0.001	0.002	0.001	0.006	0.013**	0.012**	−0.000	0.003	0.011*	0.012**	−0.000
	(0.001)	(0.002)	(0.001)	(0.002)	(0.001)	(0.007)	(0.006)	(0.005)	(0.000)	(0.003)	(0.006)	(0.006)	(0.000)
Quick Ratio	−0.056*	−0.054	−0.056**	−0.054**	−0.055**	−0.069	−0.145	−0.167***	−0.001	−0.081	−0.178	−0.189***	−0.001
	(0.028)	(0.034)	(0.025)	(0.023)	(0.025)	(0.066)	(0.111)	(0.057)	(0.001)	(0.090)	(0.145)	(0.068)	(0.000)

(Continued)

Table 9.2 (CONTINUED)

	(1)	(2)	(3)	(4)	(5)	(6)	(7)	(8)	(9)	(10)	(11)	(12)	(13)
	Number of lawsuits a company filed in a year as					A company's legal outcomes (success) in a given year as a plaintiff							
	Plaintiff	Defendant	Plaintiff	Defendant	Plaintiff	Sum. Judgm.	Perm. Injunct.	Verdicts	Monetary Awards	Sum. Judgm.	Perm. Injunct.	Verdicts	Monetary Awards
	Poisson	Poisson IV	Poisson IV	Poisson	Poisson	Poisson	Poisson	Poisson	OLS	Poisson	Poisson	Poisson	OLS
Collaboration Centr.	0.009	0.014*	0.009	0.014*	0.010**	0.026	0.018	0.008	-0.011**	0.032	0.029	0.016	-0.011**
	(0.007)	(0.008)	(0.005)	(0.008)	(0.005)	(0.038)	(0.032)	(0.010)	(0.004)	(0.031)	(0.035)	(0.011)	(0.004)
Biotechnology	1.090	-0.244	1.088*	-0.229	0.909	1.573	-0.053	0.218	-0.380**	1.852	0.508	0.221	-0.400**
	(0.940)	(0.752)	(0.630)	(0.462)	(0.606)	(1.857)	(1.378)	(1.623)	(0.180)	(1.485)	(1.226)	(1.594)	(0.183)
Patent Portfolio	0.000	0.000	0.000	0.000	0.000	-0.001	0.003	0.003**	0.002*	-0.000	0.001	0.002**	0.002*
	(0.000)	(0.000)	(0.000)	(0.000)	(0.000)	(0.003)	(0.002)	(0.001)	(0.001)	(0.002)	(0.002)	(0.001)	(0.001)
Technological Overlap	0.008	0.010	0.008	0.010	0.010*	0.029*	-0.076**	-0.010	0.002	0.041*	-0.079**	0.002	0.002
	(0.005)	(0.008)	(0.005)	(0.006)	(0.005)	(0.016)	(0.035)	(0.012)	(0.005)	(0.023)	(0.036)	(0.018)	(0.005)
Product Portfolio	0.058***	0.006	0.058***	0.005	0.064***	0.096	0.189*	0.031	-0.011	0.117*	0.223**	0.067	-0.011
	(0.011)	(0.016)	(0.014)	(0.015)	(0.015)	(0.072)	(0.099)	(0.043)	(0.025)	(0.061)	(0.110)	(0.048)	(0.025)
Patent Heterogeneity	-1.307	0.245	-1.312*	0.243	-1.495**	0.010	-0.941	-2.465	-0.007	-0.369	-1.016	-3.298	-0.028
	(1.126)	(0.635)	(0.723)	(0.516)	(0.742)	(2.936)	(2.306)	(1.849)	(0.187)	(3.390)	(2.500)	(2.482)	(0.191)

(Continued)

Table 9.2 (Continued)

	(1)	(2)	(3)	(4)	(5)	(6)	(7)	(8)	(9)	(10)	(11)	(12)	(13)
	Number of lawsuits a company filed in a year as				A company's legal outcomes (success) in a given year as a plaintiff								
	Plaintiff	Defendant	Plaintiff	Defendant	Plaintiff	Sum. Judgm.	Perm. Injunct.	Verdicts	Monetary Awards	Sum. Judgm.	Perm. Injunct.	Verdicts	Monetary Awards
	Poisson	Poisson IV	Poisson IV	Poisson	Poisson	Poisson	Poisson	Poisson	OLS	Poisson	Poisson	Poisson	OLS
Susceptibility Rate	0.004	−0.002	0.005	−0.002	0.005	−0.039	−0.034	−0.016	−0.001	−0.051	−0.022	−0.013	−0.001
	(0.004)	(0.007)	(0.004)	(0.006)	(0.004)	(0.037)	(0.045)	(0.019)	(0.001)	(0.048)	(0.036)	(0.019)	(0.001)
Infringement Rate	0.153**	0.308***	0.153	0.309***	0.140	0.477***	−2.109**	−0.705**	−0.010	0.523**	−2.344***	−0.879**	−0.012
	(0.075)	(0.053)	(0.132)	(0.066)	(0.138)	(0.157)	(0.823)	(0.313)	(0.047)	(0.213)	(0.589)	(0.357)	(0.047)
No. of Adversaries	0.008	0.012*	0.008	0.012**	0.009	0.238***	0.107***	0.061*	0.112***	0.247***	0.109***	0.067***	0.112***
	(0.009)	(0.007)	(0.008)	(0.006)	(0.008)	(0.046)	(0.034)	(0.034)	(0.018)	(0.054)	(0.027)	(0.026)	(0.017)
No. of Allies	0.037***	0.026	0.037***	0.026*	0.036***	0.049	0.263***	0.074*	−0.058	0.033	0.267***	0.069*	−0.059
	(0.012)	(0.017)	(0.014)	(0.014)	(0.014)	(0.067)	(0.075)	(0.041)	(0.041)	(0.058)	(0.065)	(0.036)	(0.041)
Year Fixed Effects	Yes	Yes	Yes	Yes	Yes	Yes	Yes	Yes	Yes	Yes	Yes	Yes	Yes

(Continued)

Table 9.2 (CONTINUED)

	(1)	(2)	(3)	(4)	(5)	(6)	(7)	(8)	(9)	(10)	(11)	(12)	(13)
	Number of lawsuits a company filed in a year as					A company's legal outcomes (success) in a given year as a plaintiff							
	Plaintiff	Defendant	Plaintiff	Defendant	Plaintiff	Sum. Judgm.	Perm. Injunct.	Verdicts	Monetary Awards	Sum. Judgm.	Perm. Injunct.	Verdicts	Monetary Awards
	Poisson	Poisson IV	Poisson IV	Poisson	Poisson	Poisson	Poisson	Poisson	OLS	Poisson	Poisson	Poisson	OLS
No. of Proximate LFOs	0.353***	-0.150	0.369***	-0.178*	0.128	-0.637*	0.299	-0.239	0.045	-0.857***	0.125	-0.620*	-0.005
	(0.101)	(0.098)	(0.113)	(0.105)	(0.167)	(0.335)	(0.380)	(0.226)	(0.032)	(0.291)	(0.413)	(0.318)	(0.039)
Uncertain Legal Env.					-2.264**					-6.747**	-12.547	-7.496	-0.280
					(1.117)					(3.140)	(9.810)	(5.260)	(0.245)
No. of Proximate LFOs X Uncertain Legal Environment					0.496**					1.129	2.159	1.486	0.085
					(0.245)					(0.741)	(1.879)	(1.062)	(0.051)
Constant	-4.658***	-2.852***	-4.729***	-2.748***	-3.562***	-0.267	-1.399	-1.229	-4.735***	1.259	-0.584	0.416	-4.553***
	(0.909)	(0.684)	(0.804)	(0.611)	(0.978)	(1.033)	(2.392)	(1.545)	(0.305)	(1.365)	(2.127)	(1.610)	(0.366)
AIC	1267.73	930.73			1264.73	144.36	150.08	202.61		143.24	149.30	202.20	
R-squared									0.185				0.186
N	1,439	1,439	1,439	1,439	1,439	1,439	1,439	1,439	1,439	1,439	1,439	1,439	1,439

Robust standard errors in parentheses, clustered by MSAs, *** p<0.01, ** p<0.05, * p<0.1 (two-tailed tests).

files in a given year. These results support this prediction. Additional tests ruled out the curvilinear effect of the *Number of Proximate LFOs*, which was insignificant and worsened model fit.

The established effects are also substantively significant. For example, when other variables are held at their means, a one standard deviation increase in the concentration of proximate law firms increases a company's litigiousness by a factor of 1.47 (Table 9.2, Model 3). Given the costs of patent litigation (AIPLA, 2011), such factor changes and the resulting extra time spent in litigation could lead an average company to incur an additional annual cost of about US$1.5 million per year just in legal expenses. Clearly, the potential costs of patent infringement litigation extend well beyond legal costs to include major organizational disruption, adverse consequences in the stock market, and losses in the company's patent and product portfolio.[7]

Four separate findings help alleviate concerns about possible endogeneity in law firms' location choices and put this effect on a firmer empirical footing. First, Model 3 in Table 9.2 established the effect of the number of proximate law firms on the frequency of litigation, while instrumenting out the location choice of law firms using IV Poisson (see Appendix 2 for first-stage results). Second, the argument test in this chapter suggests that the effect of SID by proximate lawyers should manifest for plaintiffs but not necessarily for defendants. This is because the agency for initiating and continuing litigation lies with the plaintiff. In contrast, finding a comparable effect on defendants would increase the possibility of alternative explanations. Results in Models 2 (Poisson) and 4 (IV Poisson) in Table 9.2 support this argument, suggesting that the number of proximate law firms has a positive effect on the number of lawsuits a firm files only as a plaintiff, but not as a defendant. (The 95% confidence intervals around the estimates do not overlap.) Third, Table 9.3 reports the average treatment effect of being located in areas of high density of law firm offices on the number of lawsuits a firm

7. Additional tests on the choice of litigation targets revealed that the effect of proximity to law firm offices on the company's rate of litigation is distributed homogeneously across the geography of the defendants. That is, the concentration of proximate law firm offices had no statistically discernible impact on the likelihood of the plaintiff's filing a lawsuit against a more geographically proximate defendant versus a more distant one.

Table 9.3 Propensity Score Matching Results

	Number of lawsuits filed as	
	Plaintiff	Defendant
Average treatment effect of being located in areas	0.125	0.001
with high concentration of proximate law firm	(0.054)	(0.052)
offices		
z-statistic	2.32**	0.03

Note: The table reports the average treatment effects on a firm's number of lawsuits filed as plaintiff and defendant using nearest-neighbor (with replacement) propensity score matching. The treatment effect captures the firm located in the area of high concentration of proximate law firm offices. To do so, the continuous variable *Concentration of Proximate Law Firm Offices* is split at the mean to capture areas of high (above the mean) and low (below the mean) concentration. The treatment effect is equivalent to being located in an area with above-mean concentration of proximate law firm offices. A logit-based matching model was used to estimate propensity scores using independent variables from Model 1, in Table 1. N_{obs} in the treated and control groups are 855 and 556, respectively. Robust standard errors are in parentheses; ***p<0.01, **p<0.05, *p<0.10.

files as a plaintiff and as a defendant. Consistent with the previous result, the average treatment effect is positive and significant only for the plaintiffs.

Finally, if it is indeed SID that is being captured by the number of local law firm offices, then I would expect that plaintiffs—compared to defendants—would be more likely to select proximate IP litigation firms as their legal counsel. This is because proximate IP litigation firms are likely to identify and present litigation opportunities. Figure 9.1 illustrates the cumulative distribution of external legal counsel selection by the companies in the sample. The results support this conjecture: plaintiffs prefer to work with a geographically proximate external legal counsel. More than 55% of plaintiffs' lawyers work out of offices located within a 100-mile radius of the plaintiffs' headquarters (compared to only 35% for defendants). This contrast in the preference for proximate lawyers between plaintiffs and defendants further supports the conclusion that proximate law firms may affect the principal's decision to file a lawsuit based on social influence. Also, in line with prior research (Marquis, 2003; Sorenson & Stuart, 2001), the most pronounced

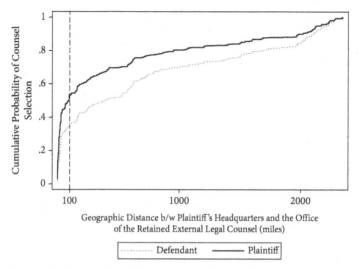

Figure 9.1 Geography of External Legal Counsel Selection

effect of distance on the formation of a tie between the company and the IP law firm is found within the 100-mile range (see Figure 9.1).

To explore the legal counsel selection further, I constructed a matched-dyadic data set, in which the actual pairings between law firm offices and plaintiffs during the period 1999 through 2006 were complemented with a random sample of non-materialized dyads, at the ratio of 1:5. As opposed to using a full risk set of all possible pairings (nearly 400,000 dyads in these data), the matched sample approach helps mitigate the issue of nonindependence of observations by reducing the number of times each company enters the sample. To correct for the bias that stems from the fact that the proportion of matches in the sample deviates from that in the population, I used the rare-events logistic regression (King & Zeng, 2001), which debiases the coefficients by using information on the rate at which the event occurs in the population. Results reported in Appendix 4a (Models 1 and 2) indicate that an IP law firm located within a 100-mile radius from the plaintiff company's headquarters has the probability of retention that is nearly seven times that of the law firm located beyond the 100-mile radius (with all other variables being held at means).

In line with the theory, I also tested whether a company that selects a geographically proximate IP litigation firm as its external legal counsel is more likely to stay in the lawsuit longer compared to a company that retains a more geographically distant IP litigation firm. The dependent variable in Models 1 and 2 (Table 9.4) is the duration of a given lawsuit in days, measured from the date on which the complaint is filed to the date of the lawsuit's adjudication. It was estimated with the Poisson regression with company-level fixed effects.[8] The results showed that companies that are geographically closer to the external legal counsel retained for a lawsuit stay in that lawsuit longer, thus supporting this prediction. These effects remained unchanged after adjusting for court-specific effects, which used the difference between the actual lawsuit duration and the mean duration of lawsuits in a particular district court (computed over filed cases, terminated cases, or both and over various time windows surrounding the focal lawsuit). Specifically, working with an IP litigation firm office located more than 100 miles from the company's headquarters reduces the lawsuit's duration by about 56 days (Table 9.4, Model 2), which can produce savings of up to US$ 400,000 in just associated legal costs, prorated based on average costs of litigation and its duration. This result indicates, therefore, that litigation is more protracted, which results from escalating legal proceedings rather than seeking an out-of-court settlement.

The Role of Legal Uncertainty

Testing for the effects of variable uncertainty can help validate the dynamics of SID. Specifically, the theory predicts that the effect of the concentration of proximate law firm offices on the number of lawsuits a firm files in a given year will be stronger for companies located in states with high legal uncertainty. The results show that the interaction of *Uncertain Legal Environment* with the measure of *Number of Proximate*

---

8. Company-level, fixed-effects estimation is possible here because, unlike the variable of the *Number of Proximate LFOs* used in Models 1 through 6 (Table 3), which varies mostly across companies, distance to the retained legal counsel also exhibits substantial variability *within* companies.

Table 9.4 EFFECTS OF PROXIMITY TO RETAINED LEGAL COUNSEL ON LAWSUIT OUTCOMES

Indep Vars/Dep Vars	(1)	(2)	(3)	(4)	(5)	(6)	(7)	(8)	(9)	(10)
	Lawsuit Duration		Win in Sum. Jdgmt.		Perm. Injunction		Claims		Monetary Award	
	Poisson		Logit		Logit		Logit		OLS	
Headcount	−0.338	−0.350*	−4.125	−17.237***	13.485	−4.488	−2.871	−3.078	−0.285	−0.289
	(0.214)	(0.210)	(17.065)	(4.554)	(67.110)	(118.229)	(2.224)	(2.147)	(0.533)	(0.531)
R&D Expenses	−0.246	−0.240	2.169	13.574	−5.115	−11.942	−0.360	−0.537	−0.301	−0.318
	(0.202)	(0.197)	(8.467)	(9.289)	(8.309)	(14.998)	(1.700)	(1.639)	(0.639)	(0.629)
Profit Margin	−0.009	−0.009	10.022	64.606	−3.119	16.058	−4.297	−4.446	−0.047	−0.047
	(0.007)	(0.007)	(48.298)	(46.129)	(27.824)	(47.177)	(3.453)	(3.582)	(0.035)	(0.035)
Quick Ratio	−0.091*	−0.091*	3.716	11.226	−1.656	−14.568	−0.535	−0.624	−0.462	−0.461
	(0.047)	(0.047)	(4.972)	(7.040)	(14.321)	(24.438)	(0.758)	(0.744)	(0.367)	(0.366)
Collaboration Centr.	0.007	0.007	−0.953	−0.676**	−1.374	−2.078	−0.163***	−0.157***	0.013	0.013
	(0.007)	(0.006)	(0.764)	(0.302)	(2.084)	(2.349)	(0.045)	(0.044)	(0.035)	(0.035)
Biotechnology	2.845**	2.830**	−294.673	−10.588	−157.664	−123.238	29.065**	27.495**	0.602	0.441
	(1.328)	(1.330)	(275.286)	(21.087)	(167.624)	(367.805)	(13.330)	(13.772)	(8.375)	(8.413)
Patent Portfolio	0.002***	0.002***	0.032**	0.286***	−0.660	−1.528	0.009**	0.009**	0.001	0.001
	(0.001)	(0.001)	(0.016)	(0.058)	(0.989)	(1.719)	(0.004)	(0.004)	(0.003)	(0.003)
Technological Overlap	−0.029	−0.029	2.149**	0.429***	7.635	14.861*	−0.188	−0.188	0.030	0.031
	(0.024)	(0.024)	(0.850)	(0.151)	(8.226)	(8.540)	(0.291)	(0.289)	(0.047)	(0.047)

(Continued)

Table 9.4 (Continued)

Indep Vars/Dep Vars	(1)	(2)	(3)	(4)	(5)	(6)	(7)	(8)	(9)	(10)
	Lawsuit Duration		Win in Sum. Jdgmt.		Perm. Injunction		Claims		Monetary Award	
	Poisson		Logit		Logit		Logit		OLS	
Product Portfolio	-0.020	-0.021	0.395	2.355***	1.543	0.966	0.266**	0.292**	-0.040	-0.040
	(0.014)	(0.014)	(0.520)	(0.270)	(8.155)	(2.973)	(0.127)	(0.127)	(0.043)	(0.044)
Patent Heterogeneity	0.108	0.157	-275.368	1,686.911***	105.534	171.002	12.996**	13.083**	1.607	1.542
	(0.958)	(0.944)	(0.000)	(314.923)	(282.078)	(370.637)	(5.683)	(5.721)	(4.780)	(4.814)
Susceptibility Rate	0.015	0.015	-2.208***	-5.926***	-1.186	-1.231	-0.143	-0.151	0.025	0.025
	(0.013)	(0.013)	(0.358)	(0.663)	(2.761)	(3.762)	(0.123)	(0.127)	(0.043)	(0.043)
Infringement Rate	-0.195*	-0.200*	4.741*	2.518***	27.208	49.926	0.481	0.470	-0.125	-0.132
	(0.104)	(0.103)	(2.830)	(0.960)	(58.643)	(83.856)	(1.042)	(1.055)	(0.394)	(0.398)
No. of Adversaries	-0.003	-0.003	0.622	-0.132	2.126	5.035	0.054**	0.053**	0.005	0.005
	(0.004)	(0.004)	(0.528)	(0.105)	(2.746)	(5.247)	(0.022)	(0.021)	(0.014)	(0.015)
No. of Allies	0.016	0.016	-0.076	0.380	-2.884	-4.575	0.125	0.121	0.015	0.016
	(0.011)	(0.011)	(0.394)	(0.288)	(3.060)	(6.139)	(0.083)	(0.082)	(0.041)	(0.041)

(Continued)

Table 9.4 (CONTINUED)

Indep Vars/Dep Vars	(1)	(2)	(3)	(4)	(5)	(6)	(7)	(8)	(9)	(10)
	Lawsuit Duration		Win in Sum. Jdgmt.		Perm. Injunction		Claims		Monetary Award	
	Poisson		Logit		Logit		Logit		OLS	
Top IP Law Firm	0.187	0.183	-1.283**	-1.203*	1.788***	1.172	-0.021	-0.032	0.419**	0.427*
	(0.129)	(0.135)	(0.646)	(0.650)	(0.567)	(0.770)	(0.403)	(0.427)	(0.192)	(0.208)
Familiarity w. Law Firm	-0.031***	-0.029***	-0.170	-0.167	-0.243***	-0.270***	0.023	0.032	-0.049	-0.029
	(0.008)	(0.010)	(0.154)	(0.168)	(0.069)	(0.077)	(0.133)	(0.132)	(0.097)	(0.082)
No. of Plaintiffs	0.079***	0.078***	0.241*	0.233*	1.900***	1.626**	-0.004	-0.009	0.350***	0.349***
	(0.016)	(0.017)	(0.140)	(0.132)	(0.627)	(0.632)	(0.308)	(0.316)	(0.072)	(0.072)
No. of Defendants	0.074**	0.076**	-0.241	-0.200	0.087	0.037	0.908***	0.914***	0.126	0.131
	(0.034)	(0.035)	(0.455)	(0.449)	(0.191)	(0.175)	(0.349)	(0.348)	(0.099)	(0.103)
Media Cvg. Focal Lawsuit	0.096	0.080	-0.107	-0.095	-0.040	-0.116	-0.342	-0.259	-0.183	-0.172
	(0.110)	(0.118)	(0.923)	(0.929)	(1.318)	(1.520)	(0.519)	(0.514)	(0.286)	(0.269)
Prior Ptshp. b/w Pltf. & Def.	0.189	0.177	0.485	0.386	3.061	3.191*	-1.994	-1.908	-0.449*	-0.438*
	(0.293)	(0.284)	(0.555)	(0.569)	(1.951)	(1.668)	(1.476)	(1.457)	(0.230)	(0.220)

(Continued)

Table 9.4 (Continued)

Indep Vars/Dep Vars	(1)	(2)	(3)	(4)	(5)	(6)	(7)	(8)	(9)	(10)
	Lawsuit Duration		Win in Sum. Jdgmt.		Perm. Injunction		Claims		Monetary Award	
	Poisson		Logit		Logit		Logit		OLS	
Year & Company Fixed Effects	Yes	Yes	Yes	Yes	Yes	Yes	Yes	Yes	Yes	Yes
Ln. Distance to Legal Counsel	-0.029*** (0.010)		-0.038 (0.107)		0.203** (0.102)		0.066 (0.058)		-0.008 (0.027)	
Distance to Legal Counsel>100mi		-0.148* (0.085)		0.217 (0.814)		-0.375 (0.853)		0.699 (0.465)		0.167 (0.271)
Constant	4.536 (3.208)	4.491 (3.190)	379.166 (312.094)	656.391 (0.000)	369.335 (0.000)	979.439 (0.000)	1.066 (32.751)	5.387 (32.233)	-19.399 (12.938)	-19.313 (12.901)
AIC/R-squared (Models 11–12)	257,989	258,742	145.73	146.08	99.50	99.74	288.87	287.74	0.415	0.416
N	854	854	451	451	496	496	562	562	854	854

Robust standard errors in parentheses, clustered by MSAs; *** $p<0.01$, ** $p<0.05$, * $p<0.1$ (two-tailed test).

LFOs has a significant positive effect on the number of lawsuits a company files (Model 5, Table 9.2). Figure 9.2 suggests that a one standard
deviation increase in the concentration of proximate law firm offices (at
means) increases the number of lawsuits a company files in a given year
by a factor of 1.67. Unexpectedly, the results suggest that the effect of
proximate lawyers does not matter in environments with a lower degree of legal uncertainty. This finding points to a potentially important
boundary condition of the theory; that is, lawyers' ability to induce
demand for their services is critically predicated on their ability to in-
termediate high levels of legal uncertainty. I further tested if the effect of
distance to the retained legal counsel on the duration of the focal lawsuit
will be stronger for companies located in states with high legal uncertainty. The interaction of *Uncertain Legal Environment* with *Ln Distance
to Legal Counsel* (Table 9.5, Model 1) and a binary variable *Distance to
Legal Counsel >100 mi* (Table 9.5, Model 2) showed a null effect. The results thus indicate that while the frequency of litigation increases under
uncertainty, its duration does not.

Increased Litigation as Economic Constraint

Does the presence and involvement of proximate lawyers in litigation
constitute SID, which imposes economic constraints on the buyers of
legal services? Results indicate that the number of proximate law firm

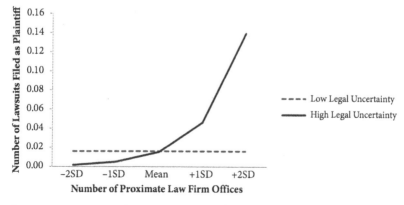

Figure 9.2 Interaction between Number of Proximate Law Firm Offices and
Legal Uncertainty

Table 9.5 Effects of Proximity to Retained Legal Counsel and Legal Uncertainty on Lawsuit Outcomes

Indep. Vars/Dep. Vars	(1)	(2)	(3)	(4)	(5)	(6)	(7)	(8)	(9)	(10)
	Lawsuit Duration		Win in Sum. Jdgmt.		Perm. Injunction		Claims		Monetary Award	
Headcount	−0.086	−0.078	−1.549**	−1.638**	0.752	0.677	0.089	0.073	0.393*	0.414*
	(0.060)	(0.061)	(0.623)	(0.703)	(0.753)	(0.753)	(0.314)	(0.317)	(0.212)	(0.223)
Org. Age	−0.002	−0.002	0.035*	0.039**	−0.037**	−0.035**	0.001	0.003	−0.001	0.000
	(0.002)	(0.002)	(0.019)	(0.019)	(0.016)	(0.014)	(0.009)	(0.010)	(0.012)	(0.012)
R&D Expenses	0.176**	0.175***	1.312***	1.405***	−0.666	−0.605	0.131	0.136	−0.353*	−0.360*
	(0.065)	(0.064)	(0.461)	(0.494)	(0.459)	(0.495)	(0.232)	(0.241)	(0.201)	(0.204)
Profit Margin	−0.001	−0.001	0.034	0.041	0.476***	0.463***	−0.013***	−0.013***	−0.016	−0.016
	(0.001)	(0.001)	(0.061)	(0.064)	(0.173)	(0.168)	(0.004)	(0.004)	(0.016)	(0.017)
Quick Ratio	−0.018	−0.017	0.125*	0.181**	−0.084	−0.096	−0.056	−0.040	−0.088	−0.083
	(0.020)	(0.020)	(0.069)	(0.083)	(0.124)	(0.110)	(0.124)	(0.126)	(0.079)	(0.081)
Collaboration Centr.	0.006	0.006	0.017	0.014	0.034*	0.029	−0.021	−0.021	−0.025*	−0.026*
	(0.004)	(0.004)	(0.011)	(0.011)	(0.020)	(0.021)	(0.016)	(0.017)	(0.013)	(0.013)

(*Continued*)

Table 9.5 (CONTINUED)

Indep. Vars/Dep. Vars	(1)	(2)	(3)	(4)	(5)	(6)	(7)	(8)	(9)	(10)
	Lawsuit Duration		Win in Sum. Jdgmt.		Perm. Injunction		Claims		Monetary Award	
Biotechnology	-0.251	-0.268	-4.535	-4.708	-2.631**	-3.087**	-1.610	-1.653	-3.923	-3.835
	(0.352)	(0.358)	(3.077)	(2.924)	(1.315)	(1.546)	(1.167)	(1.213)	(3.234)	(3.260)
Patent Portfolio	-0.001***	-0.001***	0.000	0.000	0.000	0.000	-0.001	-0.000	-0.000	-0.000
	(0.000)	(0.000)	(0.001)	(0.001)	(0.001)	(0.001)	(0.001)	(0.001)	(0.001)	(0.001)
Technological Overlap	-0.006	-0.006	0.005	-0.001	-0.135***	-0.123***	-0.040***	-0.041***	-0.019	-0.022
	(0.004)	(0.004)	(0.023)	(0.023)	(0.031)	(0.038)	(0.014)	(0.012)	(0.016)	(0.017)
Product Portfolio	0.009	0.009	0.049	0.053	0.080**	0.074***	0.004	0.003	-0.010	-0.011
	(0.009)	(0.009)	(0.065)	(0.064)	(0.031)	(0.028)	(0.025)	(0.026)	(0.045)	(0.045)
Patent	-0.573*	-0.572*	-3.731	-4.025	-0.446	-0.466	-0.156	0.039	-0.487	-0.270
	(0.342)	(0.340)	(5.447)	(5.395)	(3.787)	(3.703)	(1.665)	(1.650)	(2.082)	(2.083)
Heterogeneity										
Susceptibility Rate	-0.003	-0.004	-0.045	-0.050	0.019	0.021	-0.029*	-0.031*	-0.032	-0.033
	(0.006)	(0.006)	(0.044)	(0.042)	(0.035)	(0.036)	(0.017)	(0.016)	(0.022)	(0.022)
Infringement Rate	-0.138	-0.141	0.622	0.652	0.080	0.101	-0.297	-0.240	-0.052	-0.051
	(0.093)	(0.093)	(1.093)	(1.088)	(0.589)	(0.568)	(0.627)	(0.614)	(0.306)	(0.303)

(Continued)

Table 9.5 (Continued)

Indep. Vars/Dep. Vars	(1)	(2)	(3)	(4)	(5)	(6)	(7)	(8)	(9)	(10)
	Lawsuit Duration		Win in Sum. Jdgmt.		Perm. Injunction		Claims		Monetary Award	
No. of Adversaries	0.001 (0.003)	0.001 (0.003)	−0.006 (0.048)	−0.008 (0.049)	0.062** (0.024)	0.062** (0.025)	0.008 (0.013)	0.008 (0.013)	0.007 (0.010)	0.006 (0.010)
No. of Allies	−0.001 (0.006)	−0.001 (0.006)	0.031 (0.081)	0.044 (0.078)	0.059** (0.027)	0.060** (0.025)	0.027 (0.029)	0.030 (0.028)	−0.030 (0.030)	−0.030 (0.029)
Top IP Law Firm	0.191 (0.150)	0.185 (0.154)	−0.648** (0.283)	−0.660** (0.264)	0.646 (0.526)	0.618 (0.512)	0.683*** (0.225)	0.659*** (0.240)	0.324 (0.205)	0.323 (0.221)
Familiarity w. Law Firm	−0.015 (0.013)	−0.012 (0.014)	−0.096 (0.074)	−0.028 (0.075)	−0.195** (0.093)	−0.255*** (0.086)	0.003 (0.099)	0.012 (0.100)	−0.007 (0.105)	0.027 (0.097)
No. of Plaintiffs	0.077*** (0.016)	0.077*** (0.016)	0.069 (0.145)	0.077 (0.159)	0.920*** (0.243)	0.933*** (0.260)	0.052 (0.101)	0.056 (0.102)	0.368*** (0.087)	0.364*** (0.085)
No. of Defendants	0.048 (0.031)	0.048 (0.032)	0.533 (0.361)	0.551 (0.357)	0.118 (0.101)	0.076 (0.096)	0.347** (0.146)	0.345* (0.154)	−0.022 (0.083)	−0.009 (0.085)
Media Cvg.	0.123 (0.099)	0.113 (0.105)	0.948*** (0.362)	0.965*** (0.356)	−0.949 (0.796)	−1.047 (0.891)	−0.161 (0.498)	−0.090 (0.509)	−0.425* (0.236)	−0.403* (0.216)
Focal Lawsuit	0.184 (0.261)	0.172 (0.256)	0.607 (0.573)	0.526 (0.653)	1.919*** (0.745)	1.885** (0.789)	−0.659 (0.720)	−0.617 (0.696)	−0.576* (0.321)	−0.581* (0.320)
Prior Ptshp. b/w Pltf. & Def.										

(Continued)

Table 9.5 (CONTINUED)

Indep. Vars/Dep. Vars	(1)	(2)	(3)	(4)	(5)	(6)	(7)	(8)	(9)	(10)
	Lawsuit Duration		Win in Sum. Jdgmt.		Perm. Injunction		Claims		Monetary Award	
Uncertain Legal Env.	0.182	0.156	-0.341	-0.291	-4.629***	-3.790**	-2.365***	-2.064***	-0.305	-0.415
	(0.116)	(0.107)	(0.976)	(0.815)	(1.374)	(1.913)	(0.772)	(0.706)	(0.707)	(0.655)
Year Fixed Effects	Yes	Yes	Yes	Yes	Yes	Yes	Yes	Yes	Yes	Yes
Ln. Distance to Legal Counsel	-0.021		-0.290**		-0.139		-0.120		-0.066	
	(0.025)		(0.114)		(0.178)		(0.078)		(0.093)	
Ln. Distance to Legal Counsel X Uncertain Legal Env.	-0.004		0.381**		0.189		0.264***		0.047	
	(0.022)		(0.152)		(0.175)		(0.078)		(0.092)	

(Continued)

Table 9.5 (Continued)

Indep. Vars/Dep. Vars	(1)	(2)	(3)	(4)	(5)	(6)	(7)	(8)	(9)	(10)
	Lawsuit Duration		Win in Sum. Jdgmt.		Perm. Injunction		Claims		Monetary Award	
Distance to Legal Counsel>100mi		−0.117		−2.486***		−0.900		−0.761		−0.175
		(0.140)		(0.919)		(0.652)		(0.476)		(0.584)
Dist. to Legal Counsel>100mi X Uncertain Legal Env.		0.004		3.594**		−0.034		1.627***		0.546
		(0.114)		(1.203)		(0.625)		(0.613)		(0.603)
Constant	6.703***	6.639***	2.031	1.761	−4.835	−4.450	1.532	1.211	1.372	0.919
	(0.379)	(0.393)	(3.605)	(3.914)	(5.860)	(5.273)	(2.483)	(2.389)	(2.889)	(3.015)
AIC/R-sqaured (Models 11–12)	341,222	341,974	297.41	292.26	273.76	271.79	532.90	530.94	0.156	0.156
N	854	854	667	667	854	854	854	854	854	854

Robust standard errors in parentheses, clustered by MSAs; *** p<0.01, ** p<0.05, * p<0.1 (two-tailed tests); Models 1–2 Poisson; 3–18: Logit; 9–10: OLS.

offices decreases the number of summary judgments won (Table 9.2, Model 6) and that retaining a more proximate legal counsel decreases the odds of winning a permanent injunction in a lawsuit (Table 9.4, Model 5). The results further indicate that worse legal outcomes are even more likely under conditions of high legal uncertainty. In uncertain legal environments, retaining a more proximate legal counsel decreases the odds of winning a summary judgment (Table 9.5, Models 3 and 4) or receiving a favorable verdict (Table 9.5, Models 7 and 8). For example, in uncertain legal environments, retaining a legal counsel that is one standard deviation more proximate than the average counsel decreases the probability of a favorable summary judgment by a factor of 0.79 (see Figure 9.3) and the probability of winning at least one claim in a verdict by a factor of 0.51 (Figure 9.4).

Taken together, the results uniformly support the weak form of SID. Although the presence and involvement of proximate lawyers increase the frequency and duration of litigation, respectively, they do not contribute to legal success. As a result, the relative odds of success—defined as the likelihood of prevailing in litigation relative to lawsuits filed or days spent in litigation—decline. Even more worrisome, however, is that significant support is also found for the strong form of SID. That is, the involvement and presence of proximate lawyers not only does not increase the odds of success in litigation, but it actually decreases those

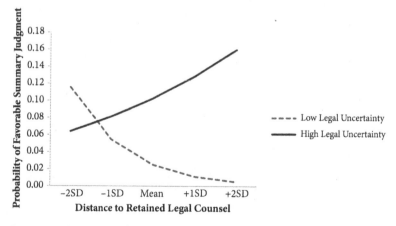

Figure 9.3 Interaction between Proximity to Retained Legal Counsel and Legal Uncertainty

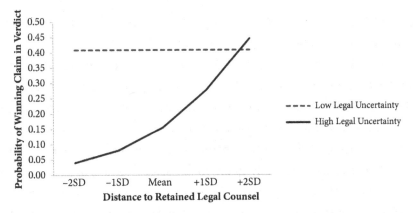

Figure 9.4 Interaction between Proximity to Retained Legal Counsel and Legal Uncertainty

odds as a range of observed legal outcomes measures. In these scenarios, the SID that manifests in increased litigiousness is most likely capturing the pursuit of especially low-quality legal opportunities.

ADDITIONAL ANALYSES AND ROBUSTNESS TESTS

In additional analyses, I explored two key alternative explanations for the effect of lawyer influence. First, it is possible that an increase in the concentration of proximate law firms can potentially lower local billing rates (due to increased competition) and thus render at least some instances of litigation more economically viable. Because information on billing rates for the specific companies in my sample was not available, I used data on billing rates from the annual survey of law firms administered by the *National Law Journal*. Specifically, for each year in the study's timeline, I first isolated the billing rates that were reported by offices located within a 100-mile range from the headquarters of each company included in the study. I then calculated the time-variant *Average Local Partner Billing Rate* and *Average Local Associate Billing Rate* for the locale of each biotechnology and pharmaceutical company. I subsequently estimated the effect of the number of local law firm offices on the local billing rates. Results reported in Appendix 3 do not support this alternative explanation: the number of proximate law firm offices has a null effect on the local billing rate for associates, and it actually increases the local billing rate for partners.[9]

Second, I explored the possibility that a company's decision (1) to retain a geographically proximate counsel and (2) to subsequently prolong a lawsuit could be driven by the economic advantages of lower communication and transportation costs. If this is the case, I would expect companies in weaker liquidity positions (as reflected by lower quick ratios [QR]) to be particularly likely to (1) select a more proximate legal counsel and (2) exhibit variation in the duration of lawsuits they file depending on the distance to the retained legal counsel. The interaction of a company's QR with distance to legal counsel, however, had no effect on counsel selection (Appendix 4a, Models 3 and 4). Similarly, the interaction of a company's QR with the distance to retained legal counsel had no effect on the duration of the lawsuit (Appendix 4b, Models 1 and 2). I obtained similar null results when examining whether smaller companies (as measured by sales and headcount) or less profitable companies (as measured by profit margins) would be more sensitive to the external legal counsel's physical proximity in selecting the firm and in managing the length of the suit. Taken together, these results do not support this alternative mechanism.

These results are not surprising. Compared to the significance of the outcomes and the lawyers' fees, communication and transportation costs are trivial. Verdicts and settlements in IP litigation in biotechnology and pharmaceuticals affect product and patent portfolios with values measured in the millions of dollars. This notwithstanding, the hourly billing rate for a partner in an IP law firm would exceed the cost of most first-class flights in the continental United States. It is therefore

---

9. The increase in the local partner billing rate could be attributed to the endogenous relationship wherein higher local billing rates could attract a greater number of law firms. In further exploratory analyses (available on request), I applied the 2SLS instrumental variable specification (using the number of local, top-tier law schools as an instrument for the number of local law firm offices), which washed out this effect entirely ($b=22.846$, $se=25.668$, $p=0.373$).

reasonable that the economic costs associated with retaining a more distant legal counsel do not substantively influence litigation dynamics.

About 20% of the lawsuits in the sample were filed under the Hatch-Waxman Act, which covers patent litigation over generic drugs (see 35 U.S.C. § 271(e)(2)). This litigation is governed under a different regulatory regime than other lawsuits; therefore, I reran all the models with the Hatch-Waxman lawsuits excluded from the sample. I also reran all the models with various controls for the intensity of regional competition, using the variables that capture the proximity to other litigious companies in the sample, proximity to newly founded biotechnology companies, as well as the intensity of the regional patenting activity. In addition, I controlled for the counts of biotechnology and pharmaceutical companies and all companies (as reported by Compustat) at the state level, using both linear and curvilinear specifications. In all these tests, the study's results remained similar.

Finally, using alternative statistical techniques, I ran a series of tests to examine the robustness of the reported effects. First, I controlled for possible selection bias by estimating a company's number of lawsuits conditional on the company entering into at least a single lawsuit (Heckman, 1979). Second, I accounted explicitly for possible autocorrelation using first-order autoregressive GLS models. Finally, the reported models account for possible spatial diffusion effects by modeling the law firms' location choice being driven in part by the local frequency of litigation. In additional analyses, I also reran the models accounting for possible diffusion effects directly by estimating the predicted effects net of the local frequency of litigation. I observed no substantive differences with the reported pattern of results.

CHAPTER SUMMARY

This chapter presents evidence supporting the strong form of supplier-induced demand in IP litigation. Specifically, it highlights a shift in the locus of control for service consumption from buyers to the geographically proximate sellers of these services. These sellers, through their close proximity and frequent interaction with buyers, exert a palpable influence over them and induce demand. Specifically, the supporting findings indicate that companies located near law firm offices tend to initiate a greater number of lawsuits. Additionally, companies retaining closer legal counsel are more likely to engage in prolonged litigation. Importantly, the heightened consumption of litigation services in these cases does not result in legal success; instead, it is more likely to lead to legal losses, indicating the strong form of supplier-induced demand. Moreover, the emergence of supplier-induced demand is not uniform. Rather, it is confined to situations characterized by particularly high levels of uncertainty, or unpredictability of lawsuit outcomes.

Appendix 1. INFRINGEMENT AND SUSCEPTIBILITY RATES

Adapting Toby E. Stuart and Waverly W. Ding's (2006) research commercializability score, the infringement rate (IR) for company (i) in year (t) can be expressed as:

$$IR_{it} = \sum_{j=1}^{k'_t} \omega_{jt} \left(\frac{p_{ijt}}{\sum_{j=1}^{k'_t} p_{ijt}} \right), \text{ where } \omega_{jt} = \sum_{i=1}^{m'_t} \left(\frac{p_{ijt}}{\sum_{j=1}^{k'_t} p_{ijt}} \right) * (p_{jt}^0)^{-1}$$

where $i = 1, ..., m'_t$ indexes the companies that have infringed on other companies' IP prior to year t; $j = 1, ..., k'_t$ lists all the product categories of companies that have infringed on others' patents prior to year t; and p_{jt}^0 is the number of times each product category, j, had been filled by companies that had not infringed prior to year t.

To compute IR_{it}, I first constructed a $m'_t * k'_t$ matrix for each year t, where m'_t reflected the number of companies in the sample that had infringed on other companies' patents in years t-5 to t-1, and where k'_t reflected all product categories in which m'_t companies were active in year t-1. Using Bioscan product descriptions, I used binary entries to delineate each company's activity in a particular product category,

$p_{ijt} = \{0; 1\}$, normalizing the entries so that each category reflected the proportion of a company's activity devoted to a particular product niche: $\left(\dfrac{p_{ijt}}{\sum_{j=1}^{k'} p_{ijt}} \right)$.

To compute ω_{jt}, I then created a vector $1 * k'_{jt}$, which reflected the sums of normalized product weights for each product category across all companies that had infringed prior to year t, where $k'_{jt} = \sum_{i=1}^{m'_t} \dfrac{p_{ijt}}{\sum_{j=1}^{k'} p_{ijt}}$.

Next, I created a similar vector for all companies that had *not* infringed on others' patents by year t, denoting it as p^0_{jt}. The interpretation of ω_{jt} then becomes straightforward: it is the frequency with which infringers participate in various product niches, adjusted for the frequency with which the non-infringing companies participate in those niches. In other words, ω_{jt} captures the *disproportionate* participation by infringers in some product niches when compared to noninfringers. To avoid endogenous calibration of IR, I removed the focal company's information when calculating ω_{jt}. In sum, the IR reflects a company's baseline propensity to infringe on other companies' patents, based on the similarity of its product portfolio to that of prior infringers.

Whereas the IR captures the focal company's baseline propensity for infringement, the susceptibility rate (SR), in turn, assesses the baseline likelihood that the company will have its IP infringed upon. The point of reference for this measure is the similarity between the focal company's patent portfolio, measured over t-1 to t-5, and the portfolios of the typical patentees in IP disputes; that is, companies that have their patent portfolio infringed upon in years t-1 to t-5.

The formula for the SR is largely analogous to the formula for the IR, but with two differences. First, p_{ijt} is a continuous variable that estimates the count of a company's patents in a given 3-digit US patent class. Second, the reference point for creating vector $1 * k'_{jt}$ becomes the list of patent classes that describe the patent portfolios of those companies whose IP was infringed. Taken together, IR and SR help control for the company's baseline propensity to be involved in patent disputes.

Appendix 2. FIRST-STAGE ESTIMATES FOR IV POISSON AND ROBUSTNESS CHECKS

	(1) No. of Proximate LFOs OLS	(2) Lawsuits Filed Poisson
Headcount	−0.006	0.577*
	(0.015)	(0.308)
Org. Age	−0.001	0.014***
	(0.004)	(0.002)
R&D Expenses	0.000	−0.000
	(0.000)	(0.000)
Profit Margin	−0.000	0.001
	(0.000)	(0.001)
Quick Ratio	−0.001	−0.057**
	(0.001)	(0.028)
Collaboration Centr.	−0.004	0.009
	(0.005)	(0.007)
Biotechnology	0.498*	1.092
	(0.288)	(0.935)
Patent Portfolio	0.000	0.000
	(0.000)	(0.000)
Technological Overlap	0.003	0.008
	(0.003)	(0.005)
Product Portfolio	0.009	0.058***
	(0.012)	(0.011)
Patent Heterogeneity	−0.271	−1.305
	(0.240)	(1.128)
Susceptibility Rate	0.001	0.004
	(0.002)	(0.004)
Infringement Rate	−0.039	0.151**
	(0.035)	(0.076)

	(1)	(2)
	No. of Proximate LFOs	Lawsuits Filed
	OLS	Poisson
No. of Adversaries	−0.006	0.008
	(0.007)	(0.009)
No. of Allies	0.004	0.037***
	(0.006)	(0.012)
No. of Proximate LFOs		0.330**
		(0.168)
No. of Proximate Top Law Schools	0.392***	0.015
	(0.091)	(0.074)
Constant	3.087***	−4.593***
	(0.383)	(1.047)
AIC		1269.66
R-Squared	0.473	
N	1,439	1,439

Robust standard errors in parentheses, clustered by MSAs; *** p<0.01, ** p<0.05, * p<0.1 (two-tailed tests).

Appendix 3. CONCENTRATION OF PROXIMATE LFOS AND LOCAL LAWYER BILLING RATES

	Model 1	Model 2	Model 3	Model 4
	Avg. Local Partner Billing Rate		Avg. Local Associate Billing Rate	
	OLS	OLS	OLS	OLS
Year Fixed Effects	Yes	Yes	Yes	Yes
State Fixed Effects	Yes	Yes	Yes	Yes

Continued

(*Continued*)

	Model 1	Model 2	Model 3	Model 4
	Avg. Local Partner Billing Rate		Avg. Local Associate Billing Rate	
	OLS	OLS	OLS	OLS
No. of Local Biotechnology Comp. founded over preceding 5 years		−4.489 (11.714)		6.949 (7.999)
No. of Patent Infringement Lawsuits filed in a company's local District Court over preceding 5 years		10.944*** (3.091)		6.305** (2.484)
No. of Local M&A Targets over preceding 5 years		−16.651 (24.051)		11.863 (12.774)
No. of Local VC Investment Targets over preceding year		−3.641 (3.443)		6.126** (2.395)
No. of Proximate LFOs	25.955*** (6.878)	36.174** (14.709)	7.808 (6.026)	−4.182 (8.089)
Constant	342.107*** (43.194)	396.495*** (107.835)	256.803*** (37.591)	115.873** (51.848)
R-squared	0.912	0.916	0.912	0.928
Operationalization	1,509	1,509	1,509	1,509

Robust standard errors in parentheses, clustered by MSAs; ***$p<0.01$, **$p<0.05$, *$p<0.1$ (two-tailed tests).

Appendix 4a. SELECTION OF EXTERNAL LEGAL COUNSEL

	(1)	(2)	(3)	(4)
	Selection of External Legal Counsel			
	Rare-Event Logit			
Headcount	0.389***	0.439***	0.389***	0.439***
	(0.083)	(0.079)	(0.083)	(0.080)
R&D Expenses	−0.000**	−0.000**	−0.000**	−0.000**
	(0.000)	(0.000)	(0.000)	(0.000)
Profit Margin	0.001	0.001	0.001	0.001
	(0.001)	(0.001)	(0.001)	(0.001)
Quick Ratio (QR)	−0.022	−0.012	−0.038	0.006
	(0.023)	(0.020)	(0.052)	(0.025)
Collaboration Centr.	0.006	0.005	0.006	0.005
	(0.008)	(0.008)	(0.008)	(0.008)
Biotechnology	1.604**	1.508*	1.595**	1.502*
	(0.778)	(0.796)	(0.777)	(0.798)
Patent Portfolio	0.001	0.000	0.001	0.000
	(0.000)	(0.000)	(0.000)	(0.000)
Technological Overlap	0.006	0.006	0.006	0.006
	(0.005)	(0.005)	(0.005)	(0.005)
Product Portfolio	0.038***	0.043***	0.039***	0.043***
	(0.014)	(0.014)	(0.014)	(0.014)
Patent Heterogeneity	−2.260**	−2.206**	−2.250**	−2.204**
	(1.042)	(1.034)	(1.040)	(1.036)
Susceptibility Rate	0.002	0.002	0.002	0.002
	(0.006)	(0.006)	(0.006)	(0.006)
Infringement Rate	−0.063	−0.087	−0.066	−0.084
	(0.150)	(0.138)	(0.149)	(0.138)
No. of Adversaries	0.018	0.017	0.018	0.017
	(0.016)	(0.015)	(0.016)	(0.015)

Continued

(*Continued*)

	(1)	(2)	(3)	(4)
	Selection of External Legal Counsel			
	Rare-Event Logit			
No. of Allies	−0.007	−0.004	−0.007	−0.003
	(0.015)	(0.015)	(0.015)	(0.015)
Top IP Law Firm	0.064	0.039	0.061	0.046
	(0.189)	(0.173)	(0.189)	(0.173)
Year Fixed Effects	Yes	Yes	Yes	Yes
Ln. Distance to Legal	−0.381***		−0.395***	
Counsel	(0.036)		(0.049)	
Distance to Legal		−2.017***		−1.913***
Counsel >100mi		(0.167)		(0.197)
Ln. Distance to Legal			0.003	
Counsel x QR			(0.008)	
Distance to Legal				−0.026
Counsel >100mi x QR				(0.031)
Constant	−3.998***	−4.932***	−3.914***	−5.000***
	(0.886)	(0.836)	(0.917)	(0.841)
N	3,444	3,444	3,444	3,444

Robust standard errors in parentheses, clustered by MSAs; *** $p<0.01$, ** $p<0.05$, * $p<0.1$ (two-tailed tests).

Appendix 4b. DURATION OF LAWSUIT

	(1)	(2)
	Lawsuit Duration	
	Poisson	
Headcount	−0.373	−0.386
	(0.247)	(0.243)
R&D Expenses	−0.174	−0.176
	(0.118)	(0.117)
Profit Margin	−0.008*	−0.008
	(0.005)	(0.005)
Quick Ratio (QR)	−0.090*	0.091*
	(0.053)	(0.053)
Collaboration Centr.	.0.007	0.008
	(0.006)	(0.006)
Biotechnology	2.980	2.972
	(1.821)	(1.809)
Patent Portfolio	0.002**	0.002**
	(0.001)	(0.001)
Technological Overlap	−0.033	−0.032
	(0.020)	(0.021)
Product Portfolio	−0.023*	−0.024*
	(0.013)	(0.014)
Patent Heterogeneity	−0.120	−0.076
	(0.846)	(0.830)
Susceptibility Rate	0.016	0.015
	(0.013)	(0.013)
Infringement Rate	−0.196	−0.201
	(0.133)	(0.133)
No. of Adversaries	−0.003	−0.003
	(0.003)	(0.003)

Continued

(*Continued*)

	(1)	(2)
	Lawsuit Duration	
	Poisson	
No. of Allies	0.015	0.015
	(0.012)	(0.012)
Top IP Law Firm	0.183**	0.178*
	(0.089)	(0.094)
Familiarity w. Law Firm	−0.032*	−0.029
	(0.017)	(0.019)
No. of Plaintiffs	0.079***	0.078***
	(0.026)	(0.026)
No. of Defendants	0.076**	0.078***
	(0.030)	(0.030)
Media Cvg. Focal Lawsuit	0.104	0.089
	(0.099)	(0.106)
Prior Ptshp. b/w Pltf. & Def.	0.179	0.168
	(0.273)	(0.264)
Year & Company Fixed Effects	Yes	Yes
Ln. Distance to Legal Counsel	−0.029**	
	(0.014)	
Ln. Distance to Legal Counsel x QR	0.000	
	(0.004)	
Distance to Legal Counsel>100mi		−0.159
		(0.111)
Distance to Legal Counsel>100mi x QR		0.009
		(0.026)
Constant	5.072*	5.146*
	(2.728)	(2.721)
AIC	255,092	255,997
N	854	854

Robust standard errors in parentheses, clustered by MSAs; *** p<0.01, ** p<0.05, * p<0.1 (two-tailed tests).

CHAPTER 10

Why Don't the Buyers Learn?

In the preceding chapter, I presented empirical evidence confirming the existence of supplier-induced demand (SID) within the realm of legal services. These findings illuminate a significant phenomenon: the physical proximity of law firms to companies notably contributes to an increase in litigation frequency. Furthermore, when a company engages the services of a nearby legal counsel for a particular lawsuit, the duration of legal proceedings tends to be prolonged, resulting in higher costs for the company. As previously discussed, this geographical proximity facilitates both intentional and spontaneous interactions between legal service providers and their clients, enabling expert influence toward taking legal action. However, it is crucial to underscore that the heightened demand for increased litigation volume and duration does not correlate with a higher likelihood of achieving favorable legal outcomes. On the contrary, it is associated with reduced legal success.

The empirical results also reveal an important caveat to these findings: the concept of SID does not universally apply to all interactions between proximate suppliers and their clients. Instead, it specifically manifests in situations characterized by significant uncertainty regarding the potential outcome of the work done by professionals. It is precisely under such circumstances that the biases ingrained in the commercial logic of service providers can exert a more potent influence on both buyers and sellers.

At this juncture, discerning readers may contemplate the following question: if SID results in no benefits and, in some cases, even harms

buyers, what impedes buyers from *learning* to avoid the grasp of
SID? A wealth of evidence suggests that organizations can accumu-
late knowledge, over time, through repeated experiences or by observing the actions of other organizations (Argote, 2013; Argote &
Miron-Spektor, 2011; Clough & Piezunka, 2020; Greve, 2003). This
knowledge indeed becomes ingrained in various ways, such as the collective cognition of the buying organizations' personnel, as well as
formal organizational procedures, informal routines, and other memory
systems.

The duty of organizational decision-makers is to harness such knowledge to enhance the performance and efficiency of their organizations.
Hence, it stands to reason that as instances of SID resurface, the buying organizations ought to acquire the capacity to detect, rectify, or
altogether abstain from transactions that fuel such behavior. In other
words, as organizations engage in recurring litigation, acquisitions, reorganizations, or marketing endeavors that external knowledge providers
facilitate, one would expect the organizations to become increasingly
adept at avoiding demand-inducing scenarios. Intriguingly, the empirical evidence fails to support this expectation. So, what could potentially
go awry?

Explorations of organizational learning have highlighted two indispensable conditions for organizational learning: the presence of multiple
comparable experiences and the availability of clear performance feedback (Argote & Miron-Spektor, 2011; March, 2010; March & Olsen,
1975; March, Sproull, & Tamuz, 1991; Popper & Lipshitz, 2000a). In my
next analysis, I will expound on the notion that these preconditions are
systematically violated within the realm of professional services. This
violation gives rise to heightened levels of causal ambiguity, which signifies the absence of clear and unequivocal connections between actions
and resulting outcomes. Such pervasive causal ambiguity severely hampers buyers' ability to learn effectively from their own experiences or
from the experiences of others. Consequently, even the most seasoned
and discerning organizations find themselves routinely vulnerable to the
adverse effects of SID.

ORGANIZATIONAL LEARNING

Organizations, much like individuals, possess a remarkable capacity for learning. In fact, organizational knowledge transcends the mere accumulation of knowledge that an organization's individual members hold. Specifically, organizational learning involves establishing and perpetuating diverse learning systems that preserve and synthesize knowledge and transfer it to those who may not have been directly involved in its creation or acquisition (Dodgson, 1993; Fiol & Lyles, 1985). In essence, while organizations may lack a singular brain, they possess intricate cognitive systems and collective memories that facilitate the acquisition and retention of knowledge.

This newfound knowledge takes shape and endures as organizational rules, procedures, forms, strategies, and technologies. Additionally, it manifests in the informal norms, beliefs, and paradigms that can complement or challenge formal processes (Hedberg, 1981; Levitt & March, 1988). Importantly, these routines can be transmitted through processes like imitation, socialization, education, professionalization, and even mergers and acquisitions (Argote & Ingram, 2000; Easterby-Smith, Lyles, & Tsang, 2008; Levitt & March, 1988; Sarala, Junni, Cooper, & Tarba, 2016). Consequently, despite the flux of employees and the transition of leadership, an organization's memories persist and continue to shape its collective actions.

Inevitably, just like individuals, organizations are bound to be imperfect learners, prone to mistakes and occasionally acquiring incorrect knowledge (Dodgson, 1993; Gino & Staats, 2015; March, 2010).[1] Despite these challenges, the aspiration to remain competitive drives organizations' continued pursuit of learning. It is precisely this imperative that compels organizations to place a heightened emphasis on organizational

1. Significantly, scholarly investigations have advanced evidence indicating that occasional organizational errors can, on certain occasions, yield serendipitous learning outcomes that contribute to positive organizational outcomes, including enhanced performance and competitiveness (Posen, Lee, & Yi, 2013). This phenomenon resembles the occurrence of random mutations in human or animal species, wherein sporadic genetic leaps can engender, at times, superior survival capabilities.

learning when they find themselves falling behind their own historical performance or the performance of their peers (Greve, 2003).[2]

So, how do organizations actually learn? At the heart of the knowledge acquisition process within organizations lies the concept of experiential learning. It encompasses the intentional or unintentional knowledge that organizations gain through direct experiences (Huber, 1991; March, 2010). Significantly, the notion of experiential organizational learning resonates with principles found in a wide array of research domains. Whether it be studies of language acquisition (Horst, 2013), cognitive psychology (Lynch & Maclean, 2000), retention of technical information (Bromage & Mayer, 1986), or the development of professional skills (Dornan, Boshuizen, King, & Scherpbier, 2007), these fields of inquiry have long recognized the intrinsic value of repetition and experience in acquiring and consolidating knowledge. The prominence of experiential learning has grown to such an extent that business schools, publications, and consultants now offer strategies and insights on how organizations can strive to become "learning organizations." These organizations are expected to harness the power of learning from their own actions to continually enhance their future performance and efficiency.

The empirical evidence supporting organizational learning from experience is undeniably compelling. One striking example is the widespread acceptance and the intellectual impact of organizational learning curves, which vividly illustrate learning as a product of accumulated experience (Argote, 2013; Argote & Epple, 1990). The concept of learning curves traces its roots back to observations made in the US Air Force Production workshops in 1936. The participants in these workshops keenly observed a significant reduction in the amount of direct labor hours required to complete a production task as the number of repetitions of that task increased. Specifically, the hours per unit decreased by a consistent percentage each time the total repetitions of the task doubled (Shrivastava, 1983).

---

2. Changes in organizational behaviors are not equivalent to learning because organizations can also acquire knowledge that is only potentially useful. Such potentially useful knowledge expands the repertoire of possible responses, some of which may only manifest in the future (Huber, 1991: 89). Similarly, not every alteration in an organization's actions inherently signifies a process of learning (Fiol & Lyles, 1985: 811).

Since then, numerous studies have meticulously documented how the unit costs of manufacturing products decline at a diminishing rate with an increasing cumulative production volume, commonly referred to as "experience" (Argote, 2013). In simpler terms, as organizations produce more units, the cost of producing an additional unit progressively decreases. A plethora of studies have subsequently presented robust evidence of learning curves in a wide range of contexts, showcasing reduced production costs for various items, including pizzas (Darr, Argote, & Epple, 1995), aircraft (Alchian, 1963), ships (Rapping, 1965), trucks (Epple, Argote, & Murphy, 1996), and semiconductors (Gruber, 1994). Repeated experience has become so central to scholarly understanding of how organizations accrue knowledge that "experience curves" have become de facto "learning curves."[3]

In circumstances where firsthand experience is either unavailable or inadequate, managers can augment their knowledge base by tapping into the experiential wisdom of other organizations (Clough & Piezunka, 2020; Levine & Argote, 2017). In such instances, organizations stand to gain from the accrued knowledge of their counterparts through the dissemination of knowledge manifested in technologies, codes, routines, practices, and procedures (Levitt & March, 1988). To illustrate, consider the study by David R. Clough and Henning Piezunka (2020), which delves into the realm of Formula One racing and explores how organizations can learn from others' experiences. The research uncovers a noteworthy pattern: when faced with underperformance, a Formula One racing company is more inclined to sever its relationship with an engine supplier if other racing companies using the same supplier also exhibit unsatisfactory performance. This finding underscores the idea that vicarious learning can serve as a powerful complement to direct experiential learning.

Networks of interpersonal and interorganizational relationships can be indispensable in validating these practices and also supporting the acquisition of tactical, complex, and contextual knowledge

---

3. Work by the Boston Consulting Group (1968) marked the advent of curves that elucidate the relationship between repeated experiences and organizational efficiency, which were aptly named "experience curves." Subsequently, these curves have been interchangeably referred to as "learning curves" in the scholarly discourse (Shrivastava, 1983).

(Centola & Macy, 2007; Sytch & Tatarynowicz, 2014; Uzzi, 1997). Accordingly, a wealth of empirical studies attests to organizations' acquiring knowledge, information, and diverse practices through networks of relationships that link organizations. To exemplify this phenomenon, consider corporate governance practices, such as anti-takeover defenses involving substantial payouts to corporate executives in the event of a hostile takeover. Such practices are known to spread through directors who serve on the boards of multiple companies, creating networks of influence and information flow (Davis, 1991; Davis & Greve, 1997). Similarly, the diffusion of total quality management practices and technological innovations often occurs through networks of strategic partnerships forged among organizations (Sytch & Tatarynowicz, 2014; Westphal, Gulati, & Shortell, 1997). Furthermore, cultural norms and principles can spread as people change employers, carrying with them the imprint of past organizational values and beliefs (Almeida & Kogut, 1999; Kane, Argote, & Levine, 2005; March, 1991; Saxenian, 1994).

The copious body of evidence supporting the notion of organizational learning suggests its potential as a powerful antidote to SID. By internalizing hard-earned wisdom derived from encounters with induced demand and subpar performance, while also gleaning insights from parallel tales of other organizations, learning organizations can be expected to promote a decline, perhaps even the complete eradication, of SID. Yet, despite these learning opportunities, SID persists, leading us to a critical question: Why don't organizations learn?

WHY DON'T ORGANIZATIONS LEARN FROM SUPPLIER-INDUCED DEMAND?

Recognizing and effectively countering SID is not just a matter of stumbling upon random adaptations or relying on trial and error.[4] It demands a higher level of learning in which decision-makers develop

---

4. This form of learning has been also described as "low-intellect" (March, 2010: 15), "stimulus-response," or "automatic" learning (Argote & Miron-Spektor, 2011: 1128), which describe situations when actions connected to success are repeated with little to no effort to understand the underlying cause.

knowledge and insights based on associations between past actions and their effectiveness. This form of learning compels decision-makers to actively wrap their heads around the underlying causal structure of the events they encounter and extract actionable insights from those experiences (Fiol & Lyles, 1985; March, 2010). These learning processes, often dubbed "mindful" (Argote & Miron-Spektor, 2011: 1128), involve conscientiously constructing explicit understandings that weave together past experiences and their outcomes into a coherent causal explanation.

Such explanations might take the shape of a natural language narrative, an analytical model, or a theoretical framework. They typically resemble what scholars refer to as double-loop learning, in which decision-makers base their explanations and corrective strategies on a comprehensive analysis of the entire organizational system, rather than on assessments of a discrete organizational activity (Argyris, 1976). Indeed, a company's decision to pursue an intellectual property (IP) lawsuit and efforts to assess its outcomes may be situated in the larger context of the company's activities. These activities may include its competitive and IP strategies, research and development efforts, market and technology projections, approach to licensing, as well as a complex assessment of the value of litigation based on the company's competitive and technological position. By the same token, assessing the need and effectiveness of acquisitions is wrapped into evaluations of the merging companies' strategies, resource synergies, regulatory implications, optimal financing models, available skills, and resources for executing integration, as well as the cultural compatibility between the merging companies.

For organizations to achieve genuine effectiveness in such complex learning processes, two fundamental prerequisites must be met without fail. First, organizations must have unfettered access to a significant collection of comparable experiences from which they can learn. Second, they must receive frequent, clear, and unambiguous performance feedback on their past actions (Argote & Miron-Spektor, 2011; Greve, 2003; March, 2010). As we delve deeper, I will shed light on the systematic violations of these conditions within the markets for professional services, which impede organizational learning from organizations' own or others' experiences in the face of SID.

Multiple Comparable Experiences and Controlled Conditions

Envision a world where organizations find themselves endowed with an invaluable reservoir of experiences—a resplendent tapestry of histori- cal data points, capable of illuminating the intricate interplay between practice and outcome. Within this world, effective learning derived from past experiences hinges on the abundance of comparable data points (March, 2010). Precisely put, organizations must possess multiple historical data points that allow them to discern the impact of alter- ations in specific practices under reasonably controlled circumstances, thereby establishing causal relationships. Consider, for example, the case of a production line involved in manufacturing pizzas or semicon- ductors. In such contexts, organizations are bestowed with a veritable cornucopia of production runs, numbering in the hundreds or even thousands, wherein incremental modifications to select aspects of the production process can be scrutinized meticulously for changes in out- comes. Crucially, these organizations can uphold the integrity of the remaining production conditions, ensuring that they remain largely un- altered. The abundance of data points serves to enhance precision in the face of potential randomness, while the controlled conditions afford organizations the capacity to isolate causal relationships.

The nature of professional service firms' work presents a striking departure from the aforementioned condition. To begin, when it comes to significant engagements, such as reorganizations, lawsuits, or merg- ers, professional service work manifests as a relatively infrequent oc- currence for many organizations. For example, in my data, an average company files a patent infringement lawsuit only once every three years. Recall also that in the fieldwork presented earlier in the book, executives consistently highlighted this infrequency as one of the main factors informing their decision not to maintain specialized expertise in-house. Learning from small samples is notoriously difficult due to their suscep- tibility to the perils of sampling errors and flawed inference (Levitt & March, 1988; March, 1991, 2010).

And even those organizations that regularly engage with professional service providers, which seemingly provides them with a sufficient sample size for learning, face a scarcity of comparable cases. This scarcity can be attributed to the very essence of professional services, be it litigation or consulting, which dictates that the conditions under which these services are delivered display significant variations. These conditions encompass fluctuations in the dynamics of competitive, technological, regulatory, and labor market landscapes, as well as disparities in organizational resources, personnel, and strategic goals (Armbrüster, 2006). Such variability describes both differences among clients seeking professional services, as well as temporal shifts within the same client.

To add further complexity, many of these conditions that vary from delivery to delivery remain beyond the purview of organizational control, rendering them, at times, unpredictable. As organizations immerse themselves in intricate professional service work within legal, financial, or consulting domains, their influence over the broader political, economic, or competitive landscape remains limited, if not altogether nonexistent. Nonetheless, the actions regulators take have the potential to exert substantial influence on the trajectory of a merger or an initial public offering; competitor responses can indelibly impact the course of litigation or the execution of a strategic rollout; and the prevailing economic climate can mold the progression and ramifications of internal restructuring endeavors. Accordingly, consumers perceive professional services as deliveries involving a "large number of features that interact in a non-simple way" (Mikolon, Kolberg, Haumann, & Wieseke, 2015: 514). Indeed, it is well-known that the presence of changing and uncontrollable conditions severely limits the applicability of learning curves (e.g., Cai, Li, & Zhou, 2021; Chambers & Johnston, 2000: 856).

A second impediment to accumulating comparable cases arises from the inherent nature of many professional service engagements, which often necessitate the *customization* of services to suit the unique context of each organization involved. For example, Richard Susskind and Daniel Susskind (2016: 130) contended that "[p]rofessionals say, with some justification, that the circumstances of the recipients of their work are always unique, so that individual solutions must be customized for each." The value creation by professional service firms is intricately tied to providing tailored services and applying professional expertise to address specific problems (Skjølsvik, Breunig, & Pemer, 2018). Nicole J. Saam (2012: 211) aptly echoes this point in the context of the consulting industry: "It is virtually impossible to purchase the same consulting package/service for the same problem again." The significant degree of customization for a given client presents a sharp contrast with the standardized operations of manufacturing sectors, which constitute much of the empirical base for research on learning curves.

Consider in this respect General Motors' approach to setting up its automobile operations:

> The company has designed the plants to look so much alike that engineers may mistake which country they are in. And the assembly lines are being set up so that a glitch in a robot in Thailand, rather than turning into an expensive engineering problem that requires an expert for each machine at each plant, may well be solved by a quick call to Rosario (Argentina) or to Shanghai, China. (Blumenstein, 1997: A1)

In much of their work, professional service firms operate vastly differently from General Motors, in part because their value proposition hinges on customization rather than standardization. Such circumstances, by their nature, diminish the comparability of professional service cases, as a significant portion of professional service work hinges upon "judgment rather than . . . repeatable processes" (Christensen, Wang, & van Bever, 2013: 114). Consequently, the variable design of service delivery presents another major challenge to organizations accumulating comparable historical data points and, therefore, learning from conventional learning curves in professional service contexts (Chambers & Johnston, 2000).

Reliable Performance Feedback

For effective learning to take place, it is essential for organizations to have valid performance feedback. This feedback should consist of verifiable, comprehensive, and unbiased information about the outcomes of services in relation to defined goals and aspirations, which buyers can comprehend and evaluate (Argote & Miron-Spektor, 2011; March, 1987, 2010; Popper & Lipshitz, 2000a). However, a significant challenge arises in the context of professional service work—the difficulty of quantifying inputs and outputs in a manner comparable to manufacturing or standardized services (Nachum, 1999).

Specifically, the inherent intangibility and immeasurability of professional service work hinder the clients' ability to assess performance accurately. Consider the insights Clayton Christensen, Dina Wang, and Derek Van Bever (2013: 108) shared regarding the field of consulting: "It's incredibly difficult for clients to judge a consultancy's performance in advance, because they are usually hiring the firm for specialized knowledge and capability that they themselves lack. *It's even harder to judge after a project has been completed* [emphasis added], because so many external factors, including quality of execution, management transition, and the passage of time, influence the outcome of the consultants' recommendations."

To be fair, professional service firms have made significant efforts in recent years to enhance the measurability of their work outcomes. For example, a senior leader in the consulting industry commented on the industry's transformation from being primarily "advice-based" to adopting an "outcome-based" approach. Many professional service firms have established dedicated roles and teams focused on measuring the impact of their work on clients. Consequently, business development efforts are riddled with statements such as, "We [professionals] do not get paid unless you [the client] make money," which has become a common refrain in the sales of a range of advisory services.

However, delving deeper into the specific measurement of outcomes in professional service engagements reveals a thorny path. During my interviews with executives, some expressed concerns about what they referred to as the "ring-fencing" of professional service firm work. In such cases, the work outcomes are so narrowly defined that they fail to consider the broader vitality of the entire organization. Worse still, these outcomes may come at the expense of the organization as a whole. As one senior executive described:

> So one thing that's clear to me and [the CEO], that we always say, which is, you know, if we save $10 over here and lose $10, over here, it's likely him and I will be out of a job at some point; it doesn't work to justify the 10 we saved if we don't have control over the whole business. However, a lot of [consultants'] models rely on what I call ring-fencing: "well, we only said we would focus on this 10, and it's very important to show that we captured the 10." I tell you this, it is so easy to capture certain values, it's so difficult to provide holistic value to the organization.

At the other end of the spectrum, professional service firms encounter resistance when they attempt to broaden the measurable scope of their impact. Clients often rebel against these efforts, perceiving professionals as taking credit for things they did not actually do. A salient example of this tension can be observed with respect to consulting firms.

Many consulting firms have developed a comprehensive approach to evaluate their clients' overall health and effectiveness. This approach typically involves a triangulation of surveys, client interviews, and data analysis to assess aspects such as the clarity of the clients' strategy, the effectiveness of their leadership and talent, the organizational culture, coordination, and innovation, among other elements.

A senior executive shared a compelling anecdote regarding their consulting services provider. The provider had included a multi-million-dollar compensation bonus in the services agreement, contingent upon a measurable increase in the client's overall organizational effectiveness, as assessed by a comprehensive approach. When the effectiveness score rose by a significant 10%, the bonus was triggered. Reflecting on this, the executive remarked, "And it's interesting, because they [the consulting firm] are connecting this 10% difference to the greatness of [consulting firm name]. The reality is that, of course, they contribute to this, but the more important change is what's happening internally."

This executive went on to detail a series of significant corporate and leadership team initiatives that were completely unrelated to the work the consulting firm had completed. These initiatives, in all like-lihood, had played a crucial role in driving the overall organizational effectiveness forward. Such revelations raise important questions that scholars have also pondered: How can one distinguish between out-comes attributed to professional service firms and those influenced by other factors, particularly the contributions of the client's manage-ment team (Sturdy, 2011: 518)? It becomes evident that drawing a clear demarcation between the specific outcomes professional service firms achieve and those that stem from other factors presents a considerable challenge.

One cannot help but feel a sense of empathy for consultants entan-gled in this predicament. They navigate a realm of work that defies easy measurement. And they find themselves trapped between the unyield-ing grip of opposing forces in measuring the outcomes of their work, striving to strike a balance that is neither too narrow nor too broad. The challenge of measuring the outcomes of knowledge-based work and offering clients unambiguous performance feedback is, of course, not exclusive to consulting services. It reverberates across the vast landscape of the professional services field.

Mats Alvesson's (1993: 1006) work sheds light on a parallel chal-lenge in the field of accounting. He reveals that in auditing, much like other knowledge-intensive domains, there exists a notable absence or, at best, the presence of highly unreliable criteria for evaluating work outcomes. Consequently, consumers of auditing services possess only a limited understanding of the quality of the work an audit firm carries out.

My interviews with professionals across various sectors of the profes-sional services industry echoed this overarching theme and reinforced this predicament. A common challenge emerged: the difficulty of isolat-ing the specific impact attributable to a particular professional service firm. To illustrate this, consider the insights a senior executive shared re-garding the role of investment bankers in the pricing of an initial public offering (IPO):

Why was that IPO successful or unsuccessful based on the market demands? Because the bankers didn't price it correctly? Because the company got bad data? It's much harder to evaluate if they did it correctly, and so I think they can get away with a lot more.

The business press pages are filled with tales of competing narratives surrounding acquisition outcomes that fell short of expectations. These stories attribute the disappointments to strategic miscalculations, botched execution, or unforeseen shifts in market conditions.

A senior legal counsel reflected on a similar challenge in assessing the performance of the work performed by an external legal counsel:

> *So we don't have clear performance metrics, clear, concrete performance metrics, we probably should, but we don't. And I would be surprised if you find a company that does, because legal services are not as . . . what's the right word? The output is harder to measure, so it's that we don't really have concrete metrics. Sometimes it's did they [the external counsel] get a successful result for us? So in an M&A deal, you know, did the deal close? And were they a part of the reason why? In litigation, did we win? And can we attribute that success to them? So I guess I would phrase it as can we attribute some of our success in that matter to the law firm? That's one way we measure it. Another way is, did they make our lives easier? That's actually a big one. So some law firms, you know, don't help the in-house counsel very much like, we still have to really do a lot of the work ourselves. And we want law firms that are going to make our lives easier and make us look good to our internal clients. So that's like the business folks that we're working with. So I think those really are the two ways that we measure success.*

One of the most intriguing revelations from my fieldwork was the discovery that clients, faced with the challenge of assessing the quality of professional service outputs, often resort to relying on weak proxies to evaluate the work. Unable to directly gauge the true quality of the outcomes, they turn to alternate indicators. Many buyers, for example, commented on the smoothness of transactions and the responsiveness of service providers:

I think there are a few things that matter. First of all, are your bosses happy? So, you know, if you're running a merger, did it go smoothly from a financial timing perspective? They don't necessarily see the legal sausage or how it's made. But do they care about the result? If so, if they're happy, you know, that's one factor. Second, you want your outside service providers to be very responsive. You know, that's a huge element, you know, how responsive they are. Do you send them an email one day, and it takes them four days to respond? Or is it within an hour or something, you know, are you getting that responsiveness?

A senior in-house counsel highlighted the significance of simple and accessible language as a crucial criterion for evaluating the quality of the external counsel's work:

So for me specifically, you know, having worked as in-house counsel for a while now, what's important is that legal advice [can] be broken down into digestible and easily understandable thoughts and paragraphs . . . So for me, it's simple language. I measure success based on that.

Another experienced in-house counsel cited the importance of good grammar and absence of factual errors, "*Another thing that can be helpful is when people turn documents back to me, they aren't riddled with typos; they are consistent with the information I gave them.*"

It may seem shocking to ponder that the evaluation of work, potentially worth millions of dollars, can hinge on seemingly trivial aspects such as spell-check accuracy or the promptness of email responses. However, these observations are not isolated incidents but emblematic of a larger phenomenon. The inherent difficulty in assessing the quality of knowledge-based work necessitates the clients' reliance on readily observable indicators that may bear little direct connection to the ultimate quality of the work.

In fact, some analysts have pointed to our collective preoccupation with email and the overwhelming influx of digital communication as an unintended consequence of the difficulties in accurately measuring the output of knowledge-based work. The speed at which individuals reply to emails and the sheer volume of email exchanges can unwittingly become stand-ins for determining the value professionals generate (Newport, 2013). These surrogate metrics, although tangential to the core essence of the work itself, become convenient substitutes in the absence of more precise and reliable means of measuring performance.

Undoubtedly, it should be acknowledged that the purchasers of professional services exhibit a concerted effort in appraising the technical quality of the work itself and endeavor to ground their assessments in tangible performance metrics. A senior buyer of legal services expressed this sentiment when they remarked:

> And then I suppose there's just the technical quality of the work, you know, was every T crossed and every i dotted? Were you able to, you know, keep up or ideally, outsmart the other side whenever you're in a confrontational or negotiation position? So, those are some of the things that would matter to me. And then, I think also costs, like [was] cost maintained, you know, did we accomplish the task within the budget that we set for ourselves . . . you'll sometimes see massive cost overruns in this type of stuff.

Interestingly, these criteria are frequently employed and raised by the buyers in conversations in the same sequence as presented within this chapter, following numerous preliminary surrogate criteria and proxies. Relying solely on project costs as a measure of performance is, at best, a limited approach. Such a measure fails to provide insight into the value derived from services (cf. Zajac & Olsen, 1993) and is typically determined with substantial input from the purchasers of professional services. In the most extreme cases, the sellers, acting as trusted expert purveyors of their domain, may even exert control over the buyer's budget. A partner in a public accounting firm shared an anecdote in which a longstanding client trusted her completely with defining the estimated costs of the work, stating, "I trust you. Just tell me how much it would cost us."

The principal predicament encountered in evaluating the technical quality of the work lies in the pervasive knowledge and information asymmetries that characterize the relationship between buyers and sellers of professional services. These asymmetries were discussed thoroughly in Chapter 4. Frequently, professional service firms serve as intermediaries in the exchange of information among multiple clients, assuming a role akin to a structural broker (Burt, 1992). Moreover, by maintaining a competitive advantage through their expertise, professional service firms make it difficult for non-experts to assess expert output (von Nordenflycht, 2010). In this context, it is essential to remember that the superior expertise of professional service firms, when compared to their clients, forms the cornerstone of their competitive advantage and it serves as the primary reason clients seek their services.

Flexible Interpretation of Performance

History will be kind to me, for I intend to write it.
—Winston Churchill

The challenges surrounding the concrete evaluation of performance in professional service work suggest that interpretations of outcomes are frequently subject to multiple possibilities. For an illustration of an exceptionally disciplined approach to performance assessment, consider Micha Popper and Raanan Lipshitz's (2000b) insightful analysis of the post-flight debriefing procedure used in the military. This procedure involves a collective debriefing session following each mission, in which participants methodically use information captured by the video cameras installed in the cockpit of every aircraft. Following the mission, the pilots collectively view the recorded footage. Subsequently, the pilots engage in a comprehensive debate and analysis of each action depicted in the films, focusing keenly on any errors.

In these debriefs, the mission leaders typically start the conversation by revealing the reasoning behind their actions, highlighting successful actions, and admitting mistakes. Other pilots actively participate by offering observations on mission aspects that may have escaped the mission pilots' attention or by challenging their diagnosis or proposed solution (Popper & Lipshitz, 2000b: 135–136). This rigorous, data-driven debate results in either a recommendation for the appropriate maneuver to undertake under similar circumstances or a broader lesson learned, which could manifest in a proposed alteration in procedures or the design of future exercises.

These organizational practices serve as a noteworthy example of processes that engender a direct, clear, and exceptionally well-structured performance assessment. Scholars often describe such processes as reflexivity, a form of collective decision-making wherein organizations rely on established mechanisms and the analysis of reliable information to understand the factors that shape performance (Levine & Argote, 2017). As explained earlier, the nature of knowledge-intensive output that professional service firms generate, which is difficult to quantify and benchmark, does not readily lend itself to such precise performance analysis. Conversely, the ambiguity that characterizes performance allows for flexible interpretation. Even worse, when fueled by the prevailing commercial institutional logic, such flexible interpretation systematically undermines the efficacy of reflexive practices in obtaining and understanding performance feedback.

At the outset, it becomes evident that the pervasive influence of the commercial institutional logic poses a significant obstacle to impartiality and transparency in professional service firms' assessment of outcomes. Under the weighty pressures imposed by the commercial logic, professional service firms often find themselves unable to fulfill their role as independent advisors. Both consciously and unconsciously, professionals are compelled to safeguard their expert status to secure new business. Consequently, minor errors and oversights tend to be downplayed or overlooked, while significant setbacks are more readily attributed to external factors.

The lens of self-justification theory offers a compelling framework for comprehending this facet of human behavior. According to this theory, decision-makers who bear responsibility for initial courses of action inevitably face pressures stemming from sunk costs, threats to their reputation, and the anticipation of regret should they admit failure. In such circumstances, the natural inclination is to seek ways to reframe questionable outcomes in a more positive light or to shift blame away from one's own skills, efforts, or foresight (Sleesman, Conlon, McNamara, & Miles, 2012). James G. March (1991: 7) said it most profoundly: "*[c]onceptions of identity in organizations tend also to be conserved by interpretations of experience.*" Indeed, experiences are often unconsciously used to strengthen individual beliefs and identities. The professionals' identities as experts who provide value to organizations pose a significant challenge when it comes to acknowledging failure.

Moreover, due to selective recruitment processes and ongoing job training, many professionals have become highly skilled in the art of influence (Stern & Westphal, 2010). They have been trained to deliver persuasive messages and cultivate executive presence. Thus, performance narratives coming from professionals are often compelling. Importantly, the pernicious effects engendered by the commercial institutional logic have likely driven much of the self-justification behavior to operate at the unconscious level. When professional success and personal identity are so closely intertwined with securing future business, avoiding failure and projecting success become almost instinctual acts of self-preservation. Indeed, among the myriad factors driving self-justification, the desire to "save face" and uphold one's reputation emerges as one of the most potent motivators (Sleesman et al., 2012).

The dynamics at play within professional service engagements can similarly describe buyers, particularly individuals who were instrumental in initiating the engagement. In my fieldwork, I witnessed an impressive array of situations wherein executives who initially harbored skepticism toward bringing in a professional service firm gradually became more enthusiastic. Remarkably, this shift in sentiment occurred in the absence of concrete performance feedback or even amidst a vehemently negative assessment of outcomes from other executives who were not involved in the decision to hire the firm. The overarching point here is that once the ink has dried on the contract, these executives find themselves ensnared. It becomes an arduous task, consciously and unconsciously, to ascend the chain of command and report that a multi-million-dollar engagement with a professional service firm has proven unsuccessful.[5]

Moreover, even in cases where buyers may hold divergent interpretations of a certain performance outcome from the professionals, the experts' advantage stemming from their superior knowledge and information can exert a formidable suppressive influence on counter-arguments and alternate interpretations. As extensively elaborated in Chapter 4, many of these dynamics can be attributed to unconscious compliance with authority. However, in certain instances, the overwhelming power a professional service firm wields can lead to the buyers' explicit self-censorship. A senior executive eloquently highlighted this phenomenon in relation to her company's engagement with a professional service provider:

We would never say anything bad—I won't even tell you who it is right now, who I think was incredibly sketchy—we would never say anything bad about them because they are such a power player in the market, that it could never get out that we were saying bad stuff about them because if they tried to blackball us or say that we were bad for some reason in an analyst report about us that was bad. We're tanked.

The elusive nature of evaluating the outcomes of professional service work, coupled with the emphasis placed on the prestige and expertise of the service provider during the selection process, creates a challenging environment for attributing failures to the professionals involved. Even

---

5. Research provides a nuanced understanding of the mechanisms through which such behaviors can manifest. Consider March's (1987: 160) penetrating insight in this respect: "Most information in organizations is collected and recorded not primarily to aid decision-making directly but as a basis for interpretations that allow coherent histories to be told. As a structure of meaning evolves from information and from the process of decision-making, specific decisions are fitted into it." In other words, a broader framework of interpretation can exert a significant influence on how subsequent organizational experiences are perceived and assimilated. Thus, by actively molding the narrative framework, executives and professionals alike can exert a powerful influence on the meaning ascribed to organizational experiences (see also Levitt & March, 1988). Pragmatically, such narrative framing enables, for example, the attribution of setbacks and failures associated with professional service work to external, uncontrollable circumstances.

when failures appear glaringly obvious, assigning responsibility to these professionals necessitates questioning the expertise that was critical in their initial selection. Consequently, it is common for poor outcomes in professional service work to be ascribed to chance or unfortunate circumstances rather than inadequate skill and advice (Ernst & Kieser, 2002). In this respect, a senior buyer of financial services observed:

> *Like the core lead banks, [bank name 1], [bank name 2], you know, they just drive such a percentage of the market. I just have never seen anything come back on them negatively, ever, even if it's clear that they have botched an IPO and that a company got screwed.*

In my empirical tests of SID, I deliberately opted to focus on legal services and litigation outcomes. This choice was driven by the inherent advantage of this domain, which offers a higher degree of tangibility and concreteness in evaluating outcomes of professional service work relative to other sectors. However, even here, one could conceivably present a competing narrative, prompting a flexible interpretation. Specifically, litigation losses could be attributed to the client's poor information disclosure or low commitment to winning in litigation. Alternatively, even a protracted yet ultimately unsuccessful lawsuit could be construed as a triumph, as it has the potential to deter future infringers, divert competitors' attention, disrupt their strategic maneuvers, or drain their financial resources. And to be candid, refuting this line of reasoning in the context of a singular lawsuit may prove to be difficult.[6]

CAUSAL AMBIGUITY

It becomes evident that the foundational conditions needed for organizational learning from experience are consistently violated in

---

6. This argument, understandably, loses much of its validity when legal losses are observed at a larger scale and can be attributed to the immediate providers of legal services who enjoy privileged access to their clients. However, acknowledging the significance of proximate external service providers in the face of uncertainty necessitates making decisions based on inferences derived from extensive samples of lawsuits, while diligently accounting for a multitude of factors that may vary across organizations—an undertaking that companies seldom pursue.

professional service work. Learning cases are scarce or not comparable, and feedback on performance is often unclear and subject to
dispute. This leads to a breakdown in learning known as causal ambiguity, where the connection between organizational actions and their
outcomes becomes, well, ambiguous (Argote, 2013; Clough & Piezunka,
2020; March, 2010; Muehlfeld, Rao Sahib, & Van Witteloostuijn, 2012).
The risk of causal ambiguity is particularly pronounced in knowledge-
based work (King & Zeithaml, 2001). As a result, breakdowns in learning
tend to obscure not only what transpired, but also why it occurred, who
bears responsibility, and how the organization should learn from it.

In the context of ambiguous experiences and the absence of reliable
performance feedback, professional service work often becomes entan-
gled in prevailing industry norms. As I highlighted in Chapter 8, there
are instances where consultants are seen as indispensable for projects
of a specific scale or complexity, or struggling companies are expected
to bring in consultants as a symbol of their commitment to transformation and advancement. This serves as a tangible example of a broader
phenomenon in which the adoption of new practices is not driven by
organizations' intentional efforts to learn and improve, but rather by
a desperate quest for legitimacy (DiMaggio & Powell, 1983; Meyer &
Rowan, 1977).

Given the many challenges associated with organizational learning
in high-touch, knowledge-based service domains, it is not astonishing
that the research findings on organizational learning in such contexts
are notably restrained (Chambers & Johnston, 2000). For example, when
examining companies' past acquisition experiences, the prevailing evidence fails to demonstrate a positive impact of cumulative learning on
future acquisition performance. In other words, engaging in more acquisitions does not necessarily result in improved proficiency. Instead, the
limited benefits of learning appear to be concentrated among a select few
organizations that undertake multiple acquisition experiences that are
similar to one another in their nature and surrounding conditions (e.g.,
Cai, Li, & Zhou, 2021; Haleblian & Finkelstein, 1999; Hayward, 2002;
Muehlfeld, Rao Sahib, & Van Witteloostuijn, 2012; Zollo & Singh, 2004).

Notwithstanding the aforementioned challenges, it is important to acknowledge the inherent difficulty in measuring acquisition performance

in empirical research. This circumstance compels scholars to resort to imperfect proxies, such as assessing stock market reactions to acquisition announcements or determining whether announced acquisitions were actually completed. Alternatively, scholars endeavor to capture associations between acquisitions and the acquirer's overall return on assets several years after the acquisition event, an approach that is plagued by intervening events.

By the same token, the findings regarding organizational learning from prior partnering experience are inconclusive. Some studies fail to identify a cumulative learning effect in partnering, whereas others observe such effects only for specific categories of companies (Hoang & Rothaermel, 2005; Zollo, Reuer, & Singh, 2002).[7] Similarly, studies investigating the impact of prior restructuring experience on the performance of subsequent restructuring events yield highly varied results, including the entire gamut of mostly null, with some negative and positive effects (Bergh & Lim, 2008). All these studies encounter similar challenges when it comes to measuring performance, which mirrors the difficulties outlined in the preceding discussion on acquisition performance. I have encountered the same challenge in my own research in measuring the performance of interorganizational partnerships (Sytch, Wohlegezogen, & Zajac, 2018).

CONCLUSION

Stepping back for a moment of broader contemplation, my central argument is that the presence of mixed evidence regarding a company's ability to learn from intricate, knowledge-based experiences is hardly

7. To provide more detail, Maurizio Zollo, Jeffrey J. Reuer, and Harbir Singh (2002) unveiled an absence of correlation between a company's prior count of strategic alliances and the performance of its focal alliance. Conversely, Hong and Rothaermel (2005) shed light on a positive impact resulting from accumulated partnering experience on R&D project performance, but only for biotechnology firms and not for pharmaceutical companies. The studies diverge in their conclusions on the effects of accumulating experience with the same partner, in which case learning from past alliances is presumed to be more partner-specific rather than general. Some studies present evidence supporting the notion of positive partner-specific learning (Zollo, Reuer, & Singh, 2002), whereas others suggest a contrary perspective, indicating a negative effect (Hoang & Rothaermel, 2005).

surprising. Acquisitions, IPOs, divestitures, strategic partnerships, litigation, reengineering, and reorganization processes—among similar knowledge-centric organizational activities typically falling in the realm of professional service firms—pose significant challenges for firms seeking to glean knowledge. These events occur infrequently and in unpredictable patterns, which hampers the accumulation of the substantial number of observations needed to effectively learn by doing. Even when these events occur more frequently, the associated services that the professional service firms provide are highly customized; that is, they are tailored to specific competitive and organizational conditions. This customization renders individual experiences daunting to compare.

Furthermore, the intrinsic complexity of these activities and of the associated professional service work erect formidable barriers to organizations consistently obtaining reliable performance feedback. This feedback is often subject to significant time delays and is vulnerable to the influence of intervening factors, which obfuscates its interpretation. Consequently, when performance feedback does eventually materialize, it becomes malleable, open to flexible interpretations, and susceptible to the emergence of conflicting narratives. These challenges are exacerbated by the constraints that limited sample sizes of organizational experiences impose, which constrain the depth and breadth of insights that can be derived.

To compound matters, the pervasive influence of the commercial institutional logic, intricately interweaving the success of professional service firms and the identity of the professionals with generating new business, systematically biases the interpretation of performance feedback. It stands to reason that such interpretations are inclined to consistently overlook setbacks or ascribe them to external or uncontrollable factors, aligning with the prevailing imperative to present an image of an infallible expert.

Buyers often further reinforce such a skewed interpretation of performance feedback. Pressures stemming from sunk financial costs, threats to ego and reputation, and the broader need for self-justification drive buying executives to validate their decisions to enlist professional service firms. Once again, this propensity is likely to color performance feedback positively, which inadvertently overlooks substantial opportunities for learning and course correction.

Consequently, understanding the outcomes of professional service work, and subsequently learning from it, often becomes an exercise in futility. It remains perplexingly ambiguous which actions contributed to observed outcomes, who bears responsibility for them, and even what the outcomes truly are, making it difficult for organizations to recover meaningful insights from their collaborations with professional service firms. In such circumstances, the potential of organizational learning to counter SID becomes exceedingly challenging, if not outright impossible.

In light of the argument and evidence presented in this chapter, it becomes abundantly clear that the chapter's title, "Why Don't the Buyers Learn?" is a misleading oversimplification. The obstacles hindering buyer learning extend beyond the buyers and infiltrate the fabric of professional service firms themselves. These firms grapple with the same impediments and struggles when navigating the intricate complexities inherent to these knowledge-based experiences. Moreover, the learning processes for professional service firms are muddled by additional factors. For example, seasoned professionals consistently echo March's (1987) early writings on the inherent ambiguities of preference within organizations, which can sometimes make it challenging to discern buyers' clear goals in certain professional service work. Furthermore, professionals frequently find themselves in situations where the necessary organizational data is either inadequately recorded or not recorded at all, rendering it useless for facilitating learning. The list of challenges goes on and on.

All these factors underscore an even truer realization: in professional service contexts, both buyers and sellers face significant limitations in their ability to learn from repeated engagements. This, in turn, weakens the effectiveness of organizational learning as a remedy for SID.

CHAPTER SUMMARY

Organizations are commonly believed to learn from experience, which theoretically should act as a potent counterforce against supplier-induced demand. In essence, if supplier-induced demand negatively affects buyers, they should gradually develop the ability to identify its occurrence and avoid it. However, in reality this does not happen. The primary reason for this discrepancy lies in the systematic violation of the two key conditions essential for organizational learning: having a large sample of comparable cases and receiving reliable performance feedback. These violations are particularly prevalent in the delivery and consumption of professional services. They arise from the infrequent nature of professional service work and its extensive customization to suit a specific client and their unique circumstances. Further complicating matters is the inherent difficulty in measuring the outcomes of knowledge-based work, which constitutes a substantial portion of professional services output. Consequently, competing narratives emerge to explain performance, leading to overall causal ambiguity, where organizational actions are ambiguously linked to outcomes. It is crucial to note that professional service providers are just as susceptible to these breakdowns in the learning cycle as their clients. Consequently, both clients and their professional service providers struggle to effectively recognize and mitigate supplier-induced demand. Altogether, these dynamics collectively hinder the ability of organizations to learn from experience and counter supplier-induced demand.

CHAPTER 11

Looking Forward

This book illuminates the significant issue of supplier-induced demand (SID) in professional services. But this is not just a story about the here and now; it's also about peering into the future. The concern at hand is far from fading away. The enabling conditions of SID—the elusive trio of problem, action, and outcome uncertainty; the sly power advantage of professionals; and the ever-present imperfections of professionals' agency—persist and amplify. The rising technical complexity of professional service work mingles with its increasing interconnectedness to numerous related areas of knowledge and expertise. This results in a bewildering sense of uncertainty, wherein the buyers might feel like they are navigating an intricate labyrinth of organizational problems and opportunities without a guiding map. The increasing reliance on professionals as chaperones, in turn, widens the rift between the buyers' and suppliers' expertise, bolstering the professionals' power advantage.

The pervasive influence of the commercial institutional logic is similarly unyielding. As professional service markets evolve into fierce competitive battlegrounds, professional service firms find themselves entangled in a fight for survival. Caught in the crossfire, they are left with little choice but to tether their hierarchies and notions of success to the sustenance and expansion of their service offerings. This perspective becomes deeply ingrained in the professionals' identities, shaping the lens through which they view the world. And through this lens, professionals see the induction of demand as the very force that propels not only the success of their employers but also their own individual self-worth.

Moreover, they view creating demand as a force that proves essential in aiding clients on their transformative journeys, enabling them to excel amidst the pressures and uncertainties of turbulent markets.

Within this context, there is an allure in motion, a seductive appeal that leads professionals and their clients toward a plethora of opportunities. But here's the catch: not all of these opportunities glitter with promise. Some are barely average; others, unfortunately, are less than stellar. You will find professionals and clients alike diving headfirst into these prospects, blinded by the allure of action. They are drawn in, not necessarily by the potential of these opportunities, but often by the sheer urgency to act, to perform, to *do* something. Anything.

And the peculiar nature of professional service work—its unique, knowledge-centric fabric—makes it difficult to see this demand as supplier-induced. The outputs of such work are a riddle in themselves. You have numerous confounding variables muddying the waters, making it a Herculean task to measure the outcomes and isolate the role professionals played in them. Thus, both buyers and sellers can be caught in a whirlpool of SID, but the swirling currents make it difficult to identify and understand. The complexity of the situation means they are struggling to learn from their experiences or find ways to lessen the impact.

In this context, SID is not a covert conspiracy, violating professional norms or skirting the edges of legality. It is not a rogue act or a mere occasional misstep. Instead, it evolves into a quotidian market dynamic, an ever-present force with significant implications for the economy at large. Such implications can be far-reaching, and one of the most critical constraints it imposes is on the buyers. This constraint can have significant ramifications for their economic growth and overall organizational effectiveness. Beyond mere misallocations of organizational resources into less promising areas, this constraint can result in buyers' purchasing services that prove to be outright detrimental.

The consequences of such decisions can be weighty. Imagine the repercussions of misguided mergers and acquisitions, leaving organizations entangled in a web of complexities and disputes, or facing the burden of costly lawsuits that drain financial resources and result in losses. Organizational transformations, in pursuit of elusive benefits, may lead to disruptions in operations, instigate reductions in personnel, and undermine morale, all while failing to yield the desired improvements in performance.

SID brings yet another compelling implication to the forefront, urging us to address the effective use of talent in labor markets. Professional service firms have long been magnets for attracting and recruiting some of the brightest minds. Yet, as the reach of SID expands, a crucial question emerges: Are we harnessing the full potential of these exceptional individuals? Indeed, a pressing concern is that some of the most promising minds may find themselves enmeshed in misdirected pursuits, toiling away on projects of little significance or, even worse, inadvertently generating harm while leaving companies in genuine need of help unattended.

Additionally, we must confront the possibility of structural misallocation of talent. The allure of professional services can draw an excessive concentration of workers into this domain, potentially diverting them from other crucial fields. As we contemplate this, we find ourselves pondering whether the economy needs the current numbers of bankers, lawyers, or consultants. Moreover, as I explain later in this chapter, we also confront a decision about who should employ these professionals: should it be the professional service firms or their corporate buyers?

As we venture further into the implications of SID, it becomes apparent that its impact is unlikely to be confined solely to the realm of professional services. Its reach can extend far beyond, casting a long-reaching shadow over various sectors of the economy. I am referring to sectors that increasingly resemble professional services in their complexity, uncertainty, and reliance on imperfect agents who influence the landscape of opportunities and challenges for buyers, while offering an array of products and services. Echoes of SID may thus reverberate through the procurement of products and services in engineering, technology, education, personal finance, healthcare, and insurance, among other sectors.

Recognizing the significance of this far-reaching impact, this closing chapter serves as both a moment of contemplation and a call to action. I first situate the conversation about SID within the context of central organizational theories. Through this exploration, we discover that the lens of SID holds the potential to inform, enrich, and advance a multitude of theoretical discourses. And in the very final leg of this journey, I aim to start a conversation about viable solutions that can help mitigate SID.

IMPLICATIONS FOR THEORY

Organizational Boundaries

The investigation into SID, detailed in this book, holds the promise to deepen and broaden the existing research on organizational boundaries. This is because the present study probes the intricate question of which activities are best maintained within an organization's boundaries, as opposed to those which could be effectively outsourced—a puzzle that has long captivated the minds of organizational researchers. Over the years, this intricate question has been analyzed using a variety of theoretical perspectives, including transaction cost economics, resource dependence, and the resource-based view.

For example, transaction cost economics approaches organization boundaries as a function of projected costs emerging from market failures and inefficiencies within legal institutions when coordinating interorganizational exchanges and resolving conflicts. This perspective suggests that specific types of transactions, such as those requiring asset-specific investments—investments that cannot be redeployed to "alternative uses and by alternative users without sacrifice of productive value" (Williamson, 1991: 282)—are particularly vulnerable to opportunistic behavior and hold up (Williamson, 1985, 1991). Consider a potential price dispute arising after a supplier has built a facility adjacent to the buyer's location in an effort to reduce shipping costs. Or when the buyer has redesigned its product around a bespoke technology provided by a single supplier. The costs related to drafting and enforcing contracts associated with such instances are viewed as too high when the transactions are left to the unpredictability of markets and the vagaries of legal systems in the event of disputes. Consequently, the prevalent wisdom within the framework of transaction cost economics advocates for the internalization of such transactions within organizational boundaries, thereby mitigating the impact of opportunism and promoting efficiency.

Similarly, the resource dependence perspective posits that organizations can and do actively manage their dependence on the suppliers of resources, which are crucial to their operations and not easily accessible from alternative sources (Pfeffer & Salancik, 1978). Following this viewpoint, an organization's survival is linked to its ability to internalize the suppliers of such critical resources, thereby ensuring operational stability and reducing dependence on external variables. Conversely, the resource-based view conceptualizes organizations as entities whose competitive advantage is integrally tied to bundles of rare resources, which competitors find challenging to replicate (Barney, 1991). Consequently, organizations are advised to delineate their boundaries primarily around these invaluable resources, which could encompass elements as diverse as advanced technology, specialized marketing expertise, or uniquely skilled personnel.

The theoretical perspective of SID provides a distinct and complementary view on the question of organizational boundaries. Notably, the exploration into SID suggests that externalizing organizational activities can, under certain conditions, *shift the locus of control* over these activities. This shift in control can subsequently impact demand, determining whether the organization procures a particular activity, and the extent to which it does. In essence, the decision regarding what to maintain within organizational boundaries transcends the traditional management of costs and uncertainties associated with markets or competition. It also encapsulates the choices the organization makes about the need for these very activities, and the examination of whether these decisions are beneficial to the organization.

From this perspective, organizing based solely on the consideration of transaction costs, for instance, appears to be markedly shortsighted. In complex organizational activities that require sophisticated expertise, the act of outsourcing such tasks essentially equates to *outsourcing expertise*, an effect that amplifies over time. This concern has been noted

by scholars who observed an expanding trend in governments outsourcing organizational activities to external consultants (Guttman &
Willner, 1976; Mazzucato & Collington, 2023). According to this research, the escalation in outsourcing by government agencies has left
these institutions bereft of the necessary expertise to perform, super-
vise, and evaluate the outsourced work. When perpetuated over time,
the outsourcing of expertise not only maintains but also widens the
expertise gap between professional service providers and their clients.
This, in turn, nurtures one of the most critical enabling conditions of
SID: the power advantage suppliers hold over buyers.

Organizing questions therefore transcend anticipations of competitors' moves or market uncertainties. The SID perspective, in turn,
advances a compelling argument for maintaining certain organizational
activities within the organization's boundaries, even in the presence
of high transaction costs or their replicability by competitors. These
activities align with the criteria of enabling conditions—namely, problem, action, and outcome uncertainty; supplier power; and imperfect
agency—and are entrenched within the commercial institutional logic
adopted by service providers. It is logical to expect that the co-existence
and intensity of these factors within a specific area of organizational
activity make a stronger economic case for more hierarchical organizational structures. In these scenarios, integrating such activities within
organizational boundaries can help reduce the expertise gap, alleviate
the conflicting roles of seller and advisor, and serve as a protective shield
against the influence of the commercial institutional logic in the field of
professional services.

Economic Agglomeration

This book unveils that SID is perpetuated by the providers of professional services who are geographically proximate to the buyers. The
effect of proximity in this context operates through expanded social
contact with co-located clients. As SID is primarily propelled by the suppliers' pursuit of revenue generation, rather than by the clients' needs,

this demand can increase the costs of economic activities in the region and, in aggregate, curtail the growth of regional clusters. Hence, this book augments the body of knowledge on economic agglomeration (Buhr & Owen-Smith, 2011; Powell, Packalen, & Whittington, 2012; Saxenian, 1994) by demonstrating how co-located specialist suppliers can increase the costs of economic activities and constrain the growth of economic clusters.

Conceptually, these findings illustrate that while specialist suppliers may initially be attracted to a specific geographical area by the demand for their services, it may be their presence that subsequently stimulates future demand, leading to an upsurge in the associated economic costs. The prospect of gaining a deeper understanding and potentially rectifying this concerning trend could reside in a more meticulous examination of local institutional contexts. This study's results indicate that the effect of geographically proximate specialist suppliers inducing demand for their services can be contingent on the degree of task uncertainty in the region, which these suppliers are tasked to alleviate. Therefore, the unique ability to manage high levels of uncertainty is likely to be a pivotal determinant of the suppliers' capacity to influence their clients.

To clarify, SID is not the only lens to reveal the constraints of economic agglomeration. Prior work has shed light on constraints emerging due to adverse selection of producers, prompted by concerns over knowledge spillovers (Kalnins & Chung, 2004; Shaver & Flyer, 2000), or due to the pressures of local competition (Sorenson & Audia, 2000). So, we have a partial answer to the question of why not all startups are located in Silicon Valley or all automotive companies in Detroit. Nonetheless, this book contrasts with and advances the conclusions of earlier research, which have generally characterized the presence of specialist suppliers as an unconditionally positive force propelling the growth of regional economies (e.g., Sorenson & Stuart, 2001; Suchman & Cahill, 1996).

In this context, it is crucial to underscore that specialist suppliers already represent an indispensable and influential element of regional economies. Moreover, their prominence is likely to intensify as firms increasingly resort to outsourcing in markets steered by specialized knowledge and expertise. Therefore, future investigations of regional economies would benefit from a comprehensive examination of the characteristics of resident specialist suppliers, as well as an in-depth understanding of the dynamics shaping their interactions with clients.

Embeddedness of Economic Action

Finally, this book informs the scholarly discourse on the embeddedness of economic action (Granovetter, 1985). The book's premise challenges the conclusions of extant theoretical work, which suggests that the increasing professionalization in our society makes human behavior disembedded (Giddens, 1990, 1991). The disembeddedness argument suggests that the development of professional systems and the concomitant universalistic standards (e.g., legal rules) extricate human behavior from the influence of local geographies and the social relationships these geographies engender. The present book's arguments and findings point to a diametrically opposite conclusion.

Consider first that the increasing professionalization of society can be accompanied by increased versus decreased uncertainty surrounding organizational activities. Applied to the evolution of the legal system in particular, Anthony D'Amato (1993: 8) stated:

> One might look at the increasing growth in reported judicial decisions, statutes, and regulations as an increasingly successful attempt to impose precision upon human activities . . . But I would regard those same volumes as a futile and sometimes mad attempt to encapsulate real-world transactions in elusive and ambiguous legal prose . . . rulemaking results in internal contradictions, a multiplication of ambiguities.

This conclusion resonates with the broader research findings that the proliferation of specialized domains of expertise, the interconnections among them, and the introduction of new terms, concepts, and frameworks—propagated in part by professional service firms—can unintentionally *give rise* to uncertainty (Groß & Kieser, 2006).

In turn, the conclusions drawn from this book suggest that the ensuing increase in task-specific uncertainty engenders opportunities for demand-inducing influence by bearers of expert knowledge. More significantly, geographic proximity to clients and the social contact such closeness facilitates, enables experts to wield this influence. Hence, this book's findings not only contest Anthony Giddens' assertions (1990; 1991) but propose that entirely converse dynamics might be at play. Specifically, a plausible scenario is that the increasing professionalization of society serves to further embed, rather than disembed, interorganizational interactions and market exchanges within local physical spaces and social relationships.

A related insight concerns how organizational actions can become "emplaced"; that is, shaped by local space. This has been a key area of exploration for scholars studying geographic communities (Marquis & Battilana, 2009; Tilcsik & Marquis, 2013; Vermeulen, Simons, & Knoben, 2012). Through both qualitative work and quantitative analyses, this book illuminates how the increased presence of specialist suppliers in close physical proximity can create opportunities for supplier influence through heightened social contact with clients. Significantly, this influence only manifests itself in institutional contexts where corporate actors perceive a substantial degree of uncertainty. This uncertainty enables suppliers to convert disparities in expertise and information with clients into powerful levers of informational influence. This finding underscores the critical importance of considering the cognitive influences of local communities (Davis & Greve, 1997; Marquis, 2003), particularly with respect to variations in local frames of reference concerning professional practices across different geographic locales.

As research into the antecedents and implications of SID evolves, one promising avenue to explore involves the precise nature of professionals' power base and their potential power advantage in interactions with clients. An enlightening perspective in this regard could be drawn from studies of mediated transactions and brokerage relationships (Burt, 1992; Fernandez-Mateo, 2007; Reagans & Zuckerman, 2008; Sytch,

Tatarynowicz, & Gulati, 2012), as well as interorganizational influence (Beckman & Haunschild, 2002; Beckman & Phillips, 2005; Gulati & Sytch, 2007). The professionals' power advantage derives from their advantages in expert knowledge within a highly specialized domain. It also derives from the professionals' privileged position relative to the buyers in the networks of knowledge, information, and economic exchange.

The privileged structural position refers to an advantageous placement within social structures that enables professional firms to scaffold different areas of the economy, thereby shaping the flow of opportunities for their client organizations (e.g., acquisition or partnership opportunities) and individual executives (e.g., jobs at other companies). A detailed investigation into the basis of power and influence, and their enactment between buyers and sellers of professional services, can offer yet another promising perspective for understanding how SID takes root, unfolds, and affects buyers.

IMPLICATIONS FOR PRACTICE

SID is not an easy problem to mitigate. The ubiquitous commercial institutional logic that is pervasive among professional service firms standardizes and normalizes the induction of demand. The professionals' associated behaviors are not unethical, malevolent, or even consciously premeditated. As previously elucidated, the act of selling—indeed, the amplification of sales of professional services—is not merely a vehicle for individual monetary gain. Rather, this practice holds a far more profound significance. It serves as the embodiment of professional self-worth, an integral facet of the professionals' identities. This worth is inextricably linked to the professionals' cardinal role of aiding corporations in their pursuit of adaptability, innovation, and advancement. In light of this, it is salient to question the efficacy of simple interventions such as modifying reward structures or expanding the scope of professional codes of ethics. Given the deep-seated nature of the problem, such remedial measures are likely to be an exercise in futility.

Standing in the way of developing ideal incentives and contracts are the significant asymmetries of knowledge and expertise characterizing the relationship between clients and professionals (Sharma, 1997; Wolinsky, 1993). A buyer often lacks the requisite knowledge of the expert seller's trade to know which and how much of the service is required or actually performed. As a result, the buyer may similarly be unable to design an adequate contract or contingency-compensation agreement. The fact that SID is difficult to detect in small samples curtails the potential for regulatory agencies or auditing bodies to mitigate SID by monitoring exchanges.

What options do buyers and sellers have then to address SID? To uncover potential solutions, we need to return to the basic framework that characterizes SID as outlined in this book. Three key conditions—uncertainty, supplier power, and imperfect agency—interact with the commercial institutional logic and barriers to learning from experience to form the bedrock of SID (see Figure 1 in Chapter 1). These factors collectively create the structural foundation of this phenomenon. Therefore, the most effective way to systematically mitigate SID involves interventions aimed at methodically dismantling these core components. By undermining these fundamental elements, we have the potential to weaken the structure of SID, thus reducing its impact. The following proposed interventions and practices are designed with this primary objective in mind.

Organizational leaders hoping for a guarantee that the strategies suggested below will definitively eliminate SID might be disappointed. Such guarantees are almost impossible to provide due to the inherent challenge of identifying SID in individual transactions or even within small batches of bespoke professional services. As a result, it is difficult to ascertain in any specific case whether the organization has been effectively protected from the potential harm of SID. However, a considerable body of social science research—covering areas such as team management, executive decision-making, and organizational leadership—offers substantial evidence that improvements in processes leading to outcomes often correlate with desirable changes in those outcomes. This same principle applies to the recommendations provided below. By promoting a more efficient management cycle for complex, knowledge-based work, we can aim to improve the consistency and quality of its outcomes.

Insourcing Certain Transactions

Addressing the issue of SID necessitates returning in-house certain organizational activities currently undertaken by professional service firms. This restructuring could effectively shield these activities from the prevailing influence of the commercial institutional logic common in professional services, along with the agency imperfections and power held by professionals. It is important to note that this does not imply a blanket dismissal of professional services. Instead, it advocates for a thoughtful and selective insourcing of tasks that may be particularly vulnerable to SID. In this regard, a key insight from this book's empirical research indicates that SID is especially likely to occur in situations characterized by extremely high outcome uncertainty. It is these transactions that should primarily be considered for potential internalization.

If complete insourcing is not feasible, organizations should, at a minimum, strive to increase their involvement in the planning, execution, and evaluation of professional service work outcomes. Both my fieldwork and empirical research have identified significant variations in the engagement level of in-house counsel during litigation, and of corporate executives in reorganizations or post-merger decisions. Often, their involvement tends to be low, with external legal counsel and consultants, respectively, primarily controlling the work. To illustrate this point, consider the following: in a review of nearly 5,000 patent infringement lawsuits, we found that in-house counsel served as counsel of record in only 5% of cases. In the remaining 95% of cases, the company's own lawyers did not officially represent the company in court (Uribe, Sytch, & Kim, 2020). Instead, litigation was handled exclusively by external legal counsel.

Undeniably, insourcing intricate, uncertain tasks that are typically managed by professional service firms is not merely a matter of adjusting organizational authority. Rather, it entails the *adjustment of expertise*. By readily outsourcing complex transactions, companies miss a crucial opportunity to cultivate requisite internal competencies. Developing such in-house expertise could potentially bridge the power gap with suppliers, a chasm primarily born out of disparities in knowledge and skillsets.

It could foster a more vibrant dialogue on the efficacy and outcomes of work and enhance experiential learning within the organization.

Indeed, during my fieldwork, many executives confessed to feeling utterly ill-equipped to even formulate the right questions to pose to professional service firms, largely due to these glaring expertise imbalances. Yet, it is these very executives who often possess invaluable insights specific to their enterprise and industry dynamics. When this insider understanding is combined with the professionals' conceptual knowledge and cross-industry expertise, it can lead to a better selection of opportunities to pursue and a more robust evaluation of those opportunities and considered courses of action.

This understanding leads to two main implications. First, the decision to outsource complex, uncertain transactions should not be determined solely, or even predominantly, based on easily identifiable, typically short-term, cost considerations. For such tasks, the question of who can complete them more inexpensively or quickly is less important. By contrast, it is vital to recognize that the outsourcing of expertise, which often accompanies the outsourcing of complex transactions, may bring significant hidden consequences due to SID.

Second, organizations could investigate various approaches to enhance their specialized expertise in-house. Doing so might require adjustments to the hiring and retention policies for full-time employees. It could also involve forming specialized, temporary "SWAT" teams[1] consisting of qualified internal employees, industry experts, independent professionals, or academics. These teams could be relied upon to assist in evaluating the discovery process, recommendations, and outcomes of professional service work. The involvement of the buyers' own employees in such teams is highly desirable as it helps organizations internalize some of that expertise (Sharma, 1997).

While few studies specifically investigate how internalizing transactions can counteract SID, the available empirical evidence generally supports the aforementioned suggestions. For example, in business

---

1. SWAT refers to "Special Weapons and Tactics." It is a specialized unit within the US police force, trained to deal with particularly complex and unusual situations.

acquisitions, companies employing specialized internal merger and acquisition staff demonstrate superior short- and long-term acquisition
performance (Gokkaya, Liu, & Stulz, 2023). Acquisition performance
was evaluated through a range of indicators such as shareholder wealth
creation related to the acquisition announcement, long-term abnormal
stock returns, shifts in long-term operating performance, changes in
analyst consensus earnings forecasts related to acquisitions, the rate
of post-acquisition divestitures, and the declaration of transactions resulting in significant shareholder wealth losses. Similarly, internalizing
expertise and establishing a dedicated alliance function has proven to be
advantageous for companies entering new strategic partnerships (Kale,
Dyer, & Singh, 2002). In healthcare, the simple act of patients seeking a
second opinion significantly reduced the overtreatment rate, lowering it
from over 70% to approximately 50% (Mimra, Rasch, & Waibel, 2016).

   To reiterate, the goal of leveraging this additional expertise is not to
ruthlessly audit the work of professional service firms with the intent
of uncovering misconduct. Instead, this intervention aims to enhance
expertise on the client side, thereby encouraging a more substantive dialogue about identifying and selecting opportunities to pursue. I understand the difficulty companies might face in accepting this step because
it could be perceived as a move that increases costs without providing
an easily identifiable benefit. However, it is not vastly different from
companies investing in initiatives with delayed and difficult-to-measure
outcomes, such as personnel training or cultural transformations. A crucial consideration in these cases also involves weighing the potential
costs and risks associated with *not implementing* these interventions.

Separating Diagnosis and Solutions Across Different Providers

This recommendation involves distributing the responsibilities of identifying problems and implementing solutions among different service
providers. In this setup, the professional service firm that diagnoses a
problem or pinpoints an opportunity will not be the one carrying out the
solution. This approach directly addresses the dual roles of professional

service firms as agents and vendors, helping to alleviate the notable flaws in their agency. It protects buyers from the pervasive influence of commercial institutional logic in professional services. It could potentially diminish the "bias to action," where professionals are inclined to suggest action in ambiguous circumstances. Similarly, it could reduce the "familiarity bias," where professionals tend to recommend solutions with which they are familiar and to which they have ready access. As previously discussed, this volatile combination often leads organizations to pursue mediocre opportunities for professional service work using less-than-optimal strategies.

The most convincing proof of this approach's effectiveness comes from the healthcare sector. While the joint provision and treatment of health services are still widespread practices in many parts of the world (Rodwin & Okamoto, 2000), several countries have introduced policies separating the two (Chen, Gertler, & Yang, 2016; Chou, Yip, Lee, Huang et al., 2003; Hayase, 2003; Kwon, 2003). Take, for instance, most of Western Europe, where the joint prescribing and dispensing of drugs by a physician have been prohibited since the 13th century (Greiner, Zhang, & Tang, 2017).[2] Scientific evidence suggests that implementing such practices generally leads to results indicative of reducing SID, such as fewer prescriptions and decreased patient spending.

Y. J. Chou and colleagues (2003) examined the gradual implementation of a policy separating drug prescription and dispensing in Taiwan, and its influence on physicians' inclination to dispense drugs. Taiwan introduced a policy to separate the prescription and provision of drugs on March 1, 1997, a process phased in over four years. Clinics with on-site pharmacists could still dispense their own drugs, while clinics without on-site pharmacists had to rely on external pharmacies. Chou et al. (2003) compared data from before and after the implementation of

2. In 1231, Holy Roman Emperor Frederic II declared in the "The Constitutions of Melfi" that: "The confectionnarii [apothecaries] will prepare medicines at their own expense, under the control of Physicians, . . . The stationarius [local apothecary] will receive money for his drugs . . . That he [the physician] must not have any partnership with confectionnarii [apothecaries] . . . . That he [the physician] could not agree to cure a patient, including the preparation of medicines for a price already determined, and that he could not have a store of his own" (Frederik II, 1231; Greiner, Zhang, & Tang, 2017: 21).

the separation policy across these two types of clinics. Their empirical results supported the hypothesis that the separation policy could be an effective tool for mitigating SID.

The study's findings indicate a decrease in drug expenditure and a reduced propensity for a physician to prescribe a drug following the implementation of the policy. Additionally, the results demonstrate that physicians did not attempt to compensate for the lost revenue by increasing other treatments or patient visits, which underscores the effectiveness of separation policies in mitigating SID. It is noteworthy that the effectiveness of the separation policy was considerably reduced in clinics with on-site pharmacists. The authors attribute this to the fact that the physicians' income in such clinics remains tied to drug dispensing.

Other studies have similarly highlighted the beneficial effects of dividing the roles of diagnosis and service provision. For instance, Ben Greiner, Le Zhang, and Chengxiang Tang (2017) used a laboratory experimental setting to assess the efficacy of separating the tasks of prescription and treatment. Their findings suggested that this separation reduces the rate of physician overtreatment. These findings resonate with the observation that physicians who have access to imaging facilities tend to order more tests than those without such facilities. Consequently, several states in the United States have imposed restrictions on physicians' ability to conduct the imaging they recommend (Dranove & Wehner, 1994).

In professional services, early signs of this change can be seen in public accounting. In the wake of the Enron and Andersen scandals, Congress passed the Sarbanes-Oxley Act of 2002. Section 201 of this Act differentiates the roles of advisors and service providers in auditing contexts (Causholli, Knechel, Lin, & Sappington, 2013). The objective of Section 201 is, therefore, to enhance auditor independence by prohibiting auditors from providing several non-audit, advisory-related services (Alles, Kogan, & Vasarhelyi, 2005). There are possibilities to promote this idea a lot further in professional services.

Consider this: you are an investment bank tasked with evaluating a company's suitability for an initial public offering (IPO). You go through the rigmarole of assessments and eventually declare the company ready. But then, in a surprising twist, you step aside. You do not manage the IPO. Now, imagine you are a law firm, pouring over a company's intellectual property portfolio, dissecting the strength of each patent. You advise, guide, and strategize. And then, if and when it is time to enforce these patents in court, you hand over the baton to someone else. What about a consulting firm identifying cost reduction measures through organizational restructuring? They map out the problem areas, devise solutions, and then . . . they pass the implementation to a different firm. And consider an executive education provider that assesses a corporate client's talent needs. They investigate, analyze, and design the program, and then step back, allowing a different entity to deliver the program. In each case, the task of diagnosing the problem and the act of executing the solution are separated.

Should policymakers, professional service firms, and the buyers of their services choose to consider separating diagnosis and implementation, we'll inevitably be confronted by a deluge of questions. Where, precisely, does diagnosis end and implementation begin? How do we separate these intertwined functions in an industry so deeply entrenched in their fusion? Many of these questions will be impossible to anticipate. This might feel like déjà vu. We have navigated similar uncharted territory before, grappling with Section 201 of the Sarbanes-Oxley Act, wrestling to define the exact contours of what auditing means in today's dynamic business landscape, and to what extent auditing and advisory services can be truly separated (Alles, Kogan, & Vasarhelyi, 2005). But these looming challenges and unanswered questions should not dissuade us from initiating the conversation.

It is important to acknowledge that professional service work is generally more intricate than, say, the process of prescribing and dispensing medicine. Its intricacies can often make the path to a diagnosis unclear and the outcomes nebulous. And yet, research suggests that even in scenarios where the efforts and results of a diagnosis are not easily observable, separating the dual roles of treatment and diagnosis can lead to more dependable outcomes for consumers (Bester & Dahm, 2018). Furthermore, professional service work is widely recognized to benefit from substantial economies of scope, where it is often more cost-effective to deliver the diagnosis and treatment as a combined service (Dulleck & Kerschbamer, 2006; Emons, 2001). Although discussions around economies of scope typically do not consider instances of SID, buyers will invariably face tradeoffs. These tradeoffs encompass the immediate cost and time benefits of having a single entity diagnose the problem and implement the solution, weighed against the less apparent long-term risks and costs of SID.

One way to address this trade-off is to recognize that not all organizational activities necessitate this separation. Specifically, the empirical results presented in this book indicate that SID is not a constant phenomenon but appears prominently when the uncertainty regarding outcomes is notably high. Therefore, activities associated with the highest levels of outcome uncertainty should be the main targets for separating the roles of diagnosis and implementation.

Another potential advantage of dividing the roles of diagnosis and implementation lies in the increased codification of knowledge. A smooth handoff of work from the diagnosing entity to the implementing one is more likely to require comprehensive documentation of information. This elevated level of knowledge codification—wherein the work is formalized into documents, rules, and policies—proves particularly beneficial for purchasing complex knowledge-based goods and services. Research has revealed that such formalization activities increased role clarity and information transparency, thereby assisting firms in managing the complexity inherent in purchasing knowledge-based goods and services. Ultimately, these efforts lead to improved organizational performance (Edwards, 2017; O'Connor, Stacey, Entwistle, Llewellyn-Thomas et al., 2003; Prior, Hitihami Mudiyanselage, & Hussain, 2022).

These findings have implications akin to those in the field of organizational learning from non-standardized tasks, such as mergers and acquisitions (M&A) and reorganizations. While there are mixed views on whether firms can learn from non-standardized tasks, one line of research has underscored the importance of explicit knowledge codification when undertaking complex work. For example, Maurizio Zollo and Harbir Singh (2004), using a sample of 228 acquisitions in the US banking industry, discovered that although the general accumulation of M&A experience does not necessarily enhance a firm's future performance, the implementation of knowledge codification strategies significantly boosts future M&A performance. In this context, much like formalizing the procurement process for complex goods and services, Zollo and Singh (2004) found that investment in specific knowledge codification tools—such as due diligence checklists, integration manuals, systems training guides, financial evaluation models, and training/self-training packages—aids firms in navigating the uncertainty inherent in professional service environments.

Leveraging Organizational Cultures to Counter the Institutional Logic

In Chapters 6 and 7, we delved into the extensive reach of the commercial institutional logic. Its grip on professional services is formidable and steadfast, showing no signs of relenting soon. However, professional service organizations can counteract its influence by strategically leveraging their cultures. Cultures are amalgamations of symbols, norms, and assumptions that dictate how work is conducted, how collaboration is fostered, and what the company values (O'Reilly & Chatman, 1996; Schein, 1985). These are often unspoken and unwritten beliefs shared by employees of a given firm. A quick review of empirical research on the topic (Cameron & Quinn, 2006), or a visit to job sites such as Indeed or GlassDoor, reveals a wide variation in organizational cultures. The key point I wish to emphasize is that the culture of a specific professional service firm could serve as a protective buffer, shielding employees from the persistent sway of the commercial institutional logic.

Instead of losing ourselves in the theoretical mazes discussing what kinds of cultures could curb SID, let me venture into the raw narratives of two real-life stories that illuminate their desired features. Our first tale whisks us off to the chilly break of a Monday morning. The backdrop is a prospective client's office, where Ajay, a senior manager of an esteemed public accounting firm, stands before an extraordinary choice. He is presented with an enticing opportunity: a multi-million-dollar project, served up by a client who selected his firm from an extremely competitive lineup of providers. Yet there he stands and *declines* the lucrative offer. You might find yourself pondering, why would he back away from such a promising prospect?

Ajay held a staunch belief that his team was not the right match to carry out the project. Adding a note of intrigue is that Ajay made this decision during a pivotal year when he was considered for a promotion to managing director (MD). Now, as a senior partner of that firm, Ajay reflects on the event, his memory echoing with the angst he felt at the time: "*I was feeling terrible about it because I was up for promotion to MD that year.*" The reason Ajay felt dreadful about his decision was that, at the time, he feared it could cost him a promotion. The story sparked a wave of attention, not just mine but also from his fellow partners. Why, you ask? Because it was unusual and daring. It is not commonplace to hear stories of partners walking away from business, and even rarer for such actions to be celebrated.

Well, in cultures equipped to resist the pressures of SID, stories like this should indeed be celebrated. Employees should not feel angst or trepidation for walking away from business. Successfully battling SID calls for cultures in which delivering value to clients might mean letting someone else do the work or even advising that no action be taken at all. Typically, senior leaders of professional service firms do not share such narratives. But they absolutely should. These stories give rise to important cultural beliefs that powerfully guide people's behaviors in situations of uncertainty.

But the story doesn't conclude there. Ajay shared that he maintained a relationship with the company, even though their exchanges were somewhat awkward at first. There came a point when the company was acquired, and Ajay's original contact at that company moved on. But before he left, he called Ajay and referred him to a new executive taking over his role. As time rolled on, this newly formed connection resulted in an influx of business that was about four times the size of the initial project that Ajay originally turned down. The new executive, at some stage, revealed how Ajay was introduced to him: "*You can trust this guy, because he'll be honest if there's something he can't do.*" This blossoming relationship, Ajay concluded, is the reason he stood in front of his colleagues as a senior partner.

The story has a habit of replaying in my mind. It serves as a captivating illustration of a blueprint for cultures that not only resist SID but actively reshape themselves against it. It demonstrates that letting go of business, a necessary cultural feature in combatting SID, does not have to equate to diminished career progression. Yet, it also makes me wonder. Had the story not resulted in such an unexpected windfall, would Ajay have shared it? Would he even still be with the firm? The true test of a desirable culture would lie right there.

My second story involves a senior partner at a technology consulting firm, who shared his sales pitch to a prospective client with me and several of his colleagues. Previously, he had worked within the government sector, a client segment he currently serves. His pitch began not with numbers, statistics, or graphs, but with a story—a vivid, achingly human tale from his days as a government official. It was a story of a technology implementation project that had spiraled into a complete disaster. He painted a picture of the ordeal in breathtaking detail—the initial optimism giving way to tension until it became unbearable, and finally, the unmasked failure and the bitter pill of public humiliation. He conveyed that the failure was of such magnitude that the project earned a spot on the list of the year's most monumental technological debacles.

He argued that the critical piece missing from this chaotic puzzle was an "independent advisor." Someone who could have assessed the landscape with a dispassionate eye and warned the client that they were woefully unprepared for implementation. Now, he claimed, he was ready to be that missing piece for his potential clients. The narrative he wove was so compelling, so captivating, that I found myself drawn in. Yet, as he spoke, a single word began to echo in my mind: "independent." It seemed at odds with the overarching commercial logic that pervaded the sector, a logic that positioned professional service firm employees not just as advisors but also as executors of the plans they devised. And just as he had drawn the story to a close, a fellow partner blurted out,

"Well, now I really want to know if we got the business." The statement hung in the air, embodying much of what I have been trying to articulate. Can independence truly coexist with the driving question: "Have we secured the business?"

This story highlights another set of desirable cultural attributes that underscore developing a comprehensive understanding of SID on the part of both buyers and sellers. We collectively need to fathom the evolution of professional services over the past half a century. Not only have the services themselves morphed, but the very essence of what it means to be a professional has been reshaped in their wake. We are then drawn to consider the circumstances in which SID is most likely to stir. It is an awareness that can make the difference between being led and leading, between informed decisions and blind acquiescence. We need to consider the professional standing at the intersection of advisor and seller, acting out what we term an "imperfect agency."

In this duality, independence becomes a tightrope, walked all too often without the professionals' conscious realization of the precarious balancing act. Desirable cultures within professional service firms would not deny this reality but rather openly acknowledge it, assisting professionals in understanding their vulnerable position. Furthermore, in such a culture, dialogues regarding the confines of independence would not remain secluded within the walls of service providers. Instead, they would reach out to clients, endeavoring to craft optimal strategies to mitigate the perils of SID. My aspiration is that this book will empower both buyers and sellers to spark these crucial conversations.

CHAPTER SUMMARY

The implications of a systematic examination of supplier-induced demand for organizations are substantial, including considerations for managerial control and vertical integration, the economics of agglomeration, and the embeddedness of the economy. For instance, they unveil a fresh set of criteria necessary for determining the locus of control over organizational activities and suggest that the growing professionalization of the economy could heighten organizations' reliance on social relationships as conduits of expert influence. On a broader scale, supplier-induced demand prompts inquiries into the allocation of talent to professional services relative to other sectors of the economy. A principled approach to mitigating supplier-induced demand involves systematically undercutting the conditions conducive to its emergence. Rather than universally applying such measures to all transactions, they should be targeted toward those at higher risk. Specific strategies to contemplate in this regard include selectively insourcing certain transactions, bolstering in-house expertise for identifying opportunities and evaluating solutions, and separating the roles of diagnosis and implementation among different professional service providers. Additionally, professional service firms might explore harnessing organizational cultures as bulwarks against supplier-induced demand.

ACKNOWLEDGMENTS

The seeds of the ideas presented here, along with much of the empirical groundwork, were sown during my time at the Kellogg School of Management at Northwestern University. I am indebted to my advisors at Kellogg—Ranjay Gulati, Edward Zajac, Paul Hirsch, and Shane Greenstein—for their encouragement and guidance. The initial exploration of these concepts, captured in a paper, was honored with the Best Paper Award from the Organization and Management Theory Division at the Academy of Management.

During my tenure at the Ross School of Business at the University of Michigan, a host of colleagues played pivotal roles in shaping the ideas within this book. Among them are Norm Bishara, Ron Burt, Jerry Davis, Sendil Ethiraj, Ranjay Gulati, Exequiel Hernandez, Andy Hoffman, Michael Jensen, Jason Owen-Smith, Lance Sandelands, George Siedel, Olav Sorenson, Jose Uribe, Jim Walsh, Jim Westphal, and Ezra Zuckerman. Their insightful discussions and meticulous reviews enriched the content immeasurably. Special mention goes to Jerry Davis, Andy Hoffman, and Ranjay Gulati, whose input not only strengthened the book's substance but also provided invaluable advice on navigating the academic publishing landscape. I would not have been able to write this book without the continuous support of my colleagues at the Ross School of Business at the University of Michigan. I am grateful for their ideas, feedback, and friendship.

I am deeply grateful for the opportunities to present and refine the concepts discussed in this book at various academic institutions and conferences worldwide. These engagements, particularly those hosted by the University of California at Irvine, University of Chicago, London Business School, INSEAD, MIT, New York University, Stanford University, Tilburg University, University of Pennsylvania, and Washington University in St. Louis, have been instrumental in honing the clarity and persuasiveness of the arguments presented in this book.

In the journey of crafting this book, Madison Erdall's contribution as a research assistant was nothing short of remarkable. Her genuine curiosity about ideas, coupled with an analytical mind that never ceased to probe deeper, breathed life into the research process. Madison's unwavering diligence and meticulous attention to detail ensured that every aspect of the work was thoroughly scrutinized.

My collaboration with Oxford University Press, and in particular with my editor, James Cook, has been immensely rewarding. James's keen insight and unwavering support have been invaluable assets throughout this journey. I extend my gratitude to the anonymous reviewers at Oxford University Press whose thorough feedback contributed significantly to the refinement of the manuscript.

I am indebted to scores of professionals and business leaders who generously shared their time and insights during interviews conducted for this book. While confidentiality agreements prevent me from naming them, their contributions have been integral to enriching the empirical foundations of this work.

Above all, my deepest gratitude goes to my parents, Elena Bogach and the late Vitaly Sytch. They not only instilled in me a boundless curiosity about the world and a hunger for knowledge but also served as living examples of the joy found in crafting and sharing ideas. To my beloved wife, Svetla, I extend heartfelt thanks for her unwavering support throughout this endeavor, and especially for her candid feedback, which often served as the litmus test for the relevance and significance of the book's content.

Financial support from the Ross School of Business and the Kellogg School of Management's Dispute Resolution Research Center has been instrumental in realizing this project. Additionally, the Ross School of Business provided me with the invaluable gift of sabbatical time in Europe, allowing me the uninterrupted focus needed to bring this book to fruition. For this, I am profoundly grateful.

REFERENCES

Abbott, A. 1981. Status and status strain in the professions. *American Journal of Sociology*, 86(4): 819–835.

Abbott, A. 1988. *The system of professions: An essay on the division of expert labor.* Chicago: University of Chicago Press.

Abelson, R. P., Frey, K. P., & Gregg, A. P. 2014. *Experiments with people: Revelations from social psychology.* New York:Taylor and Francis.

Addams, L., Davis, B., Mano, R., & Nycum, V. 1997. Why are partners and managers leaving the big six? *Journal of Applied Business Research*, 13(4): 75–82.

Adler, P. S., & Seok-Woo, K. 2002. Social capital: Prospects for a new concept. *Academy of Management Review*, 27(1): 17–40.

Agrawal, A., & Mandelker, G. N. 1987. Managerial incentives and corporate investment and financing decisions. *Journal of Finance*, 42(4): 823–827.

Ahuja, G. 2000. The duality of collaboration: Inducements and opportunities in the formation of interfirm linkages. *Strategic Management Journal*, 21(3): 317–343.

Ahuja, G. 2022. *You get what you pay for: The rise of the index fund and exploration in R&D.* Working Paper. Hong Kong University of Science and Technology.

Ahuja, G., Soda, G., & Zaheer, A. 2012. The genesis and dynamics of organizational networks. *Organization Science*, 23(2): 434–448.

American Intellectual Property Law Association (AIPLA). 2011. *Annual Economic Survey.*

Alchian, A. 1963. Reliability of progress curves in airframe production. *Econometrica*, 31(4): 679–693.

Allan, S. M., Faulconbridge, J. R., & Thomas, P. 2019. The fearful and anxious professional: Partner experiences of working in the financialized professional services firm. *Work, Employment and Society*, 33(1): 112–130.

Alles, M. G., Kogan, A., & Vasarhelyi, M. A. 2005. Implications of section 201 of the Sarbanes–Oxley act: The role of the audit committee in managing the informational costs of the restriction on auditors engaging in consulting. *International Journal of Disclosure and Governance*, 2(1): 9–26.

Almeida, P., & Kogut, B. 1999. Localization of knowledge and the mobility of engineers in regional networks. *Management Science*, 45(7): 905–917.

Alvarez, G., Vermeulen, K., & Zimmon, V. 2020. The social law firm index. *Good2bSocial*. Accessed May 10, 2022.

Alvehus, J., & Spicer, A. 2012. Financialization as a strategy of workplace control in professional service firms. *Critical Perspectives on Accounting*, 23(7): 497–510.

Alvesson, M. 1993. Organizations as rhetoric: Knowledge-intensive firms and the struggle with ambiguity. *Journal of Management Studies*, 30(6): 997–1015.

Alvesson, M., Karreman, D., & Sullivan, K. 2015. Professional service firms and identity. In L. Empson, D. Muzio, J. Broschack, & B. Hinings (Eds.), *Oxford handbook of professional service firms*. New York:Oxford University Press.

Anagol, S., Cole, S., & Sarkar, S. 2017. Understanding the advice of commissions-motivated agents: Evidence from the Indian life insurance market. *Review of Economics and Statistics*, 99(1): 1–15.

Argote, L. 1982. Input uncertainty and organizational coordination in hospital emergency units. *Administrative Science Quarterly*, 27(3): 420–434.

Argote, L. 2013. *Organizational learning: Creating, retaining and transferring knowledge* (2nd ed.). New York:Springer Science & Business Media.

Argote, L., & Epple, D. 1990. Learning curves in manufacturing. *Science*, 247(4945): 920–924.

Argote, L., & Ingram, P. 2000. Knowledge transfer: A basis for competitive advantage in firms. *Organizational Behavior and Human Decision Processes*, 82(1): 150–169.

Argote, L., McEvily, B., & Reagans, R. 2003. Managing knowledge in organizations: An integrative framework and review of emerging themes. *Management Science*, 49(4): 571–582.

Argote, L., & Miron-Spektor, E. 2011. Organizational learning: From experience to knowledge. *Organization Science*, 22(5): 1123–1137.

Argyle, M., & Dean, J. 1965. Eye contact, distance, and affiliation. *Sociometry*, 28(3): 289–304.

Argyris, C. 1976. Single-loop and double-loop models in research on decision making. *Administrative Science Quarterly*, 21(3): 363–375.

Armbrüster, T. 2006. *The economics and sociology of management consulting*. Cambridge: Cambridge University Press.

Arrow, K. J. 1963. Uncertainty and the welfare economics of medical care. *American Economic Review*, 53: 941–973.

Ashforth, B. E., & Mael, F. 1989. Social identity theory and the organization. *Academy of Management Review*, 14(1): 20–39.

Ashforth, B. E., Rogers, K. M., & Corley, K. G. 2011. Identity in organizations: Exploring cross-level dynamics. *Organization Science* 22: 1144–1156.

Ashley, L., & Empson, L. 2013. Differentiation and discrimination: Understanding social class and social exclusion in leading law firms. *Human Relations*, 66(2): 219–244.

Ashley, L., & Empson, L. 2016. Explaining social exclusion and the "war for talent" in the UK's elite professional service firms. In D. B. Wilkins, R. L. Nelson,
R. Dinovitzer, & S. Headworth (Eds.), *Diversity in practice: Race, gender, and
class in legal and professional careers*: 114–138. Cambridge: Cambridge University
Press.

Bain. 2014. Bain & company time management study and impact on organizations. http://managersmagazine.com/wp-content/uploads/2014/09/2014.05.
05-Time-Management-Study.pdf.

Baker, G., & Parkin, R. 2006. The changing structure of the legal services industry
and the careers of lawyers. *North Carolina Law Review*, 84(5): 1635–1682.

Balafoutas, L., & Kerschbamer, R. 2020. Credence goods in the literature: What
the past fifteen years have taught us about fraud, incentives, and the role of
institutions. *Journal of Behavioral and Experimental Finance*, 26: 100285.

Balland, P.-A., Belso-Martínez, J. A., & Morrison, A. 2016. The dynamics of technical
and business knowledge networks in industrial clusters: Embeddedness, status, or
proximity? *Economic Geography*, 92(1): 35–60.

Bank of America. 2022. What we do. https://business.bofa.com/en-us/content/about-
us.html#whatwedo. Accessed April 22, 2022.

Barnard, N., & Underhill, D. 2022. ABA formal opinion approves lawyers' passive investment in law firms with nonlawyer owners. September 21. https://www.jdsupra.
com/legalnews/aba-formal-opinion-approves-lawyers-7208920/. Accessed April
5, 2022.

Barney, J. 1991. Firm resources and sustained competitive advantage. *Journal of
Management*, 17(1): 99–120.

Barney, J. B. 1999. How a firm's capabilities affect boundary decisions. *MIT Sloan
Management Review*, 40(3): 137.

Barry, J. 2018. Non-CPA firm ownership: From nice to have to have to have.
March. https://www.cpajournal.com/2018/03/23/non-cpa-firm-ownership-nice/.
Accessed April 28, 2023.

Bartlett, C. 2000. McKinsey & company: Managing knowledge and learning. *Harvard Business School Case 9-396-357*. Cambridge, MA: Harvard Business School
Press.

Bates v. State Bar of Arizona, 433 U.S. 350. 1977. In *433 U.S. 350*: U.S. Supreme Court.

Bathelt, H., Malmberg, A., & Maskell, P. 2004. Clusters and knowledge: Local
buzz, global pipelines and the process of knowledge creation. *Progress in Human
Geography*, 28(1): 31–56.

Bauer, W., Hämmerle, M., Schlund, S., & Vocke, C. 2015. Transforming to a hyper-
connected society and economy–towards an "industry 4.0." *Procedia Manufacturing*, 3: 417–424.

Bazerman, M., & Neale, M. 1992. Nonrational escalation of commitment in negotia-
tion. *European Management Journal*, 10(2): 163–168.

Bebchuk, L. A. 1984. Litigation and settlement under imperfect information. *RAND
Journal of Economics*, 15(3): 404–415.

Beckman, C. M., & Haunschild, P. R. 2002. Network learning: The effects of part-ners' heterogeneity of experience on corporate acquisitions. *Administrative Science Quarterly*, 47(1): 92–124.

Beckman, C. M., & Phillips, D. J. 2005. Interorganizational determinants of pro-motion: Client leadership and the attainment of women attorneys. *American Sociological Review*, 70: 678–701.

Benford, R. D., & Snow, D. A. 2000. Framing processes and social movements: An overview and assessment. *Annual Review of Sociology*: 611–639.

Bergh, D. D., & Lim, E. N.-K. 2008. Learning how to restructure: Absorptive capac-ity and improvisational views of restructuring actions and performance. *Strategic Management Journal*, 29(6): 593–616.

Bester, H., & Dahm, M. 2018. Credence goods, costly diagnosis and subjective evaluation. *Economic Journal*, 128(611): 1367–1394.

Bhattacharjee, Y. 2013. The mind of a con man. New York Times. April 26: 44–52.

Bielen, S., & Marneffe, W. 2018. Testing the lawyer-induced litigation hypothesis in Europe. *Applied Economics*, 50(16): 1837–1851.

Binning, G. 1950. Perturbations in childhood. *Canadian Medical Association Journal*, 63(5): 461.

Blackburn, R. 2006. Finance and the fourth dimension. *New Left Review*, 39(39): 39–72.

Blau, P. M. 1977. A macrosociological theory of social structure. *American Journal of Sociology*, 83(1): 26–54.

Blau, P. M. 1977. *Inequality and heterogeneity: A primitive theory of social structure.* New York: Free Press.

Bloom, P. 1984. Effective marketing for professional services, *Harvard Business Review*, September: 102–110.

Bloor, M. 1976. Bishop Berkeley and the adenotonsillectomy enigma: An explo-ration of variation in the social construction of medical disposals. *Sociology*, 10(1): 43–61.

Blumberg, M., & Pringle, C. D. 1982. The missing opportunity in organizational research: Some implications for a theory of work performance. *Academy of Management Review*, 7(4): 560–569.

Blumenstein, R. 1997. GM is building plants in developing nations to woo new markets. *Wall Street Journal*. August 4: A1.

Bogg, L., Diwan, V., Vora, K. S., & DeCosta, A. 2016. Impact of alternative maternal demand-side financial support programs in India on the cesarean section rates: In-dications of supplier-induced demand. *Maternal and Child Health Journal*, 20(1): 11–15.

Bossard, J. H. S. 1932. Residential propinquity as a factor in marriage selection. *American Journal of Sociology*, 38(2): 219–224.

Boston Consulting Group. 1968. *Perspectives on experience*. Boston: Boston Consult-ing Group Inc.

Bottger, P. C. 1984. Expertise and air time as bases of actual and perceived influence in problem-solving groups. *Journal of Applied Psychology*, 69: 214–221.

Bourdieu, P. 1977. *Outline of a theory of practice*. Cambridge: Cambridge University Press.

Boussebaa, M., & Faulconbridge, J. R. 2018. Professional service firms as agents of economic globalization: A political perspective. *Journal of Professions and Organization*, 6(1): 72–90.

Brivot, M. 2011. Controls of knowledge production, sharing and use in bureaucratized professional service firms. *Organization Studies*, 32(4): 489–508.

Brock, D. M. 2006. The changing professional organization: A review of competing archetypes. *International Journal of Management Reviews*, 8(3): 157–174.

Bromage, B. K., & Mayer, R. E. 1986. Quantitative and qualitative effects of repetition on learning from technical text. *Journal of Educational Psychology*, 78: 271–278.

Broschak, J. P. 2015. Client relationships in professional service firms. In L. Empson, D. Muzio, J. Broschack, & B. Hinings (Eds.), *Oxford handbook of professional service firms*: 304–326. New York:Oxford University Press.

Brown, J., & Minor, D. B. 2012. *Misconduct in credence good markets*. Washington, DC: National Bureau of Economic Research.

Browne, R. 2019. Banks must behave "more like technology companies" to survive, finance execs say. *CNBC, East Tech West*. https://www.cnbc.com/2019/11/18/banks-must-behave-like-tech-companies-to-survive-amid-fintech-threat.html#:~:text=Sberbank's%20Rafalovsky%20said%20that%20the,And%20WeBank's%20Ma%20agreed. November 18. Accessed June 10, 2022.

Bucher-Koenen, T., & Koenen, J. 2015. *Do Seemingly Smarter Consumers Get Better Advice?* Munich:Max Planck Institute for Social Law and Social Policy.

Buhr, H., & Owen-Smith, J. 2011. Networks as institutional support: Law firm and venture capitalist relations and regional diversity in high technology IPOs. *Research in Sociology of Work*, 21: 95–126.

Bulcroft, R. A., & Bulcroft, K. A. 1993. Race differences in attitudinal and motivational factors in the decision to marry. *Journal of Marriage and Family*, 55(2): 338–356.

Bull, R., & Robinson, G. R. 1981. The influence of eye-gaze, style of dress, and locality on the amount of money donated to charity. *Human Relations*, 34: 895–905.

Burns, L. 2018. *Autonomy: The quest to build the driverless car—And how it will reshape our world*. New York:Harper Collins.

Burt, R. 2022. Structural holes: Capstone, cautions, and enthusiasms In M. L. Small, B. L. Perry, B. Pescosolido, & E. Smith (Eds.), *Personal networks: Classic readings and new directions in egocentric analysis*. Cambridge:Cambridge University Press.

Burt, R. S. 1982. *Toward a structural theory of action: Network models of social structure, perception and action*. New York: Academic Press.

Burt, R. S. 1992. *Structural holes: The social structure of competition*. Cambridge, MA: Harvard University Press.

Burt, R. S. 2004. Structural holes and good ideas. *American Journal of Sociology,* 110(2): 349–400.

Business Research Company. 2022. *Professional services global market report 2022.* https://www.thebusinessresearchcompany.com/report/professional-services-global-market-report#.

Cai, C., Li, H., & Zhou, H. 2021. Learning by doing in mergers and acquisitions. *Accounting and Finance,* 62(S1): 1189–1229.

Cain, D. M., Loewenstein, G., & Moore, D. A. 2005. The dirt on coming clean: Perverse effects of disclosing conflicts of interest. *Journal of Legal Studies,* 34(1): 1–25.

Cameron, K. S., & Quinn, R. E. 2006. *Diagnosing and changing organizational culture: Based on the competing values framework.* Hoboken, NJ: Jossey-Bass.

Campbell, I., & Charlesworth, S. 2012. Salaried lawyers and billable hours: A new perspective from the sociology of work. *International Journal of the Legal Profession,* 19(1): 89–122.

Canbäck, S. 1998. Transaction cost theory and management consulting: Why do management consultants exist? Working Paper No. 9810002. Henley: Henley Management College. https://econwpa.ub.uni-muenchen.de/econ-wp/io/papers/9810/9810002.pdf. Accessed July 22, 2022.

Capron, L., & Mitchell, W. 2012. *Build, borrow, or buy: Solving the growth dilemma.* New York:Harvard Business Review Press.

Carlson, M. 2004. The vanishing partnership carrot: Where did it go? What does it mean for law firms? *Law Practice.* April 30: 31–34.

Carmignani, A., & Giacomelli, S. 2010. Too many lawyers? Litigation in Italian civil courts. Working Paper No. 745. February 22. Bank of Italy Temi di Discussione. https://ssrn.com/abstract=1669988.

Carmody, D., Vamadevan, T., & Cooper, S. M. 1982. Post tonsillectomy hemorrhage. *Journal of Laryngology and Otology,* 96(7): 635–638.

Carnahan, S., Rabier, M., & Uribe, J. 2022. Do managers' affiliation ties have a negative relationship with subordinates' interfirm mobility? Evidence from large us law firms. *Organization Science,* 33(1): 353–372.

Carreyrou, J. 2018. *Bad blood: Secrets and lies in a silicon valley startup.* New York: Knopf.

Cartwright, B. C., & Shwartz, R. D. 1973. The invocation of legal norms: An empirical investigation of Durkheim and Weber. *American Sociological Review,* 38: 340–353.

Casciaro, T. 1998. Seeing things clearly: Social structure, personality, and accuracy in social network perception. *Social Networks,* 20(4): 331–351.

Casciaro, T., Carley, K. M., & Krackhardt, D. 1999. Positive affectivity and accuracy in social network perception. *Motivation and Emotion,* 23(4): 285–306.

Causholli, M., Knechel, W. R., Lin, H., & Sappington, D. E. 2013. Competitive procurement of auditing services with limited information. *European Accounting Review,* 22(3): 573–605.

Cavusgil, S. T., van der Vegt, S., Dakhli, M., De Farias, S., Doria, E., Eroglu, S., & Wang, E. Y. 2021. International business in an accelerated VUCA world: Trends, disruptions, and coping strategies. *Rutgers Business Review*, 6(3): 219–243.

Centola, D., & Macy, M. 2007. Complex contagions and the weakness of long ties. *American Journal of Sociology*, 113(3): 702–734.

Chambers, S., & Johnston, R. 2000. Experience curves in services: Macro and micro level approaches. *International Journal of Operations & Production Management*, 20(7): 842–859.

Chappel, F. W. 1889. Examination of the throat and nose of two thousand children to determine the frequency of certain abnormal conditions. *American Journal of Medical Science*, 97: 148–154.

Chatman, J., & Cha, S. 2003. Leading by leveraging culture. *California Management Review*, 45(4): 20–33.

Chen, B. K., Gertler, P. J., & Yang, C.-Y. 2016. Physician ownership of complementary medical services. *Journal of Public Economics*, 144: 27–39.

Chen, F., Huang, J., Ma, M., & Yu, H. 2021. In-house deals: Agency and information asymmetry perspectives. *Corporate Ownership and Control*, 18(2): 8–19.

Chiappori, P. A., Salanié, B., & Weiss, Y. 2017. Partner choice, investment in children, and the marital college premium. *American Economic Review*, 107(8): 2109–2167.

Chieffallo, Bethany. 2019. "The Evolution of Legal Marketing." National Law Forum. https://nationallawforum.com/2019/12/19/the-evolution-of-legal-marketing/. Accessed November 29, 2022.

Chou, Y. J., Yip, W. C., Lee, C.-H., Huang, N., Sun, Y.-P., & Chang, H.-J. 2003. Impact of separating drug prescribing and dispensing on provider behaviour: Taiwan's experience. *Health Policy and Planning*, 18(3): 316–329.

Christensen, C. M., Wang, D., & van Bever, D. 2013. Consulting on the cusp of disruption, *Harvard Business Review*, 91: 106–114.

Cialdini, R. B. 1993. *Influence: Science and practice.* New York: Addison-Wesley Pub Co.

Clare, R. J. 2016. "Fit to fight?" How the physical condition of the conscripts contributed to the manpower crisis of 1917–18. *Journal of the Society for Army Historical Research*, 94(379): 225–244.

Clough, D. R., & Piezunka, H. 2020. Tie dissolution in market networks: A theory of vicarious performance feedback. *Administrative Science Quarterly*, 65(4): 972–1017.

Coffey, A. J. 1994. "Timing is everything:" Graduate accountants, time and commitment. *Sociology*, 28(4): 943–956.

Cohen, L., Gurun, U. G., & Kominers, S. D. 2016. The growing problem of patent trolling. *Science*, 352(6285): 521–522.

Collins, H., & Evans, R. 2007. *Rethinking expertise.* Chicago: University of Chicago Press.

Collins, H., & Pinch, T. 2005. Tonsils: Diagnosing and dealing with uncertainty. In *Dr Golem: How to think about medicine*: 61–83. Chicago: University of Chicago Press.

Consulting Group. 2013. *2013 lateral hiring study*. Chicago:Koltin Consulting Group.

Consulting Report. 2023. EY and KPMG push back-office teams to return to the office. April 3. https://www.theconsultingreport.com/ey-and-kpmg-push-back-office-teams-to-return-to-the-office/.

Cooper, D. J., Hinings, B., Greenwood, R., & Brown, J. L. 1996. Sedimentation and transformation in organizational change: The case of Canadian law firms. *Organization Studies*, 17(4): 623–647.

Cragg, J. G., & Donald, S. G. 1993. Testing identifiability and specification in instrumental variable models. *Econometric Theory*, 9: 222–240.

Cravath [@Cravath]. (n.d). Tweets. [Twitter profile]. https://twitter.com/cravath. Accessed March 26,2024.

Cyert, R. M., & March, J. G. 1963. *A behavioral theory of the firm*. Englewood Cliffs, NJ: Prentice-Hall.

D'Amato, A. 1993. Legal uncertainty. *California Law Review*, 71(1): 1–55.

Dacin, M. T. 1997. Isomorphism in context: The power and prescription of institutional norms. *Academy of Management Journal*, 40(1), 46–81.

Darby, M. R., & Karni, E. 1973. Free competition and the optimal amount of fraud. *Journal of Law and Economics*, 16(1): 67–88.

Darley, J. M., & Berscheid, E. 1967. Increased liking as a result of anticipating personal contact. *Journal of Personality and Social Psychology*, 20: 29–40.

Darr, E. D., Argote, L., & Epple, D. 1995. The acquisition, transfer, and depreciation of knowledge in service organizations: Productivity in franchises. *Management Science*, 41(11): 1750–1762.

Davis, G. F., & Greve, H. R. 1997. Corporate elite networks and governance changes in the 1980s. *American Journal of Sociology*, 103: 1–37.

Davis, G. F. 1991. Agents without principles? The spread of the poison pill through the intercorporate network. *Administrative Science Quarterly*, 36(4): 583–613.

Davis, G. F. 2011. *Managed by the markets: How finance re-shaped America*. New York: Oxford University Press.

Davis, J. P., Eisenhardt, K. M., & Bingham, C. B. 2009. Optimal structure, market dynamism, and the strategy of simple rules. *Administrative Science Quarterly*, 54: 413–452.

Deloitte Legal. 2020. *A changing world requires a new approach to law*. Deloitte.

Demski, J. S. 2003. Corporate conflicts of interest. *Journal of Economic Perspectives*, 17(2): 51–72.

Department of Justice. 2021. Federal contractor agrees to pay more than $6 million to settle overbilling allegations. February 19. https://www.justice.gov/opa/pr/federal-contractor-agrees-pay-more-6-million-settle-overbilling-allegations.

Department of Justice. 2022. Former CEO of Souktel, inc., agrees to pay $100,000 to settle false claims act allegations. September 1. https://www.justice.gov/usao-dc/pr/former-ceo-souktel-inc-agrees-pay-100000-settle-false-claims-act-allegations.

Dezalay, Y. 1992. *Marchands de droit*. Paris: Fayard.

Dhiwakar, M., Clement, W. A., Supriya, M., & McKerrow, W. 2008. Antibiotics to reduce post-tonsillectomy morbidity. *Cochrane Database of Systematic Reviews* (2).

DiMaggio, P. J., & Powell, W. W. 1983. The iron cage revisited: Institutional isomorphism and collective rationality in organizational fields. *American Sociological Review*, 48(2): 147–160.

Dingwall, R. 1983. Introduction. In R. Dingwall & P. S. C. Lewis (Eds.), *The sociology of the professions: Lawyers, doctors and others*. London: Macmillan.

Dodgson, M. 1993. Organizational learning: A review of some literatures. *Organization Studies*, 14(3): 375–394.

Dornan, T., Boshuizen, H., King, N., & Scherpbier, A. 2007. Experience-based learning: A model linking the processes and outcomes of medical students' workplace learning. *Medical Education*, 41(1): 84–91.

Dranove, D. & Wehner, P. 1994. Physician-induced demand for childbirths. *Journal of Health Economics*, 13(1): 61–73.

Drucker, J. 2022. Officials balked at a drug company's tax shelter. Auditors approved it anyway. New York Times. July 7. https://www.nytimes.com/2022/07/07/business/perrigo-omeprazole-taxes-ey.html. Accessed July 3, 2023.

Dulleck, U., & Kerschbamer, R. 2006. On doctors, mechanics, and computer specialists: The economics of credence goods. *Journal of Economic Literature*, 44(1): 5–42.

Durkheim, É. 1949. *Division of labor in society* (G. Simpson, Trans.). Glencoe, IL: Free Press.

Dwyer-Hemmings, L. 2018. "A wicked operation?" Tonsillectomy in twentieth-century Britain. *Medical History*, 62(2): 217–241.

Easterby-Smith, M., Lyles, M. A., & Tsang, E. W. K. 2008. Inter-organizational knowledge transfer: Current themes and future prospects. *Journal of Management Studies*, 45(4): 677–690.

Eddy, D. 1984. Variations in physician practice: The role of uncertainty. *Health Affairs*, 3(2): 74–89.

Edelman, L. B., & Suchman, M. C. 1997. The legal environments of organizations. *Annual Review of Sociology*, 23: 479–515.

Edelman, L. B., Uggen, C., & Erlanger, H. S. 1999. The endogeneity of legal regulation: Grievance procedures as rational myth. *American Journal of Sociology*, 105(2): 406–454.

Editorial Board. 1928. Tonsillectomy in the United States. *Journal of the American Medical Association*, 91(16): 1195–1197.

Edwards, B. P. 2017. The professional prospectus: A call for effective professional disclosure. *Washington & Lee Law Review*, 74: 1457.

Egan, M. 2019. Brokers versus retail investors: Conflicting interests and dominated products. *Journal of Finance*, 74(3): 1217–1260.

Eisen, B. 2022. Wells Fargo to pay record CFPB fine to settle allegations it harmed customers. *Wall Street Journal*. December 20. https://www.wsj.com/articles/wells-fargo-reaches-3-7-billion-deal-with-regulators-over-consumer-banking-11671546132. Accessed June 12, 2022.

Eisenberg, T. 2009. U.S. Chamber of commerce liability survey: Inaccurate, unfair, and bad for business. *Journal of Empirical Legal Studies*, 6(4): 969–1002.

Eisenhardt, K. M. 1989. Agency theory: An assessment and review. *Academy of Management Review*, 14(1): 57–74.

EIU. 2018. In brief: Operational complexity. Accessed December 9, 2022.

Ellsberg, D. 1961. Risk, ambiguity, and the savage axioms. *Quarterly Journal of Economics*, 75(4): 643–669.

Emerson, R. M. 1962. Power-dependence relations. *American Sociological Review*, 27(1): 31–41.

Emerson, R. M. 1981. Social exchange theory. In M. Rosenberg & R. H. Turner (Eds.), *Social psychology: Sociological perspectives*: 30–65. New York: Basic Books.

Emons, W. 2001. Credence goods monopolists. *International Journal of Industrial Organization*, 19(3–4): 375–389.

Empson, L., & Chapman, C. 2006. Partnership versus corporation: Implications of alternative forms of governance in professional service firms. In R. Greenwood & R. Suddaby (Eds.), *Professional service firms*: 139–170. Bingley, UK: Emerald Group Publishing Limited.

Epple, D., Argote, L., & Murphy, K. 1996. An empirical investigation of the microstructure of knowledge acquisition and transfer through learning by doing. *Operations Research*, 44(1): 77–86.

Epstein, A. M., Begg, C. B., & McNeil, B. J. 1986. The use of ambulatory testing in prepaid and fee-for-service group practices. Relation to perceived profitability. *New England Journal of Medicine*, 314(17): 1089–1094.

Ernst, B. & Kieser, A. 2002. Consultants as agents of anxiety and providers of managerial control. *Academy of Management Proceedings*, 2002(1): C1–C6.

Ertugrul, M. & Krishnan, K. 2014. Investment banks in dual roles: Acquirer M&A advisors as underwriters. *Journal of Financial Research*, 37(2): 159–189.

Evans, R. G. 1974. Supplier-induced demand: Some empirical evidence and implications. In M. Perlman (Ed.), *The economics of health and medical care*: 162–173. Camden, UK: Palgrave Macmillan.

Ezzamel, M., Willmott, H., & Worthington, F. 2008. Manufacturing shareholder value: The role of accounting in organizational transformation. *Accounting, Organizations and Society*, 33(2–3): 107–140.

Fahlenbrach, R., Low, A., & Stulz, R. 2010. Why do firms appoint CEOs as outside directors? *Journal of Financial Economics*, 97: 12–32.

Falk, E. B., Berkman, E. T., Mann, T., Harrison, B., & Lieberman, M. D. 2010. Predicting persuasion-induced behavior change from the brain. *Journal of Neuroscience*, 30(25): 8421–8424.

Fama, E. F., & Jensen, M. C. 1983. Separation of ownership and control. *Journal of Law & Economics*, 26(2): 301–325.

Fama, E. F. 1980. Agency problems and the theory of the firm. *Journal of Political Economy*, 88(2): 288–307.

Farr, C. 2019. The inside story of why Amazon bought PillPack in its effort to crack the $500 billion prescription market. CNBC. May 10.

Faulconbridge, J. R., & Muzio, D. 2009. The financialization of large law firms: Situated discourses and practices of reorganization. *Journal of Economic Geography*, 9(5): 641–661.

Faulconbridge, J. R., & Muzio, D. 2016. Global professional service firms and the challenge of institutional complexity: "Field relocation" as a response strategy. *Journal of Management Studies*, 53(1): 89–124.

Feld, S. L. 1981. The focused organization of social ties. *American Journal of Sociology*, 86(5): 1015–1035.

Fernandez, R. M., & Gould, R. V. 1994. A dilemma of state power: Brokerage and influence in the national health policy domain. *American Journal of Sociology*, 99(6): 1455–1491.

Fernandez-Mateo, I. 2007. Who pays the price of brokerage? Transferring constraint through price setting in the staffing sector. *American Sociological Review*, 72: 291–317.

Festinger, L. 1950. Informal social communication. *Psychological Review*, 57(5): 271–282.

Festinger, L., Schachter, S., & Back, K. 1950. *Social pressures in informal groups: A study of human factors in housing*. New York: Harper.

Financial Times. 2021. The changing face of professional services. https://professional.ft.com/_/view_pdf/file/1142/bf8bbf7081c/-.

Fiol, C. M., & Lyles, M. A. 1985. Organizational learning. *Academy of Management Review*, 10(4): 803–813.

Fish and Richardson. 2016. Fish & Richardson named #1 top patent litigation firm for 13th consecutive year by corporate counsel magazine. *Fish & Richardson*. June 7. https://www.fr.com/news/top-patent-lit-firm-year-13-06-07-2016/. Accessed September 13, 2024.

Fish and Richardson. 2023. Lex Machina ranks Fish & Richardson most active firm for patent defense and PTAB work. *Fish & Richardson*. March 2. https://www.fr.com/news/lex-machina-ranks-fish-richardson-most-active-firm-for-patent-defense-and-ptab-work-03-02-2023/. Accessed September 13, 2024.

Folland, S., Goodman, A. C., & Stano, M. 2016. *The economics of health and health care*. New York: Routledge.

Forsythe, M., & Bogdanich, W. 2022. McKinsey charged in South African corruption case. New York Times. September 30.

Fortney, S. S. 2000. Soul for sale: An empirical study of associate satisfaction, law firm culture, and the effects of billable hour requirements. *UMKC Law Review*, 69(2): 239–309.

Fortune. 2019. Fortune 500. *Fortune*. https://fortune.com/fortune500/2019/. Accessed November 9, 2022.

Frederik II. 1231. Liber augustalis. Titulus 46: Novae *constitutiones regni siciliae*.

French, J., & Raven, B. 1959. The bases of social power. In D. Cartwright (Ed.), *Studies in social power*, vol. 7: 150–167. Ann Arbor, MI: Institute for Social Research.

Friedland, R., & Alford, R. R. 1991. Bringing society back in: Symbols, practices, and institutional contradictions. In W. W. Powell & P. J. DiMaggio (Eds.), *The new institutionalism in organizational analysis*. 232–267. Chicago: University of Chicago Press.

Fuchs, V. R. 1978. The supply of surgeons and the demand for operations. *Journal of Human Resources*, 13: 35–56.

Funk, R. J., Sytch, M., & Nahm, P. 2023. Shared social contexts and the dynamics of inequality in social networks. Under Review.

Furusten, S. 2009. Management consultants as improvising agents of stability. *Scandinavian Journal of Management*, 25(3): 264–274.

Gaba, V., & Terlaak, A. 2013. Decomposing uncertainty and its effects on imitation in firm exit decisions. *Organization Science*, 24(6): 1847–1869.

Galanter, M., & Palay, T. 1990. Why the big get bigger: The promotion-to-partner tournament and the growth of large law firms. *Virginia Law Review*, 76: 747.

Galbraith, J. R. 1971. Matrix organizational design. *Business Horizons*, 14(1): 29–40.

Galbraith, J. R. 1973. *Designing Complex Organizations*. Reading, MA: Addison-Wesley Pub. Co.

Gao, C., & McDonald, R. 2022. Shaping nascent industries: Innovation strategy and regulatory uncertainty in personal genomics. *Administrative Science Quarterly*, 67(4), 915–967.

Gardner, H. K., Anand, N., & Morris, T. 2008. Chartering new territory: Diversification, legitimacy, and practice area creation in professional service firms. *Journal of Organizational Behavior*, 29(8): 1101–1121.

Giddens, A. 1984. *The constitution of society: Outline of the theory of structuration*. Berkeley: University of California Press.

Giddens, A. 1990. *The consequences of modernity*. Cambridge: Polity.

Giddens, A. 1991. *Modernity and self-identity*. Cambridge: Polity.

Gilbert, B. B. 1965. Health and politics: The British physical deterioration report of 1904. *Bulletin of the History of Medicine*, 39(2): 143–153.

Gino, F., & Staats, B. 2015. Why organizations don't learn, *Harvard Business Review*, 93(11): 110–118.

Glover, J. A. 1938. The incidence of tonsillectomy in school children: (Section of epidemiology and state medicine). *Proceedings of the Royal Society of Medicine*, 31(10): 1219–1236.

Gokkaya, S., Liu, X., & Stulz, R. M. 2023. Do firms with specialized M&A staff make better acquisitions? *Journal of Financial Economics*, 147(1): 75–105.

Goldman, M., Kiyohara, O., & Pfannensteil, D. A. 1984. Interpersonal touch, social labeling, and the foot-in-the-door effect. *Journal of Social Psychology*, 125: 143–147.

Gopalkrishnan, N., & Babacan, H. 2007. Ties that bind: Marriage and partner choice in the Indian community in Australia in a transnational context. *Identities: Global Studies in Culture and Power*, 14(4).

Granovetter, M. 1985. Economic action and social structure: The problem of embeddedness. *American Journal of Sociology*, 91(3): 481–510.

Greenberg, D. S. 1972. Don't ask the barber whether you need a haircut. The Saturday Review, November 25: 58–59.

Greenwood, R., & Empson, L. 2003. The professional partnership: Relic or exemplary form of governance? *Organization Studies*, 24(6): 909–933.

Greenwood, R., Li, S. X., & Deephouse, D. L. 2002. *Does governance matter?* Working Paper. School of Business, University of Alberta.

Greenwood, R., Li, S. X., Prakash, R., & Deephouse, D. L. 2005. Reputation, diversification, and organizational explanations of performance in professional service firms. *Organization Science*, 16(6): 661–673.

Greiner, B., Zhang, L., & Tang, C. 2017. Separation of prescription and treatment in health care markets: A laboratory experiment. *Health Economics*, 26(S3): 21–35.

Greve, H. R. 2003. *Organizational learning from performance feedback: A behavioral perspective on innovation and change*. New York: Cambridge University Press.

Greve, H. R., Rowley, T., & Shipilov, A. 2014. *Network advantage: How to unlock value from your alliances and partnerships*. New York: Jossey-Bass.

Grey, C. 1994. Career as a project of the self and labour process discipline. *Sociology*, 28(1): 479–497.

Griffin, J. M. 2021. Ten years of evidence: Was fraud a force in the financial crisis? *Journal of Economic Literature*, 59(4): 1293–1321.

Griffiths, C. 2005. From profit per equity partner to earnings per partner: A new indicator of financial health. The Lawyer.com. September 13. https://www.thelawyer.com/uk100/2005/eppvpep.html.

Grimshaw, J. M., Patey, A. M., Kirkham, K. R., Hall, A., Dowling, S. K., Rodondi, N., Ellen, M., Kool, T., van Dulmen, S. A., Kerr, E. A., Linklater, S., Levinson, W., & Bhatia, R. S. 2020. De-implementing wisely: Developing the evidence base to reduce low-value care. *BMJ Quality & Safety*, 29(5): 409–417.

Grob, G. N. 2007. The rise and decline of tonsillectomy in twentieth-century America. *Journal of the History of Medicine and Allied Sciences*, 62(4): 383–421.

Grol, R., & Grimshaw, J. 2003. From best evidence to best practice: Effective implementation of change in patients' care. *Lancet*, 362(9391): 1225–1230.

Groß, C., & Kieser, A. 2006. Are consultants moving towards professionalization? In R. Greenwood & R. Suddaby (Eds.), *Professional service firms*, vol. 24: 69–100. Bingley, UK: Emerald Group Publishing Limited.

Grossmann, C. 2022. Why alternative legal service providers are on the rise. January 4. https://www.ey.com/en_hr/tax/why-alternative-legal-service-providers-are-on-the-rise. Accessed April 21, 2022.

Groysberg, B. 2010. *Chasing stars*. Princeton, NJ: Princeton University Press.

Groysberg, B., Lee, L. E., & Nanda, A. 2008. Can they take it with them? The portability of star knowledge workers' performance. *Management Science*, 54(7): 1213–1230.

Gruber, H. 1994. The yield factor and the learning curve in semiconductor production. *Applied Economics*, 26(8): 837–843.

Grumet, L.. 2007. Should non-CPAs be allowed to co-own CPA firms? May. http://archives.cpajournal.com/2007/507/perspectives/p7.htm. Accessed April 27, 2023.

Grytten, J., & Sørensen, R. 2001. Type of contract and supplier-induced demand for primary physicians in Norway. *Journal of Health Economics*, 20(3): 379–393.

Gulati, R. 1995. Social structure and alliance formation patterns: A longitudinal analysis. *Administrative Science Quarterly*, 40(4): 619–652.

Gulati, R. 2007. *Managing network resources: Alliances, affiliations, and other relational assets*. Oxford: Oxford University Press.

Gulati, R. 2009. *Reorganize for resilience*. Cambridge, MA: Harvard Business School Press.

Gulati, R. 2022. *Deep purpose: The heart and soul of high-performance companies*. Penguin UK.

Gulati, R., & Gargiulo, M. 1999. Where do interorganizational networks come from? *American Journal of Sociology*, 104(5): 1439–1493.

Gulati, R., & Kletter, D. 2005. Shrinking core, expanding periphery: The relational architecture of high-performing organizations. *California Management Review*, 47(3): 77–104.

Gulati, R., & Nickerson, J. 2008. Interorganizational trust, governance choice, and exchange performance. *Organization Science*, 19(5): 669–806.

Gulati, R., & Srivastava, S. B. 2014. Bringing agency back into network research: Constrained agency and network action. In *Contemporary perspectives on organizational social networks*: 73–93. Bingley, UK: Emerald Group Publishing Limited.

Gulati, R., & Sytch, M. 2007. Dependence asymmetry and joint dependence in interorganizational relationships: Effects of embeddedness on exchange performance. *Administrative Science Quarterly*, 52: 32–69.

Gulati, R., & Sytch, M. 2008. Does familiarity breed trust? Revisiting the antecedents of trust. *Managerial and Decision Economics*, 29: 165–190.

Gulati, R., Sytch, M., & Tatarynowicz, A. 2012. The rise and fall of small worlds: Exploring the evolutionary dynamics of social structure. *Organization Science*, 23(2): 449–471.

Gunz, H. P., & Gunz, S. P. 2006. Professional ethics in formal organizations. In R. Greenwood & R. Suddaby (Eds.), *Professional service firms*, vol. 24: 257–281. Bingley, UK: Emerald Group Publishing Limited.

Guttman, D., & Willner, B. 1976. *The shadow government: The government's multi-billion-dollar giveaway of its decision-making powers to private management consultants, "experts," and think tanks.* New York:Pantheon Books.

Haleblian, J., & Finkelstein, S. 1999. The influence of organizational acquisition experience on acquisition performance: A behavioral learning perspective. *Administrative Science Quarterly*, 44(1): 29–56.

Hall, D. T., Schneider, B., & Nygren, H. T. 1970. Personal factors in organizational identification. *Administrative Science Quarterly*, 15(2): 176–190.

Hamilton, R. W. 1995. Registered limited liability partnerships: Present at the birth (nearly). *University of Colorado Law Review*, 66: 1065–1074.

Hans, V. P., & Eisenberg. 2011. The predictability of juries. *DePaul Law Review*, 60(2): 375–396.

Hargadon, A., & Sutton, R. I. 1997. Technology brokering and innovation in a product development firm. *Administrative Science Quarterly*, 42(December): 716–749.

Hargadon, A. B. 2002. Brokering knowledge: Linking learning and innovation. *Research in Organizational Behavior*, 24: 41–85.

Harvey, J. B. 1974. The Abilene paradox: The management of agreement. *Organizational Dynamics*, 3(1): 63–80.

Haslem, B. 2005. Managerial opportunism during corporate litigation. *Journal of Finance*, LX(4): 2013–2041.

Haunschild, P. R., & Miner, A. S. 1997. Modes of interorganizational imitation: The effects of outcome salience and uncertainty. *Administrative Science Quarterly*, 42(3): 472–500.

Haveman, H. A., & Rao, H. 1997. Structuring a theory of moral sentiments: Institutional and organizational coevolution in the early thrift industry. *American Journal of Sociology*, 102: 1606–1651.

Haveman, H. A. 2022. *The power of organizations: A new approach to organizational theory.* Princeton, NJ: Princeton University Press.

Hayase, Y. 2003. Problems of the separation of prescription and dispensing. *Yakugaku Zasshi: Journal of the Pharmaceutical Society of Japan*, 123(3): 121–132.

Hayward, M. L. A. 2002. When do firms learn from their acquisition experience? Evidence from 1990–1995. *Strategic Management Journal*, 23(1): 21–39.

Heckman, J. J. 1979. Sample selection bias as a specification error. *Econometrica*, 47: 153–161.

Hedberg, B. 1981. How organizations learn and unlearn. In P. Nystrom & W. Starbuck (Eds.), *Handbook of organizational design: Adapting organisations to their environment*: 3–27. Oxford: Oxford University Press.

Henisz, W. J., & Delios, A. 2001. Uncertainty, imitation, and plant location: Japanese multinational corporations, 1990–1996. *Administrative Science Quarterly*, 46(3): 443–475.

Henisz, W. J., & Delios, A. 2004. Information or influence? The benefits of experience for managing political uncertainty. *Strategic Organization*, 2(4): 389–421.

Hewitt, L. L. 2005. *Patent infringement litigation.* Boston, MA: Aspatore Inc.

Hickson, G. B., Altemeier, W. A., & Perrin, J. M. 1987. Physician reimbursement by salary or fee-for-service: Effect on physician practice behavior in a randomized prospective study. *Pediatrics*, 80(3): 344–350.

Higgins, T. 2023. Elon Musk revives old banking dream in pursuing $250 billion Twitter valuation. *Wall Street Journal*. April 1.

Hirsch, P. M. 1986. From ambushes to golden parachutes: Corporate takeovers as an instance of cultural framing and institutional integration. *American Journal of Sociology*, 91(4): 800–837.

Hirst, E., & Schweitzer, M. 1990. Electric-utility resource planning and decision making. *Risk Analysis*, 10: 137–146.

Hoang, H., & Rothaermel, F. T. 2005. The effect of general and partner-specific alliance experience on joint R&D project performance. *Academy of Management Journal*, 48(2): 332–345.

Hogg, M. A., Adelman, J. R., & Blagg, R. D. 2010. Religion in the face of uncertainty: An uncertainty-identity theory account of religiousness. *Personality and Social Psychology review*, 14(1): 72–83.

Horst, J. S. 2013. Context and repetition in word learning. *Frontiers in Psychology*, 4: 149.

Hsu, M., Bhatt, M., Adolphs, R., Tranel, D., & Camerer, C. F. 2005. Neural systems responding to degrees of uncertainty in human decision-making. *Science*, 310(5754): 1680–1683.

Huber, G. P. 1991. Organizational learning: The contributing processes and the literatures. *Organization Science*, 2(1): 88–115.

Indeed. 2012. "If you're not a partner, you don't count." *McGladrey Reviews* (blog), *Indeed.com*. April 18. https://www.indeed.com/cmp/Mcgladrey/reviews/if-you-re-not-a-partner-you-don-t-count?id=3df4f6f60737b572.

Indeed. 2013. "Productive and results driven environment." *JPMorgan Chase & Co Reviews* (blog), *Indeed.com*. November 12. https://www.indeed.com/cmp/JP Morgan-Chase-&-Co-7555c073/reviews/productive-and-results-driven-envirom ent?id=7a4ef7e599507976.

Indeed. 2013a. "Churn and burn." *JPMorgan Chase & Co Reviews* (blog), *Indeed.com*. July 16. https://www.indeed.com/cmp/JPMorgan-Chase-&-Co-7555c073/ reviews/churn-and-burn?id=bb7acd6737f111a3.

Indeed. 2013b. "Productive and results-driven environment." *JPMorgan Chase & Co Reviews* (blog), *Indeed.com*. November 12. https://www.indeed.com/cmp/ JPMorgan-Chase-&-Co-7555c073/reviews/productive-and-results-driven-envir oment?id=7a4ef7e599507976.

Indeed. 2016. "Productive and challenging workplace." *Deloitte Reviews* (blog), *Indeed.com*. April 27. https://www.indeed.com/cmp/Deloitte/reviews/productive-and-challenging-workplace?id=4739470a49bcf26b.

Indeed. 2017a. "Culture has significantly deteriorated over the years." *EY Reviews* (blog), *Indeed.com*. December 14. https://www.indeed.com/cmp/Ey/ reviews/culture-has-significantly-deteriorated-over-the-years?id=7ae23c07b 1466e23.

Indeed. 2017b. "Not what you think." *Deloitte Reviews* (blog), *Indeed.com*. September 2. https://www.indeed.com/cmp/Deloitte/reviews/not-what-you-think?id=9d50ba8bfcf5d4b2.

Indeed. 2018a. "Avoid at all costs." *EY Reviews* (blog), *Indeed.com*. July 18. https://www.indeed.com/cmp/Ey/reviews/avoid-at-all-costs?id=54b6b29508886f8a.

Indeed. 2018b. "Great company to work for." *JPMorgan Chase & Co Reviews* (blog), *Indeed.com*. October 9. https://www.indeed.com/cmp/JPMorgan-Chase-&-Co-7555c073/reviews/great-company-to-work-for?id=64b34f4ac676be68.

Indeed. 2018c. "Not for everyone." *PwC Reviews* (blog), *Indeed.com*. January 3. https://www.indeed.com/cmp/Pwc/reviews/not-for-everyone?id=08b96f85c08c6048.

Indeed. 2019a. "Bait and Switch." *PwC Reviews* (blog), *Indeed.com*. June 28. https://www.indeed.com/cmp/Pwc/reviews?fcountry=US&ftext=sell#.

Indeed. 2019a. "Good organization." *Deloitte Reviews* (blog), *Indeed.com*. January 9. https://www.indeed.com/cmp/Deloitte/reviews/good-organization?id=99c5e0be eb271a61.

Indeed. 2019b. "Cutting edge projects and employee development." *KPMG Reviews* (blog), *Indeed.com*. March 25. https://www.indeed.com/cmp/Kpmg-0828bc85/reviews/cutting-edge-projects-and-employee-development?id=356a0f35be6e 9dfe.

Indeed. 2019b. "Gotta sell to be successful." *KPMG Reviews* (blog), *Indeed.com*. December 21. https://www.indeed.com/cmp/Kpmg-0828bc85/reviews/gotta-sell-to-be-successful?id=36ef52ae0f50fc99.

Indeed. 2019c. "Good organization." *Deloitte Reviews* (blog), *Indeed.com*. January 9. https://www.indeed.com/cmp/Deloitte/reviews/good-organization?id=99c5e0be eb271a61.

Indeed. 2019d. "Sell or don't get promoted." *KPMG Reviews* (blog), *Indeed.com*. April 3. https://www.indeed.com/cmp/Kpmg-0828bc85/reviews/sell-or-don-t-get-promoted?id=1fbe3866efe99fb7.

Indeed. 2020a. "Difficult to advance." *JPMorgan Chase & Co Reviews* (blog), *Indeed.com*. April 29. https://www.indeed.com/cmp/JPMorgan-Chase-&-Co-7555c073/reviews/difficult-to-advance?id=65d48f518ab10977.

Indeed. 2020b. "Management lies about expectations." *EY Reviews* (blog), *Indeed.com*. July 30. https://www.indeed.com/cmp/Ey/reviews/management-lies-about-expectations?id=83f63a5d05fb51fe.

Indeed. 2021. "Stressful and professionally dangerous." *Morgan Stanley Reviews* (blog), *Indeed.com*. August 16. https://www.indeed.com/cmp/Morgan-Stanley/reviews/stressful-and-professionally-dangerous?id=96f4f1bbec139fe3.

Indeed. 2022. "Do not recommend to work here unless you are fresh out of school. Great co-workers and training." *Bank of America Reviews* (blog), *Indeed.com*. February 23. https://www.indeed.com/cmp/Bank-of-America/reviews/do-not-recommend-to-work-here-unless-you-are-fresh-out-of-school-great-co-workers-and-training?id=88ccc956fdd6ffcd.

IP Law & Business. 2009. August/September.

Jacobs, J. 2023. Exxonmobil boosts energy trading ambitions to compete against peers. *Financial Times*. February 9: 4–18.

Jacquart, P., & Antonakis, J. 2015. When does charisma matter for top-level leaders? Effect of attributional ambiguity. *Academy of Management Journal*, 58(4): 1051–1074.

Janis, I. L., & Mann, L. 1977. *Decision-making: A psychological analysis of conflict, choice and commitment*. New York: Free Press.

Jensen, M. C., & Meckling, W. H. 1976. Theory of the firm: Managerial behavior, agency costs and ownership structure. *Journal of Financial Economics*, 3(4): 305–360.

Jetten, J., Hogg, M. A., & Mullin, B.-A. 2000. In-group variability and motivation to reduce subjective uncertainty. *Group Dynamics: Theory, Research, and Practice*, 4(2): 184.

Johs, Allison C. 2020. 2020 websites & marketing. American Bar Association. https://www.americanbar.org/groups/law_practice/resources/tech-report/archive/websites-marketing/Koltin. Accessed November 29, 2022.

Jones, Leigh. 2017. "A look back at big law advertising from A to ZZZZZ." *Law.com*. https://www.law.com/2017/06/14/a-look-back-at-big-law-advertising-from-a-to-zzzzz/. Accessed February 13, 2024.

Kabo, F., Hwang, Y., Levenstein, M., & Owen-Smith, J. 2015. Shared paths to the lab: A sociospatial network analysis of collaboration. *Environment and Behavior*, 47(1): 57–84.

Kakkar, H., & Sivanathan, N. 2017. When the appeal of a dominant leader is greater than a prestige leader. *Proceedings of the National Academy of Sciences*, 114(26): 6734–6739.

Kale, P., Dyer, J. H., & Singh, H. 2002. Alliance capability, stock market response, and long-term alliance success: The role of the alliance function. *Strategic Management Journal*, 23(8): 747–767.

Kalnins, A., & Chung, W. 2004. Resource-seeking agglomeration: A study of market entry in the lodging industry. *Strategic Management Journal*, 25: 689–699.

Kane, A. A., Argote, L., & Levine, J. M. 2005. Knowledge transfer between groups via personnel rotation: Effects of social identity and knowledge quality. *Organizational Behavior and Human Decision Processes*, 96(1): 56–71.

Karreman, D., & Alvesson, M. 2009. Resisting resistance: Counter-resistance, consent and compliance in a consultancy firm. *Human Relations*, 62(8): 1115–1144.

Kelly, J. 2022. Bosses are winning the battle to get workers back to the office. *Forbes*. September 20. https://www.forbes.com/sites/jackkelly/2022/09/20/bosses-are-winning-the-battle-to-get-workers-back-to-the-office/?sh=79d99309783e. Accessed May 10, 2023.

Kerschbamer, R., Neururer, D., & Sutter, M. 2019. Credence goods markets and the informational value of new media: A natural field experiment. Max Planck Institute for Research on Collective Goods (SSRN Electronic Journal). MPI Collective Goods Discussion Paper, No. 2019/3.

Kesner, I. F., Shapiro, D. L., & Sharma, A. 1994. Brokering mergers: An agency theory perspective on the role of representatives. *Academy of Management Journal*, 37(3): 703–721.

Kieser, A. 2001. Applying theories of fashion to management consulting: How consultants turn concepts into fashions and sell them to managers. *Academy of Management Proceedings*, 2001(1): A1–A6.

King, A. W., & Zeithaml, C. P. 2001. Competencies and firm performance: Examining the causal ambiguity paradox. *Strategic Management Journal*, 22(1): 75–99.

King, G., & Zeng, L. 2001. Logistic regression in rare events data. *Political Analysis*, 9: 1371–1363.

King-Casas, B., Tomlin, D., Anen, C., Camerer, C. F., Quartz, S. R., & Montague, P. R. 2005. Getting to know you: Reputation and trust in a two-person economic exchange. *Science*, 308(5718): 78–83.

Klucharev, V., Smidts, A., & Fernández, G. 2008. Brain mechanisms of persuasion: How "expert power" modulates memory and attitudes. *Social Cognitive and Affective Neuroscience*, 3(4): 353–366.

Knappenberger, B. (2024). *Turning Point: The Bomb and the Cold War*. [Documentary series, Episode 3, Institutional Insanity]. *Netflix*. https://www.netflix.com/

Knight, F. H. 1921. *Risk, uncertainty and profit*. Boston: Houghton Mifflin.

Knyazeva, A., Knyazeva, D., & Masulis, R. W. 2013. The supply of corporate directors and board independence. *Review of Financial Studies*, 26(6): 1561–1605.

Kosnik, R. D., & Shapiro, D. L. 1997. Agency conflicts between investment banks and corporate clients in merger and acquisition transactions: Causes and remedies. *Academy of Management Perspectives*, 11(1): 7–20.

KPMG International. 2011. Confronting complexity: Research findings and insights: 1–41. Amstelveen: KPMG. https://ub-sachdokpdf.ub.unibas.ch/sachdok/2011/BAU_1_5663533.pdf.

KPMG International. 2022. Together for better: KPMG p/s annual report. April 14. https://assets.kpmg/content/dam/kpmg/dk/pdf/dk-2022/dk-KPMG-annual-report-2021.pdf.

Krishna, P., & Lee, D. 2001. Post-tonsillectomy bleeding: A meta-analysis. *Laryngoscope*, 111(8): 1358–1361.

Kwon, S. 2003. Pharmaceutical reform and physician strikes in Korea: Separation of drug prescribing and dispensing. *Social Science & Medicine*, 57(3): 529–538.

Labelle, R., Stoddart, G., & Rice, T. 1994. A re-examination of the meaning and importance of supplier-induced demand. *Journal of Health Economics*, 13(3): 347–368.

Larson, M. S. 1977. *The rise of professionalism: A sociological analysis*: Berkeley: University of California Press.

Latane, B. 1981. The psychology of social impact. *American Psychologist*, 36: 343–356.

Latane, B., Liu, J. H., Nowak, A., Bonevento, M., & Zheng, L. 1995. Distance matters: Physical space and social impact. *Personality and Social Psychology Bulletin*, 21(8): 795–805.

Lavie, D. 2006. The competitive advantage of interconnected firms: An extension of the resource-based view. *Academy of Management Review*, 31(3): 638–658.

Law Firm Associates. 2021.Is the brass ring of partnership tarnished for young lawyers? *Law.com*. November 20. https://www.law.com/americanlawyer/2021/11/30/is-the-brass-ring-of-partnership-tarnished-for-young-lawyers/.

Lawler, E. J., & Yoon, J. 1993. Power and the emergence of commitment behavior in negotiated exchange. *American Sociological Review*, 58(4): 465–481.

Lawler, E. J., & Yoon, J. 1998. Network structure and emotion in exchange relationships. *American Sociological Review*, 63(6): 871–894.

Lawler, E. J., Thye, S. R., & Yoon, J. 2000. Emotion and group cohesion in productive exchange. *American Journal of Sociology*, 106(3): 616–657.

Lawrence, T. B., Malhotra, N., & Morris, T. 2012. Episodic and systemic power in the transformation of professional service firms. *Journal of Management Studies*, 49(1): 102–143.

Leicht, K. T., & Lyman, E. C. W. 2006. Markets, institutions, and the crisis of professional practice. In R. Greenwood & R. Suddaby (Eds.), *Professional service firms*, vol. 24: 17–44: Bingley, UK: Emerald Group Publishing Limited.

Levine, J. M., & Argote, L. 2017. Group and organizational learning: Past, present, and future. In L. Argote & J. M. Levine (Eds.), *Oxford handbook of group and organizational learning*: 3–20. New York:Oxford University Press.

Levitt, B., & March, J. G. 1988. Organizational learning. *Annual Review of Sociology*, 14(1): 319–338.

Levitt, T. 2004. Marketing myopia. *Harvard Business Review*, 82(7/8): 138–149.

Lipshitz, R., & Strauss, O. 1997. Coping with uncertainty: A naturalistic decision-making analysis. *Organizational Behavior and Human Decision Processes*, 69(2): 149–163.

Littlepage, G. E., Schmidt, G. W., Whisler, E. W., & Frost, A. G. 1995. Input-process-output analysis of influence and performance in problem-solving groups. *Journal of Experimental Social Psychology*, 68: 877–889.

Liu, X., & Mills, A. 2007. Supplier-induced demand and unnecessary care. In A. Preker & V. Velenyi (Eds.), *Public ends, private means: Strategic purchasing of health services*: 279–310. Chicago: World Bank Publications.

Lorrain, F., & White, H. C. 1971. Structural equivalence of individuals in social networks. *Journal of Mathematical Sociology*, 1: 49–80.

Løwendahl, B. 2005. *Strategic management of professional service firms*. Frederiksberg:Copenhagen Business School Press DK.

Lowry, M., & Shu, S. 2002. Litigation risk and IPO underpricing. *Journal of Financial Economics*, 65: 309–335.

Lupu, I., & Empson, L. 2015. Illusion and overwork: Playing the game in the accounting field. *Accounting, Auditing & Accountability Journal*, 28(8): 1310–1340.

Lynch, T., & Maclean, J. 2000. Exploring the benefits of task repetition and recycling for classroom language learning. *Language Teaching Research*, 4(3): 221–250.

Macaulay, S. 1963. Non-contractual relations in business: A preliminary study. *American Sociological Review*, 28: 55

Maclnnis, D. J., Moorman, C., & Jaworski, B. J. 1991. Enhancing and measuring consumers' motivation, opportunity, and ability to process brand information from ads. *Journal of Marketing*, 55(4): 32–53.

Mael, F. 1988. *Organizational identification: Construct Redefinition and a Field Application with Organizational Alumni.* Detroit: Wayne State University.

Malhotra, N., Morris, T., & Hinings, C. R. 2006. Variation in organizational form among professional service organizations. In R. Greenwood & R. Suddaby (Eds.), *Professional service firms*, vol. 24: 171–202. Bingley, UK: Emerald Group Publishing Limited.

Marcec, D. 2018. CEO tenure rates. February 18. https://corpgov.law.harvard.edu/2018/02/12/ceo-tenure-rates/. Accessed May 4, 2023.

March, J. G. 1987. Ambiguity and accounting: The elusive link between information and decision making. *Accounting, Organizations and Society*, 12(2): 153–168.

March, J. G. 1991. Exploration and exploitation in organizational learning. *Organization Science*, 2(1): 71–87.

March, J. G. 2010. *The ambiguities of experience.* Ithaca, NY: Cornell University Press.

March, J. G., & Olsen, J. P. 1975. The uncertainty of the past: Organizational learning under ambiguity. *European Journal of Political Research*, 3(2): 147–171.

March, J. G., & Simon, H. A. 1958. *Organizations.* New York: John Wiley & Sons.

March, J. G., Sproull, L. S., & Tamuz, M. 1991. Learning from samples of one or fewer. *Organization Science*, 2(1): 1–13.

Margolick, D. 1993. They're selling lawyers on selling their services. New York Times. March 26: D16.

Maroulis, S., Sytch, M., & Cifuentes, C. 2024. From spark to spotlight: The emergence of the most valuable ideas in networks. Under Review.

Marquis, C., & Battilana, J. 2009. Acting globally but thinking locally? The enduring influence of local communities on organizations. *Research in Organizational Behavior*, 29: 283–302.

Marquis, C. 2003. The pressure of the past: Network imprinting in intercorporate communities. *Administrative Science Quarterly*, 48: 655–689.

Mayer, R. C., Davis, J. H., & Schoorman, F. D. 1995. An integration model of organizational trust. *Academy of Management Review*, 20(3): 709–734.

Mazzucato, M., & Collington, R. 2023. *The big con: How the consulting industry weakens our businesses, infantilizes our governments, and warps our economies.* New York: Penguin.

McDonald, D. 2014. *The firm: The story of McKinsey and its secret influence on American business.* New York: Simon and Schuster.

McEvily, B., Jaffee, J., & Tortoriello, M. 2012. Not all bridging ties are equal: Network imprinting and firm growth in the Nashville legal industry 1933–1978. *Organization Science*, 23(2): 547–563.

McEvily, B., Perrone, V., & Zaheer, A. 2003. Trust as an organizing principle. Organization Science, 14(1), 91–103.

McGavin, L. H. 1903. A note on tonsillar enlargements and their treatment. *Lancet*, 162(4178): 876–878.

McLaughlin, R. M. 1996. Adverse contract incentives and investment banker reputation: Target firm tender offer fees. *Journal of Financial Research*, 19(1): 135–156.

Merket, R., & Swidan, H. 2019. Flying with(out) a safety net: Financial hedging in the airline industry. *Transportation Research Part E: Logistics and Transportation Review*, 127: 206–219.

Meshi, D., Biele, G., Korn, C. W., & Heekeren, H. R. 2012. How expert advice influences decision making. *PLoS One*, 7(11): e49748.

Meyer, J. W., & Rowan, B. 1977. Institutionalized organizations: Formal structure as myth and ceremony. *American Journal of Sociology*, 83(2): 340–363.

Michaels, D., & Gryta, T. 2020. GE to pay $200 million to settle SEC accounting probe. *Wall Street Journal*. December 9.

Michel, A. 2011. Transcending socialization: A nine-year ethnography of the body's role in organizational control and knowledge workers' transformation. *Administrative Science Quarterly*, 56(3): 325–368.

Mikolon, S., Kolberg, A., Haumann, T., & Wieseke, J. 2015. The complex role of complexity: How service providers can mitigate negative effects of perceived service complexity when selling professional services. *Journal of Service Research*, 18(4): 513–528.

Milgram, S. 1963. Behavioral study of obedience. *Journal of Abnormal & Social Psychology*, 67(4): 371–378.

Milgram, S. 1965. Some conditions of obedience and disobedience to authority. *Human Relations*, 18(1): 57–76.

Miller, F. J. W., Court, S. D. M., Walton, W. S., & Knox, E. G. 1960. *Growing up in Newcastle upon Tyne: A continuing study of health and illness in young children within their families*. London: Oxford University Press.

Milliken, F. J. 1987. Three types of perceived uncertainty about the environment: State, effect, and response uncertainty. *Academy of Management Review*, 12(1): 133–143.

Mimra, W., Rasch, A., & Waibel, C. 2016. Second opinions in markets for expert services: Experimental evidence. *Journal of Economic Behavior & Organization*, 131: 106–125.

Mitchell, V., & Harvey, W. S. 2015. Marketing and reputation within professional service firms. In L. Empson, D. Muzio, J. Broschak, & B. Hinings (Eds.), *Oxford handbook of professional service firms*: 279–303. New York:Oxford University Press.

Moeller, S. B., Schlingemann, F. P., & Stulz, R. M. 2005. Wealth destruction on a massive scale? A study of acquiring-firm returns in the recent merger wave. *Journal of Finance*, 60(2): 757–782.

Mohammadshahi, M., Yazdani, S., Olyaeemanesh, A., Akbari Sari, A., Yaseri, M., & Emamgholipour Sefiddashti, S. 2019. A scoping review of components of physician-induced demand for designing a conceptual framework. *Journal of Preventive Medicine and Public Health*, 52(2): 72–81.

Molm, L. D., & Cook, K. S. 1995. Social exchange and exchange networks. In K. S. Cook, G. A. Fine, & J. House (Eds.), *Sociological perspectives on social psychology*: 209–235. Boston: Allyn and Bacon.

Mooney, G., & Ryan, M. 1993. Agency in health care: Getting beyond first principles. *Journal of Health Economics*, 12(2): 125–135.

Moore, K. A. 2000. Judges, juries, and patent cases-an empirical peek inside the black box. *Michigan Law Review*, 99, 365.

Morris, T., & Empson, L. 1998. Organization and expertise: An exploration of knowledge bases and the management of accounting and consulting firms. *Accounting, Organizations and Society*, 23(5): 609–624.

Morris, T., & Pinnington, A. 1998. Promotion to partner in professional service firms. *Human Relations*, 51(1): 3–24.

Morrison, A. D., & Wilhelm Jr, W. J. 2008. The demise of investment banking partnerships: Theory and evidence. *Journal of Finance*, 63(1): 311–350.

Muehlfeld, K., Rao Sahib, P., & Van Witteloostuijn, A. 2012. A contextual theory of organizational learning from failures and successes: A study of acquisition completion in the global newspaper industry, 1981–2008. *Strategic Management Journal*, 33(8): 938–964.

Mullahy, J. 1997. Instrumental-variable estimation of count data models: Applications to models of cigarette smoking behavior. *Review of Economics and Statistics*, 79(4): 586–593.

Mullainathan, S., Noeth, M., & Schoar, A. 2012. *The market for financial advice: An audit study*:1–32. Washington, DC: National Bureau of Economic Research.

Mullin, B.-A., & Hogg, M. A. 1999. Motivations for group membership: The role of subjective importance and uncertainty reduction. *Basic and Applied Social Psychology*, 21(2): 91–102.

Nachum, L. 1999. Measurement of productivity of professional services. *International Journal of Operations & Production Management*, 19(9): 922–950.

National Association of State Boards of Accountancy. 2018. *Uniform accountancy act standards for regulation* (8th ed.). Nashville, TN: National Association of State Boards of Accountancy.

Nelson, R. L. 1988. *Partners with power: Social transformation of the large law firm*. Berkeley: University of California Press.

Nelson, R. L., & Nielson, L. B. 2000. Cops, counsel, and entrepreneurs: Constructing the role of inside counsel in large corporations. *Law & Society Review*, 34(2): 457–494.

Newport, C. 2013. *Deep work: Rules for focused success in a distracted world*. New York:Little Brown.

Nguyen, L., & Nishant, N. 2023. JP Morgan asks senior bankers to return to office for five days a week—Memo. *Reuters*. April 12. https://www.reuters.com/business/finance/jpmorgan-managing-directors-asked-work-office-five-days-week-memo-2023-04-12/. Accessed May 10, 2023.

Nohria, N., & Eccles, R. G. 1992. *Networks and organizations: Structure, form, and action*. Boston: Harvard Business School Press.

O'Connor, A. M., Stacey, D., Entwistle, V., Llewellyn-Thomas, H., Rovner, D., Holmes-Rovner, M., Tait, V., Tetroe, J., Fiset, V., Barry, M., & Jones, J. 2003. Decision aids for people facing health treatment or screening decisions. *Cochrane Database of Systematic Reviews* (2): Cd001431.

O'Reilly, C. A., & Chatman, J. A. 1996. Culture as social control: Corporations, cults, and commitment. *Research in organizational behavior*, vol. 18: 157. Amsterdam: Elsevier Science.

Oh, S. T. 2022. *Competition as the key mechanism in the co-evolution of technology and society: The case of autonomous vehicles*. Working Paper.

Ordóñez, L. D., Schweitzer, M. E., Galinsky, A. D., & Bazerman, M. H. 2009. Goals gone wild: The systematic side effects of overprescribing goal setting. *Academy of Management Perspectives*, 23: 6–16.

Ozmel, U., Reuer, J. J., & Wu, C. W. 2017. Interorganizational imitation and acquisitions of high-tech ventures. *Strategic Management Journal*, 38(13): 2647–2665.

Packard, M. D., & Clark, B. B. 2020. On the mitigability of uncertainty and the choice between predictive and nonpredictive strategy. *Academy of Management Review*, 45(4): 766–786.

Packard, M. D., Clark, B. B., & Klein, P. G. 2017. Uncertainty types and transitions in the entrepreneurial process. *Organization Science*, 28(5): 840–856.

Padgett, J. F., & Powell, W. W. 2012. *The emergence of organizations and markets*. Princeton, NJ: Princeton University Press.

Pahnke, E. C., Katila, R., & Eisenhardt, K. M. (2015). Who takes you to the dance? How partners' institutional logics influence innovation in young firms. *Administrative Science Quarterly*, 60(4), 596–633.

Parker, C., & Ruschena, D. 2011. The pressures of billable hours: Lessons from a survey of billing practices inside law firms. *University of St. Thomas Law Journal*, 9(2): 619–664.

Parsons, T. 1968. Professions. In D. Sills (Ed.), *International encyclopedia of the social sciences*, vol. 12: 536–547. New York: Macmillan, Free Press.

Parvinen, P., & Tikkanen, H. 2007. Incentive asymmetries in the mergers and acquisitions process*. *Journal of Management Studies*, 44(5): 759–787.

Patterson, M. L. 1976. An arousal model of interpersonal intimacy. *Psychological Review*, 83: 235–245.

Pentland, B. T. 1993. Getting comfortable with the numbers: Auditing and the microproduction of macro-order. *Accounting, Organizations and Society*, 18(7–8): 605–620.

Peters, T. J., & Waterman, R. H. 1982. *In search of excellence: Lessons from America's best-run companies.* New York: Harper & Row.

Pfarrer, M. D., Pollock, T. G., & Rindova, V. P. 2010. A tale of two assets: The effects of firm reputation and celebrity on earnings surprises and investors' reactions. *Academy of Management Journal*, 53(5): 1131–1152.

Pfeffer, J., & Salancik, G. R. 1978. *The external control of organizations: A resource dependence perspective.* New York: Harper and Row.

Pfeffer, J., Salancik, G. R., & Leblebici, H. 1976. The effect of uncertainty on the use of social influence in organizational decision making. *Administrative Science Quarterly*, 21(2): 227–245.

Pinnington, A., & Morris, T. 2003. Archetype change in professional organizations: Survey evidence from large law firms. *British Journal of Management*, 14(1): 85–99.

Pitchbook. 2018. Changing roles in a changing landscape: How (and why) investment banks are reinventing themselves. June 10. https://pitchbook.com/blog/changing-roles-in-a-changing-landscape-how-and-why-investments-banks-are-reinventing-themselves. Accessed September 20, 2022.

Polinsky, A. M., & Rubinfeld, D. L. 2003. Aligning the interests of lawyers and clients. *American Law and Economics Review*, 5(1): 165–188.

Popper, M., & Lipshitz, R. 2000a. Organizational learning: Mechanisms, culture, and feasibility. *Management Learning*, 31(2): 181–196.

Popper, M., & Lipshitz, R. 2000b. Installing mechanisms and instilling values: The role of leaders in organizational learning. *Learning Organization*, 7(3): 135–145.

Posen, H. E., & Levinthal, D. A. 2012. Chasing a moving target: Exploitation and exploration in dynamic environments. *Management Science*, 58(3): 587–601.

Posen, H. E., Lee, J., & Yi, S. 2013. The power of imperfect imitation. *Strategic Management Journal*, 34: 149–164.

Poulfelt, F., & Olson, T. H. 2018. *Management consulting today and tomorrow.* New York: Routledge.

Powell, W. W. 1998. Learning from collaboration: Knowledge and networks in the biotechnology and pharmaceutical industries. *California Management Review*, 40(3): 228–240.

Powell, W. W., Packalen, K. A., & Whittington, K. B. 2012. Organizational and institutional genesis: The emergence of high-tech clusters in the life sciences. In J. F. Padgett & W. W. Powell (Eds.), *The emergence of organization and markets*: 434–465. Princeton, NJ: Princeton University Press.

Priest, G. L., & Klein, B. 1984. The selection of disputes for litigation. *Journal of Legal Studies*, 13: 1–55.

Prior, D. D., Hitihami Mudiyanselage, L. K., & Hussain, O. K. 2022. Does formalization or centralization mitigate uncertainty in knowledge-intensive procurement? *Journal of Business & Industrial Marketing*, 37(2): 433–446.

Puranam, P., & Vanneste, B. S. 2016. *Corporate strategy: Tools for analysis and decision-making.* New York: Cambridge University Press.

Pustorino, A., & Rabinowitz, A. 1998. Recent developments in non-CPA ownership of CPA firms. *CPA Journal*, 68(2): 12–13.

Ramarajan, L. 2014. Past, present and future research on multiple identities: Toward an intrapersonal network approach. *Academy of Management Annals*, 8: 589–659.

Rao, H. 2008. *Market rebels*. Princeton, NJ: Princeton University Press.

Rao, H., Greve, H. R., & Davis, G. F. 2001. Fool's gold: Social proof in the initiation and abandonment of coverage by Wall Street analysts. *Administrative Science Quarterly*, 46: 502–526.

Rao, H., Yue, L. Q., & Ingram, P. 2011. Laws of attraction: Regulatory arbitrage in the face of activism in right-to-work states. *American Sociological Review*, 76(3): 365–385.

Rapping, L. 1965. Learning and World War II production functions. *Review of Economics and Statistics*, 47(1): 81–86.

Rau, R. 2000. Investment bank market share, contingent fee payments, and the performance of acquiring firms. *Journal of Financial Economics*, 56(2): 293–324.

Rauch, J. 2006. Own company stock in defined contribution pension plans: A takeover defense? *Journal of Financial Economics*, 81: 379–410.

Raymond, N. 2016. Ex-McKinsey partner arrested for fraudulent invoices, expenses. January 4. https://www.reuters.com/article/us-usa-crime-mckinsey/ex-mckinsey -partner-arrested-for-fraudulent-invoices-expenses-idUSKBN0UI1ZJ20160105. Accessed March 26, 2023.

Reagans, R., & McEvily, B. 2003. Network structure and knowledge transfer: The effects of cohesion and range. *Administrative Science Quarterly*, 48: 240–267.

Reagans, R., & Zuckerman, E. 2008. Why knowledge does not equal power: The network redundancy trade-off. *Industrial and Corporate Change*, 17(5): 904–944.

Reed, M. I. 1996. Expert power and control in late modernity: An empirical review and theoretical synthesis. *Organization Studies*, 71(4): 573–597.

Reid, M. 2008. Contemporary marketing in professional services. *Journal of Services Marketing*, 22(5): 374–384.

Replogle, T. J. 2017. The business of law: Evolution of the legal services market. *Michigan Business and Entrepreneurial Law Review*, 6(2): 287–304.

Richardson, J. R., & Peacock, S. J. 2006. Supplier-induced demand: Reconsidering the theories and new Australian evidence. *Applied Health Economics Health Policy*, 5(2): 87–98.

Rider, C. 2014. Educational credentials, hiring, and intra-occupational inequality: Evidence from law firm dissolutions. *SSRN Electronic Journal*. https://papers.ssrn.com/sol3/papers.cfm?abstract_id=1881028.

Rider, C. I., & Tan, D. 2015. Labor market advantages of organizational status: A study of lateral partner hiring by large us law firms. *Organization Science*, 26(2): 356–372.

Riketta, M. 2005. Organizational identification: A meta-analysis. *Journal of Vocational Behavior*, 66(2): 358–384.

Rindova, V. P., Pollock, T. G., & Hayward, M. L. A. 2006. Celebrity firms: The social construction of market popularity. *Academy of Management Review*, 31(1): 50–71.

Rindova, V. P., Williamson, I. O., & Petkova, A. P. 2010. Reputation as an intangible asset: Reflections on theory and methods in two empirical studies of business school reputations. *Journal of Management*, 36(3): 610–619.

Rindova, V. P., Williamson, I. O., Petkova, A. P., & Sever, J. M. 2005. Being good or being known: An empirical examination of the dimensions, antecedents, and consequences of organizational reputation. *Academy of Management Journal*, 48(6): 1033–1049.

Rivera, L. A. 2011. Ivies, extracurriculars, and exclusion: Elite employers' use of educational credentials. *Research in Social Stratification and Mobility*, 29(1): 71–90.

Rivera, L. A. 2012. Hiring as cultural matching: The case of elite professional service firms. *American Sociological Review*, 77(6): 999–1022.

Rivera, L. A. 2016. *Pedigree: How elite students get elite jobs*. Princeton, NJ: Princeton University Press.

Rizzo, J. A., & Blumenthal, J. A. 1996. Is the target income hypothesis an economic heresy? *Medical Care Research and Review*, 53(3): 243–266; discussion 267–293.

Robinson, N. 2016. When lawyers don't get all the profits: Non-lawyer ownership, access, and professionalism. *Georgetown Journal of Legal Ethics*, 29(1): 1–62.

Rodwin, M. A., & Okamoto, A. 2000. Physicians' conflicts of interest in Japan and the United States: Lessons for the United States. *Journal of Health Politics, Policy and Law*, 25(2): 343–376.

Roemer, M. 1961. Bed supply and hospital utilization: A natural experiment. *Hospitals*, 35: 36–42.

Rogelberg, S. G., Scott, C., & Kello, J. 2007. The science and fiction of meetings. *MIT Sloan Management Review*, 48(2): 18–21.

Ross, W. G. 1996. *The honest hour: The ethics of the time-based billing by attorneys*. Durham, NC: Carolina Academic Press.

Roth, M. 2020. Regulating the future: Autonomous vehicles and the role of government. *Iowa Law Review* 105(3): 1411–1446.

Rubino, K. 2022. Reminder: Billing more than 24 hours in a day is a pretty obvious red flag. November 9. https://abovethelaw.com/2022/11/reminder-billing-more-than-24-hours-in-a-day-is-a-pretty-obvious-red-flag/. Accessed March 25, 2023.

Saam, Nicole J. 2012. Economics approaches to management consulting. In T. Clark & M. Kipping (Eds.), *The Oxford handbook of management consulting*: 207–224. Oxford: Oxford University Press.

Saint-Charles, J., & Mongeau, P. 2009. Different relationships for coping with ambiguity and uncertainty in organizations. *Social Networks*, 31(1): 33–39.

Sanchez-Burks, J., & Sytch, M. 2021. Reimagining the office for immensely human interactions. *MIT Sloan Management Review*, 62: 1–4.

Sarala, R. M., Junni, P., Cooper, C. L., & Tarba, S. Y. 2016. A sociocultural perspective on knowledge transfer in mergers and acquisitions. *Journal of Management*, 42(5): 1230–1249.

Saxenian, A. 1994. *Regional advantage: Culture and competition in Silicon Valley and Route 128.* Cambridge, MA: Harvard University Press.

Schein, E. H. 1985. *Organizational culture and leadership: A dynamic view.* Jossey-Bass.

Schneider, H. S. 2012. Agency problems and reputation in expert services: Evidence from auto repair. *Journal of Industrial Economics,* 60(3): 406–433.

Scott, E. S. 2000. Social norms and the legal regulation of marriage. *Virginia Law Review,* 86: 1901–1970.

Scott, R. W., & Davis, G. F. 2007. *Organizations and organizing: Rational, natural, and open system perspectives.* Upper Saddle River, NJ: Prentice Hall.

Segal, D. 1998. In the business of billing? *Washington Post.* March 22. https://www.washingtonpost.com/wp-srv/business/longterm/ethics/ethics2.htm. Accessed January 17, 2022.

Sewell, W. 1992. A theory of structure: Duality, agency, and transformation. *American Journal of Sociology,* 98(1): 1–29.

Seymour, W. N. 1992. Cheaper, faster civil justice. New York Times. January 7: A15.

Shafer, W. E., Lowe, D. J., & Fogarty, T. J. 2002. The effects of corporate ownership on public accountants' professionalism and ethics. *Accounting Horizons,* 16(2): 109–124.

Shah, V. 2022. The tech companies that want to build cars. *Car Expert.* January 15. https://www.carexpert.com.au/car-news/the-tech-companies-that-want-to-build-cars.

Sharma, A. 1997. Professional as agent: Knowledge asymmetry in agency exchange. *Academy of Management Review,* 22(3): 758–798.

Shaver, M., & Flyer, F. 2000. Agglomeration economies, firm heterogeneity, and foreign direct investment in the United States. *Strategic Management Journal,* 21: 1175–1193.

Shek, D. T., Chung, P. P., & Leung, H. 2015. Manufacturing economy vs. Service economy: Implications for service leadership. *International Journal on Disability and Human Development,* 14(3): 205–215.

Shigeoka, H., & Fushimi, K. 2014. Supplier-induced demand for newborn treatment: Evidence from Japan. *Journal of Health Economics,* 35: 162–178.

Shipilov, A., & Gawer, A. 2020. Integrating research on interorganizational networks and ecosystems. *Academy of Management Annals,* 14(1): 92–121.

Shrivastava, P. 1983. A typology of organizational learning systems. *Journal of Management Studies,* 20(1): 7–28.

Shubik, M. 1971. The dollar auction game: A paradox in noncooperative behavior and escalation. *Journal of Conflict Resolution,* 15(1): 109–111.

Siemsen, E., Roth, A., & Balasubramanian, S. 2008. How motivation, opportunity, and ability drive knowledge sharing: The constraining-factor model. *Journal of Operations Management,* 26(3): 426–445.

Simmel, G. 1955. *Conflict* (K. H. Wolf, Trans.). Glencoe, IL: Free Press.

Simon, N., & Taylor, M. 2016. Insights on the profession: How the consulting process is mastering increased complexity. *Consulting Magazine.* November 6. https://

www.consultingmag.com/sites/cmag/2016/11/06/insights-on-the-profession-ho
w-the-consulting-process-is-mastering-increased-complexity/?slreturn=202208
05185806. Accessed December 1, 2022.

Skjølsvik, T., Breunig, K. J., & Pemer, F. 2018. Digitalization of professional services: The case of value creation in virtual law firms. In P. Andersson, S. Movin,
M. Mähring, R. Teigland, & A. K. Wennberg (Eds.), *Managing digital transformation*: 155–174. Stockholm: Stockholm School of Economics Institute for
Research.

Sleesman, D. J., Conlon, D. E., McNamara, G., & Miles, J. E. 2012. Cleaning up the big
muddy: A meta-analytic review of the determinants of escalation of commitment.
Academy of Management Journal, 55(3): 541–562.

Small, M. L., & Adler, L. 2019. The role of space in the formation of social ties. *Annual
Review of Sociology*, 45(1): 111–132.

Sorenson, O., & Audia, P. G. 2000. The social structure of entrepreneurial activity: Geographic concentration of footwear production in the United States, 1940–1989.
American Journal of Sociology, 106(2): 424–461.

Sorenson, O., & Stuart, T. E. 2001. Syndication networks and the spatial distribution of venture capital investments. *American Journal of Sociology*, 106(6):
1546–1588.

Sorenson, O., & Waguespack, D. M. 2006. Social structure and exchange: Self-
confirming dynamics in Hollywood. *Administrative Science Quarterly*, 51(4):
560–589.

Spence, M. 1973. Job market signaling. *Quarterly Journal of Economics*, 87(3):
355–374.

Spier, K. 2007. Litigation. In M. A. Polinsky & S. Shavell (Eds.), *The handbook of law
and economics*, Vol1 (1st ed.): 259–342. Amsterdam: Elsevier.

Staw, B. M., & Ross, J. 1989. Understanding behavior in escalation situations. *Science*,
246(4927): 216–220.

Staw, B. M. 1997. The escalation of commitment: An update and appraisal. In Z.
Shapira (Ed.), *Organizational decision making*: 191–215. New York: Cambridge
University Press.

Stempel, J. 2022. Racketeering lawsuit against McKinsey revived by U.S.
appeals court. *Reuters*. January 19. https://www.reuters.com/legal/government/
racketeering-lawsuit-against-mckinsey-revived-by-us-appeals-court-2022-01-19
/. Accessed March 23, 2023.

Sterling, A., & Boxall, P. 2013. Lean production, employee learning and workplace
outcomes: A case analysis through the ability-motivation-opportunity framework.
Human Resource Management Journal, 23(3): 227–240.

Stern, I., & Westphal, J. D. 2010. Stealthy footsteps to the boardroom: Executives' backgrounds, sophisticated interpersonal influence behavior, and board
appointments. *Administrative Science Quarterly*, 55: 278–319.

Stock, J. H., & Yogo, M. 2002. *Testing for weak instruments in linear iv regression*.
NBER Technical Working Paper 284.

Storey, G. O. 2004. James Alison Glover (1874–1963). *Journal of Medical Biography*, 12(2): 77–81.

Stuart, T. E., & Ding, W. W. 2006. When do scientists become entrepreneurs? The social structure antecedents of commercial activity in the academic life sciences. *American Journal of Sociology*, 112(1): 97–144.

Stuart, T. E., & Sorenson, O. 2003. The geography and opportunity: Spatial heterogeneity in founding rates and the performance of biotechnology firms. *Research Policy*, 32: 229–253.

Sturdy, A. 2011. Consultancy's consequences? A critical assessment of management consultancy's impact on management. *British Journal of Management*, 22(3): 517–530.

Sturdy, A. J., Kirkpatrick, I., Reguera, N., Blanco-Oliver, A., & Veronesi, G. 2020. The management consultancy effect: Demand inflation and its consequences in the sourcing of external knowledge. *Public Administration*, 100(3): 488–506.

Sturdy, A. J., Kirkpatrick, I., Reguera, N., Blanco-Oliver, A., & Veronesi, G. 2020. "The management consultancy effect: Demand inflation and its consequences in the sourcing of external knowledge." *Public Administration* 100(3): 488–506. doi:10.1111/padm.12712.

Suchman, M. C., & Cahill, M. L. 1996. The hired gun as facilitator: Lawyers and the suppression of business disputes in Silicon Valley. *Law & Social Inquiry*, 21(3): 679–712.

Suchman, M. C. 1998. Working without a net: The sociology of legal ethics in corporate litigation. *Fordham Law Review*, 67(2): 837–874.

Suchman, M. C. 2000. Dealmakers and counselors: Law firms as intermediaries in the development of Silicon Valley. In M. Kenney (Ed.), *Understanding Silicon Valley*: 69–97. Berlin: Walter de Gruyter.

Susskind, R., & Susskind, D. 2016. *The future of the professions: How technology will transform the work of human experts*. Oxford: Oxford University Press.

Sutton, T., Devine, R. A., Lamont, B. T., & Holmes, R. M. J. 2021. Resource dependence, uncertainty, and the allocation of corporate political activity across multiple jurisdictions. *Academy of Management Journal*, 64(1): 38–62.

Sytch, M., & Kim, Y. H. 2020. Want to win someone over? Talk like they do. *Harvard Business Review*.

Sytch, M., & Kim, Y. H. 2021. Quo vadis? From the schoolyard to the courtroom. *Administrative Science Quarterly*, 66(1): 177–219.

Sytch, M., & Tatarynowicz, A. 2014. Exploring the locus of invention: The dynamics of network communities and firms' invention productivity. *Academy of Management Journal*, 57(1): 249–279.

Sytch, M., Kim, Y., & Page, S. 2022. Supplier-selection practices for robust global supply chain networks: A simulation of the global auto industry. *California Management Review*, 64(2): 119–142.

Sytch, M., Tatarynowicz, A., & Gulati, R. 2012. Toward a theory of extended contact: Incentives and opportunities for bridging across network communities. *Organization Science*, 23: 1658–1681.

Sytch, M., Wohlegezogen, F., & Zajac, E. J. 2018. Collaborative by design? How matrix organizations see/do alliances. *Organization Science*, 29(6): 1130–1148.

Tadros, E. 2023. EY cuts poor performing, misbehaving partners. Financial Review. December 18. https://www.afr.com/companies/professional-services/ey-cuts-poor-performing-misbehaving-partners-20231218-p5es4g#:~:text=More%20tha n%2040%20partners%20have,and%20those%20with%20behavioural%20issues.

Tatarynowicz, A., Sytch, M., & Gulati, R. 2016. Environmental demands and the emergence of social structure: Technological dynamism and interorganizational network forms. *Administrative Science Quarterly*, 61(1): 52–86.

Tate, N. 1963. Deaths from tonsillectomy. *Lancet*, 2(7317): 1090–1091.

The Times. 1919. Defects of grade in men. The Times, 7.

Thomiak, M. 1917. Breaking through the complexity barrier. December 9, 2022.

Thornton, P. H., & Ocasio, W. 1999. Institutional logics and the historical contingency of power in organizations: Executive succession in the higher education publishing industry, 1958–1990. *American Journal of Sociology*, 105(3): 801–843.

Thornton, P. H., Ocasio, W., & Lounsbury, M. 2012. *The institutional logics perspective: Foundations, research, and theoretical elaboration.* New York: Oxford University Press.

Tilcsik, A., & Marquis, C. 2013. Punctuated generosity: How mega-events and natural disasters affect corporate philanthropy in U.S. communities. *Administrative Science Quarterly*, 58(1): 111–148.

Townsend, D. M., Hunt, R. A., McMullen, J. S., & Sarasvathy, S. D. 2018. Uncertainty, knowledge problems, and entrepreneurial action. *Academy of Management Annals*, 12(2): 659–687.

Treem, J. W. 2012. Communicating expertise: Knowledge performances in professional-service firms. *Communication Monographs*, 79(1): 23–47.

Turner, J. C. 1982. Towards a cognitive redefinition of the social group. In H. Tajfel (Ed.), *Social identity and intergroup relations*: 15–40. Cambridge, UK: Cambridge University Press.

Turner, John C. 1991. *Social influence.* Pacific Grove, CA:Thomson Brooks/Cole Publishing Co.

Turner, J. C., Hogg, M. A., Oakes, P. J., Reicher, S. D., & Wetherell, M. S. 1987. *Rediscovering the social group: A self-categorization theory.* Cambridge, MA: Basil Blackwell.

UK Competition and Markets Authority. 2019. **Annual report and accounts 2018/19.** London, UK: United Kingdom Government.

Uribe, J., Sytch, M., & Kim, Y. H. 2020. When friends become foes: Collaboration as a catalyst for conflict. *Administrative Science Quarterly*, 65(3), 751–794.

Uzzi, B. 1997. Social structure and competition in interfirm networks: The paradox of embeddedness. *Administrative Science Quarterly*, 42: 35–67.

van Dijk, C. E., van den Berg, B., Verheij, R. A., Spreeuwenberg, P., Groenewegen, P. P., & de Bakker, D. H. 2013. Moral hazard and supplier-induced demand: Empirical evidence in general practice. *Health Economics*, 22(3): 340–352.

Van Doorslaer, E., & Geurts, J. 1987. Supplier-induced demand for physiotherapy in the Netherlands. *Social Science & Medicine*, 24(11): 919–925.

Vedula, S., York, J. G., Conger, M., & Embry, E. 2022. Green to gone? Regional institutional logics and firm survival in moral markets. *Organization Science*, 33(6): 2085–2540.

Vermeulen, G. A. M., Simons, T., & Knoben, J. 2012. A community-level theory of organizational resistance to anti-smoking regulation. Academy of Management Best Proceedings Papers, 21(1).

Villasenor, J. 2022. Patents and AI inventions: Recent court rulings and broader policy questions. *Brookings Institute*. August 25. https://www.brookings.edu/blog/techtank/2022/08/25/patents-and-ai-inventions-recent-court-rulings-and-broader-policy-questions/. Accessed December 9, 2022.

Voisin, A. 2022. Consultants fined, disqualified for submitting inflated invoices to state's underground tank cleanup fund. *California Water Boards*. November 7. https://www.waterboards.ca.gov/press_room/press_releases/2022/pr11072022-fraud-unit-enforcement.pdf.

von Nordenflycht, A. 2010. What is a professional service firm? Toward a theory and taxonomy of knowledge-intensive firms. *Academy of Management Review*, 35(1): 155–174.

Wald, E. 2020. Getting in and out of the house: The worlds of in-house counsel, big law, and emerging career trajectories of in-house lawyers. *Fordham Law Review*, 88: 1765–1800.

Walsman, M. C. 2022. Operational adaptation and innovation during COVID-19: Lessons learned from consulting and a road map for the future. *Service Science*, 14(2): 195–212.

Watts, B. V., Shiner, B., Klauss, G., & Weeks, W. B. 2011. Supplier-induced demand for psychiatric admissions in northern New England. *BMC Psychiatry*, 11(1): 146.

Weaver, C. 2022. Theranos investors react with sadness and satisfaction. *Wall Street Journal*. November 18.

Weiss, D. C. 2010. Ohio lawyer suspended for billing more than 24 hours in a day. *ABA Journal*. August 25. https://www.abajournal.com/news/article/ohio_lawyer_suspended_for_billing_more_than_24_hours_a_day. Accessed March 26, 2023.

Wennberg, J. E., Barnes, B. A., & Zubkoff, M. 1982. Professional uncertainty and the problem of supplier-induced demand. *Social Science & Medicine*, 16(7): 811–824.

Westphal, J., & Park, S. H. 2020. *Symbolic management: Governance, strategy, and institutions*. New York: Oxford University Press.

Westphal, J. D. 1998. Board games: How CEOs adapt to increases in structural board independence from management. *Administrative Science Quarterly*, 43(3): 27.

Westphal, J. D., Gulati, R., & Shortell, S. M. 1997. Customization or conformity? An institutional and network perspective on the content and consequences of TQM adoption. *Administrative Science Quarterly*, 42(2): 366–394.

Whalen, P. J. 1998. Fear, vigilance, and ambiguity: Initial neuroimaging studies of the human amygdala. *Current Directions in Psychological Science*, 7(6): 177–188.

Whitson, J. A., & Galinsky, A. D. 2008. Lacking control increases illusory pattern perception. *Science*, 322: 115–117.

Wilensky, G. R., & Rossiter, L. F. 1983. The relative importance of physician-induced demand in the demand for medical care. *Milbank Memorial Fund Quarterly: Health and Society*, 61(2): 252–277.

Wilkins, D. B., & Ferrer, M. J. E. 2018. The integration of law into global business solutions: The rise, transformation, and potential future of the big four accountancy networks in the global legal services market. *Law & Social Inquiry*, 43(3): 981–1026.

Williamson, O. E. 1975. *Markets and hierarchies: Analysis and antitrust implications.* New York: Free Press.

Williamson, O. E. 1981. The economics of organization: The transaction cost approach. *American Journal of Sociology*, 87(3): 548–577.

Williamson, O. E. 1985. *The economic institutions of capitalism: Firms, markets, relational contracting.* New York: Free Press.

Williamson, O. E. 1991. Comparative economic organization: The analysis of discrete structural alternatives. *Administrative Science Quarterly*, 36(2): 269–296.

Wistrich, A. J., & Rachlinski, J. J. 2013. How lawyers' intuitions prolong litigation. *Southern California Law Review*, 86(3): 571–636.

Wittreich, W. J. 1966. How to buy/sell professional services. *Harvard Business Review*. March. 127–138.

Wolinsky, A. 1993. Competition in a market for informed experts' services. *RAND Journal of Economics*, 24(3): 380–398.

Wood, B., Wong, Y. K., & Theodoridis, C. G. 1972. Pediatricians look at children awaiting adenotonsillectomy. *Lancet*, 300(7778): 645–647.

Wooldridge, A. 1997. The advice business. *Economist*. March 22: 3–5.

Wooten, M., & Hoffman, A. J. 2017. Organizational fields: Past, present and future. In R. Greenwood, C. Oliver, T. B. Lawrence, & R. E. Meyer (Eds.), *SAGE handbook of organizational institutionalism*, vol. 2: 55–74. Thousand Oaks, CA: SAGE.

Wu, Y., Balasubramanian, S., & Mahajan, V. 2004. When is a preannounced new product likely to be delayed? *Journal of Marketing*, 68(2): 101–113.

Yakura, E. K. 2001. Billables: The valorization of time in consulting. *American Behavioral Scientist*, 44(7): 1076–1095.

Yu, S., & Kilduff, G. J. 2020. Knowing where others stand: Accuracy and performance effects of individuals' perceived status hierarchies. *Journal of Personality and Social Psychology*, 119(1): 159–184.

Zajac, E. J., & Olsen, C. P. 1993. From transaction cost to transactional value analysis: Implications for the study of interorganizational strategies. *Journal of Management Studies*, 30(1): 131–145.

Zipf, G. K. 1949. *Human behavior and the principle of least effort: An introduction to human ecology.* Cambridge, MA: Addison-Wesley.

Zollo, M., & Singh, H. 2004. Deliberate learning in corporate acquisitions: Post-acquisition strategies and integration capability in us bank mergers. *Strategic Management Journal*, 25(13): 1233–1256.

Zollo, M., Reuer, J. J., & Singh, H. 2002. Interorganizational routines and performance in strategic alliances. *Organization Science*, 13(6): 701–703.

Zweifel, P., & Manning, W. G. 2000. Moral hazard and consumer incentives in health care. In A. J. Culyer & J. P. Newhouse (Eds.), *Handbook of health economics*, vol. 1: 409–459. Amsterdam: Elsevier.

Tables and figures are indicated by an italic *t* and *f* following the paragraph number.

For the benefit of digital users, indexed terms that span two pages (e.g., 52–53) may, on occasion, appear on only one of those pages.